WESTMAR COLLE

THE
NORTHERN TEACHER
IN THE SOUTH

1862–1870

THE
NORTHERN TEACHER
IN THE SOUTH

1862–1870

By

HENRY LEE SWINT

1967
OCTAGON BOOKS, INC.
New York

INTRODUCTION TO THE OCTAGON EDITION

The events of the twenty-five years which have passed since the publication of this book have sharpened, rather than blunted, the edge of a phrase in its concluding sentence: ". . . the education of the Negro became a point of conflict in the reconstruction of the South." But the arena of conflict has expanded; the education of the Negro has become the center of bitter controversy throughout most of the nation.

In the period 1862-1870 the Yankee schoolma'am, the Southern white, and the Negro understood the fact that education was not an end in itself. It was the force by which social political power was to be maintained, the lever by which social and economic changes were to be wrought. Many of the teachers, idealistic and impatient, went to the South expecting to bring about a sudden, dramatic transformation in the Negro. Negro faith in education as the open sesame to wealth, political power, and social position did not end with the gradual waning of Northern enthusiasm which became quite evident by 1870 nor did Southern opposition to "abolitionist" ideas end with the withdrawal of Federal troops. The problems with which the Northern teachers grappled in the postwar period have grown in complexity, even since 1941.

Much important material now available to the historian was unavailable or practically unknown twenty-five years ago. For example, the records of the Bureau of Refugees, Freedmen, and Abandoned Lands, a massive and rich source, are now in the National Archives, and the American Missionary Association collection, at Fisk University, is now open to the student. Several scholars have used these sources in the preparation of works on various aspects of the history of the period 1862-1900. Were I to revise *The Northern Teacher* I would rely on these works in making minor changes but, in my opinion, no substantial reinterpretation of the major thesis would be necessary. Education alone was not enough in 1866; it is not the complete answer in 1966. The Northern teachers understood

the vicious cycle, ignorance—lack of skill-poverty-ignorance—
in which the Negro was caught a century ago. Some of them
attempted, without dramatic success, to break the cycle. Despite the enthusiasm of many Negroes and the conscientious
and devoted efforts of many teachers, the Northern politicians
who planned and administered reconstruction did not bring
about radical changes in the economy of the South, such as
that embodied in the well-known phrase, "forty acres and a
mule," which were necessary if freedom was to be meaningful.
The determination of the dominant Southern white group to
regain political control, resistance to any trend toward social
equality, and a decline in crusading fervor which was noticeable in the North by 1870 were among the factors which made
the Negro a casualty of the march along the "road to reunion."

In 1966, as in 1866, the Negro vote is important; now, as
then, zealous champions of individualism demand, in the name
of democracy, legal enforcement of egalitarian concepts, while
equally vociferous champions of individualism, North and
South, condemn legislative encroachment on the sacred rights
of property. The Negro is a more powerful force in 1966 than
he was in 1866, of course; he is more powerful in 1966 than
he was in 1941. But this fact does not invalidate the general
conclusions presented in *The Northern Teacher in the South.*

The location of contemporary personal records, such as
Dear Ones at Home, a group of letters written by Northern
teachers working in the South during and immediately after
the Civil War, recently published by the Vanderbilt University
Press, would help historians in their effort to understand the
complex nature of the problems which vexed the Negro and
his friends a century ago and which again have become a topic
for debate, often as acrimonious now as then, and conflict,
bloody now, as it was then.

HENRY LEE SWINT

October, 1966

PREFACE

DURING the last years of the Civil War and throughout the period of reconstruction several thousand Northern teachers, selected and supported by aid societies and educational associations, entered the South and established schools for Negroes and whites. Abolitionist in sentiment and equalitarian in practice, these men and women represented a philosophy which was anathema to the Southern white, and the program which they introduced met with hearty and active opposition.

Immediately after the collapse of the Confederacy many Southern leaders advocated the education of the freedmen, but they insisted that such education be carried out by the Southerner rather than by the "Yankee schoolmarm." As the political controversy progressed from bitterness to violence the Northern teacher became the object of social ostracism, persecution, and physical assault.

In the belief that this phase of the sectional controversy is worthy of more study than it has hitherto received, I have examined the attitudes and ideals of many of the teachers who saw active service in the field, and have investigated the lives of many of the men who selected and supported the teachers. I have attempted to discover the motivating factors behind this movement, to determine the forces which impelled the teachers to go into the South, and which caused thousands of individuals throughout the North to contribute to their support.

This study is not intended to be definitive, but, on the contrary, should be considered as an introductory statement. It is a study of those individuals who engaged in teaching the freedmen of the South during the period 1862–1870; of their motives, their attitudes, and their experiences. It does not deal with the work of contemporary educational institutions for Negroes, nor does it enter the lists either with those who see in the work of the Northern teachers and politicians the origin of the public school system of the South, or with those who bitterly deny this contention. It is merely an examination of the genesis of a movement and does not purport to be an evaluation of the social significance of recent extra-regional contributions to education in the South.

I am aware that the work of the missionary associations and aid societies did not cease with the defeat of Radical Reconstruction, and that their work has extended to the education of both the white and the Negro. Schools, colleges, and hospitals have been supported by various Northern benevolent groups and associations since the close of the period with which I am concerned. The work of such bodies as the Peabody Fund, the Rosenwald Fund, the Slater Fund, the Jeanes Foundation, the General Education Board, and similar organizations has been increasingly important.

I wish to express my appreciation to Professor Dan M. Robison, of Vanderbilt University, in whose seminar the basis for this study was laid; to Professor Frank L. Owsley, also of Vanderbilt, whose encouragement and inspiration have been invaluable; to Professor William C. Binkley, Chairman of the Department of History at Vanderbilt, who has been ever ready with patient assistance and sound advice; and to Dr. John E. Pomfret, Dean of the Senior College and the Graduate School of Vanderbilt University, for assistance in arranging for the publication of this volume.

Grateful acknowledgement is made to the National Society of Colonial Dames of America in Tennessee, to whom I am indebted for the use of certain microfilm now on deposit at Vanderbilt University, and to the Institute of Research and Training in the Social Sciences, Vanderbilt University, which sponsored the publication of this volume. I am also indebted to the Julius Rosenwald Fund, whose generous assistance made possible the collection of a portion of the material upon which this study was based; to the officials of the Organization and Old Records Division, Adjutant General's Office, United States War Department; and to certain officials of the National Archives and of the Library of Congress. I am especially grateful for the assistance given by the officials and staff of the libraries of Vanderbilt University and Fisk University.

Dr. Charles Summersell and Mr. Frank Futrell called my attention to certain valuable information. Mr. Merton England has given valuable assistance by his careful and critical reading of the manuscript. My wife, Elizabeth Welter Swint, assisted in the location and collection of data and in the preparation of the manuscript. Conventional expressions of my appreciation of her constant assistance and co-operation are completely inadequate.

HENRY LEE SWINT

Vanderbilt University
April 20, 1941

CONTENTS

ix

THE
NORTHERN TEACHER
IN THE SOUTH

CHAPTER I

FREEDMEN'S AID SOCIETIES AND ASSOCIATIONS

EARLY in the Civil War, as the Federal armies occupied Southern territory, teachers and missionaries from the Northern states moved into the South in great numbers and established schools in almost every city and town and on many plantations. According to one author, "The Yankee teacher entered the South on the heels of the soldier. Whenever a foothold had been secured by the Federal Army . . . the . . . philanthropic organizations sent out schoolmasters."[1] After Appomattox the teachers spread rapidly over the South, until, by 1867, few cities and towns were without a "nig school" supported by Northern associations and administered by Northern teachers.

The movement for the education of the freedmen aroused great interest in the North. Although no absolutely accurate statement can be made concerning the money spent in supporting the Yankee teachers, it is probable that between $5,000,000 and $6,000,000 were used for this purpose in the period from 1862 to 1872. In 1869 there were 9,503 teachers in freedmen's schools in the South. Some of these teachers were Southerners, but the majority were natives of Northern states.

The Northern teachers were selected and supported by a number of freedmen's aid societies, aid commissions, and educational associations. Some of the societies were organized as relief agencies, their principal object being the alleviation of suffering among the freedmen and the white refugees of the South. When the most pressing needs of the people had been met these societies also established schools and commissioned teachers, thus following the example of the "educational commissions." In their work in the South, both in relief and in education, all of the societies co-oper-

[1]Ellis P. Oberholtzer, *A History of the United States Since the Civil War* (5 vols., New York, 1917–1937), I, 89.

3

ated with the Bureau of Refugees, Freedmen, and Abandoned Lands, better known as the Freedmen's Bureau.

⟨The Freedmen's Bureau was the result of Congressional response to the demands of the public, led by the officers of the Freedmen's Aid Associations. It is impossible to state with any certainty where the idea of a central organization for freedmen originated. It has been attributed to E. L. Pierce, of Boston,[2] and also to Josephine Sophie White Griffing, an active abolitionist and agent of the underground railroad, who, in 1861, went to Washington to work with the National Women's Loyal League in freedmen's aid.[3] Here she "counseled with" President Lincoln and Secretary Stanton in regard to freedmen's relief and urged the establishment of a bureau.[4] Her plan was supported by Charles Sumner, B. F. Wade, Henry Wilson, T. D. Eliot, and others. Whether or not Mrs. Griffing was responsible for the idea of a Freedmen's Bureau, her efforts in support of such an organization were of sufficient value to bring strong recommendation that she be appointed to the chief clerkship of the Bureau in 1865.[5]

A petition asking for the establishment of the Freedmen's Bureau was presented to the Senate on January 12, 1863, by Senator Wilson.[6] A bill for the establishment of a bureau was introduced into the House by Eliot, of Massachusetts. These measures were defeated, however, and Eliot introduced a second bill in December, 1863.[7] A long and heated debate ensued, and on March 1 the bill passed the House. The bill as passed by the House was unacceptable to the Senate, but under pressure from many prominent men in the North and from the aid societies of the West, the two houses finally reached an agreement, on March 3, 1865. At the head of the new Bureau was placed General O. O. Howard, a

[2] W. E. Burghardt DuBois, "The Freedmen's Bureau," *Atlantic Monthly*, LXXXVII (March, 1901), 354.

[3] *Dictionary of American Biography*, Allen Johnson and Dumas Malone, editors (20 vols., New York, 1929–1936), VII, 622–623.

[4] Elizabeth Cady Stanton, Susan B. Anthony, and Matilda Joslyn Gage, *History of Woman Suffrage* (6 vols., New York, 1881–1922), II, 28–29.

[5] *Ibid.*, II, 33. Ida H. Harper says that "full credit" belongs to Mrs. Griffing. *The Life and Work of Susan B. Anthony* (3 vols., Indianapolis, 1898–1909), I, 239.

[6] Paul S. Peirce, *The Freedmen's Bureau* (Iowa City, 1904), *State University of Iowa, Studies in Sociology, Economics, Politics and History*, III, 1, p. 34.

[7] *Ibid.*, 35.

graduate of Bowdoin and West Point, and formerly commander of the Army of the Tennessee.

The work of the Bureau included the relief of freedmen through medical and hospital service and supplies; the establishment of schools; the supervision of labor contracts; and the control of all confiscated or abandoned lands. In carrying out these great aims much was left to the discretion of the subordinate officials.

For the purposes of this study only the relief and educational work of the Bureau need be examined. The pressing problem of relief for the destitute refugees, freedmen, and citizens was met through rationing depots, hospitals, and camps. In 1866 the Bureau issued to refugees and freedmen "rations" to the enormous total of 9,456,482. In his study of the Freedmen's Bureau, Peirce estimates "the actual expense" of the food and clothing dispensed by the Bureau between January, 1865, and September, 1871, as $4,500,000.[8] Further, before September, 1866, over 2,000 white refugees had been furnished transportation to their homes and, by 1870, 30,000 Negroes had been transported. Another phase of direct relief was the establishment of hospitals and asylums. In September, 1867, there were forty-five hospitals under the jurisdiction of the Bureau. The total expenditure of the medical department of the Bureau "must have approximated $2,000,000!" says Peirce.[9]

General Howard was especially interested in the work of the schools. He believed that "the most urgent want of the freedmen was education." In a report he said, "From the first I have devoted more attention to this than to any other branch of my work."[10] The educational work of the Freedmen's Bureau was carried out in co-operation with the benevolent and philanthropic associations of the North. By the Act of July 16, 1866, the Bureau was empowered to sell or lease any property which had belonged to the Confederate government, and to use the money thus realized to lease and construct school buildings. The Bureau estab-

[8] *Ibid.*, 99.
[9] *Ibid.*, 93.
[10] *House Executive Documents,* 41 Cong., 2 Sess., No. 142 (Serial 1417), 10. Report of O. O. Howard, Commissioner, Bureau of Refugees, Freedmen, and Abandoned Lands, October 20, 1869, and February 15, 1870.

lished schools all over the South. In addition to establishing and supporting its own schools, the Bureau was charged with the responsibility of protecting the schools maintained by the benevolent associations. Teachers were often chosen by the associations and their transportation and quarters supplied by the Bureau. The Bureau paid rentals on buildings "quarterly . . . at the rate of ten dollars per month for each teacher actually engaged in instructing an average of thirty or more scholars." [11]

In addition to the Bureau schools, whether conducted by teachers from the associations or selected by the Bureau, there were many important schools entirely under the control of the benevolent associations. Thus there were, in effect, two types of schools in operation in the South, those maintained by the Freedmen's Bureau and those controlled by the associations. The agents of the Bureau were not required to report the schools taught by association teachers, nor even those taught by resident teachers but sustained and operated by Northern societies. All such teachers reported directly to their societies and to J. W. Alvord, the Superintendent of Schools of the Freedmen's Bureau, and not to the Superintendent of Education of the Freedmen's Bureau in the state in which the school was located. [12]

No definite statement of the number of teachers sent South by the associations is at present possible. The official reports give the following totals of teachers in the field.

January 1, 1867	972 white
June 30, 1867	1,388 white
January 1, 1868	2,948 white
January 1, 1869	7,840 white and colored
July 1, 1869	9,503 white and colored
July 1, 1870	9,307 white and colored [13]

[11] J. W. Alvord to Rev. J. Haight, May 12, 1869. Manuscripts of the Educational Division, Bureau of Refugees, Freedmen, and Abandoned Lands. Hereinafter cited as B.R.F.A.L. MSS. See, also, E. Whittlesey to Rev. S. C. Logan, November 4, 1868, B.R.F.A.L. MSS.

[12] Circular of G. L. Eberhart, State Superintendent of Education B.R.F.A.L., Savannah, Georgia, January 25, 1867. B.R.F.A.L. MSS.

[13] J. W. Alvord, *Semi-annual Reports on Schools and Finances for Freedmen, 1866–1870* (Washington, 1866–1870), January 1, 1867, p. 2; July 1, 1867, p. 2; January 1, 1868, pp. 12–14; January 1, 1869, pp. 6–9; July 1, 1869, pp. 6–9; July 1, 1870, p. 4; and *House Executive Documents,* 41 Cong. 3 Sess. No. 1 (Serial 1450), part 4, pp. 338–339. Report of O. O. Howard, July 1, 1870, in Report of Commissioner of Education, 1870.

These figures cannot be accepted as including all the teachers who were engaged in work in association schools, private schools, and denominational schools, and there seems to be no possible way to determine with exactness the number who may have gone out independently, or who were supported by a single church or local society.

On the other hand, the figures given in Alvord's reports are misleading, because Alvord, in giving the number of pupils in attendance, as for example, 247,333 in 1870, counts as "total enrollment" all those who attended any type of school—day, night, Sabbath, or industrial. As he said in his *Report* of July 1, 1870, "Individuals are often duplicated in our aggregate of pupils in the different kinds of schools; we refer to previous explanations of this fact. The total amount of *teaching,* however, is accurately represented by the number of pupils given." [14] Evidently it was possible for a student to be counted twice, or even four times; it does not appear whether a teacher who was employed in a day school, night school, and Sabbath school, was counted once, twice, or thrice, in the final tabulation.

Furthermore, many of the Bureau schools merited that name by courtesy only, since the teachers were often hardly less illiterate than the pupils whom they professed to teach. To many of the Bureau teachers the school was a business enterprise, and it is possible that some of the lesser Bureau officers did not refrain from connivance with such teachers. H. R. Pease, Superintendent of Education of Mississippi, described the condition clearly in a personal letter to Alvord:

In some cases teachers (these were colored) presented fraudulent accounts and others started schools for the purpose of obtaining the pay offered who were entirely incompetent to teach a primary school in several cases the teachers could neither read nor write they managed to get someone to make out their monthly reports. These schools were located in the interior counties of the state. The Bureau Agents have recognized these teachers and schools and in many cases they have been paid. I have inspected these schools and where I found them entirely incompetent I have refused to pay them. The result of which is, that certain colored men who were interested in a grand swindling enterprise in Natchez, (the case Gen. Small was

[14] Alvord, *Report,* July 1, 1870, p. 4.

directed to investigate, in which investigation, I assisted him) are making a great howdee [?], and have reported, (so I have been informed) to Gen Howard that I refused to recognize colored teachers. The difficulty is in this;—inefficient Bureau Agents have recognized these teachers without even taking the pains to ascertain whether they were morally or otherwise qualified to teach, and now since matters have come under my control I have been obliged to reject a number of this class of teachers. . . . Schools of this class are springing up like mushrooms all over the state since the teachers have learned that the Bureau will pay them more than they can earn at any other business.[15]

Illiterate Negro teachers were not confined to Mississippi, as the following letters show.

Hamilton Martin co N. C.
June the 5, 1869

Sir general Howard

Will you Please healpe the School of Hamilton Col) to Some Books Heare is a Large School and no Books and that not able to get them at this Time Please furnish for them Second Redars Third and 4 Reder and Primer and Geography Arithmetic and High Branches. Please Excuse my Pen for I have not any Better Pen and it is Bad. We is Wating for Books Excuse our Povity [?]

Techer is me

Your most And obt
Rev. J. M. Brand [16]

Montgomery Co
Va. July 11, 1870

My Dear Sir and general

i take my pen in hand to Write a few lines to you to inform you that I am Teachen a day Day School in the State of Virginia in montgomery County aBout 22 miles from Crishtenburg and a very poor part of the country i went there to Preach the gospel of our lord and Saviour and when i Commence my labores i found a great meney children Who was toue [?] years a goe Without the Spelling Book and know Nothing a bout the Spelling Book nor Reading and nowe they Can Read and Write and Pass geography well and are good in all there Studey i have done the very best i can for the people in this part of Virginia my field of labor being Very Poor therefore i am compeld to ask the ade of the Education Bureau to assit me in this grate work for heare is a grate number of Children must Be taught and i hope you will do all in your Power for me . . . the School is giting

15 H. R. Pease, Vicksburg, Mississippi, to J. W. Alvord, April 24, 1868, B.R.F.A.L. MSS.
16 B.R.F.A.L. MSS.

a long very Well in the ways of learning but the People is so very Poor that they can not pay for there children Schoolin i have taught this School a bout 14 months and i have Riscived 44 dollars in the way of Schooling and i now ask the ade of the Education Bureau to give me the Some of $10 dollars Per month. . . .

Yours in christ the lord
Rev. Richard gassaway

Sind your letter to Central depot
Montgomery co Va [17]

The reports of Alvord and Howard cannot be accepted without question. The official printed reports were made up of selections from the reports of the subordinate officers and of the teachers. Doubtless this selection was done with an eye to increasing the prestige of the Bureau and demonstrating the necessity of its schools. An examination of the manuscripts of the Educational Division of the Bureau shows many instances of careful editing of the manuscripts which were used as bases for official reports.

In fact, the reports were not always accepted at their face value by the friends of the freedmen. For example, Yardley Warner, of Germantown, Pennsylvania, wrote Alvord on January 18, 1869, concerning a statement in the report of July, 1868, that 5,712 freedmen were in "the higher branches." He desired to know the meaning of the term "higher branches"; whether arithmetic was the dividing line, and if so, how many of these pupils could compute interest, and how many were studying algebra and geometry.[18] Alvord replied on January 21, but his explanation was evidently unsatisfactory, for Warner wrote: "I am obliged for the explanation of 'higher branches'—in thy letter of 21 inst. But I can scarcely credit the statement that over 5,000 Freedmen are beyond Arithmetic. Is this thy understanding? or that 5,000 are in *some study higher than some study* enumerated in the table or report? We are moving, or taking measures to move in Normal Schools and some definite knowledge is needed to predicate intelligent action upon." [19]

[17] *Ibid.*
[18] Yardley Warner, Germantown, Pennsylvania, to J. W. Alvord, January 18, 1869, B.R.F.A.L. MSS.
[19] Yardley Warner, Germantown, Pennsylvania, to J. W. Alvord, January 29, 1869, B.R.F.A.L. MSS.

There was also controversy among the officials of the associations over these reports. For instance, George Whipple, Secretary of the American Missionary Association, wrote Alvord in 1867, insisting that the official Bureau report, which credited the American Freedmen's Union Commission with seven hundred teachers, was incorrect. He declared that he knew his reports to be correct, and that if the statement made by the American Freedmen's Union Commission was correct Alvord's reports must be erroneous.[20] Secretary Whipple asserted that evidently the reports were not understood in the same way; that it was difficult to secure "definite information"; and that it was impossible to tell whether the American Freedmen's Union Commission had "10—15— 100—or 458 teachers in the field at any time since the summer of 1866."[21] At the same time D. C. Haynes, of the American Freedmen's Union Commission, wrote Alvord that he had noticed that the American Missionary Association had been credited with "353 teachers and *preachers.*" "How many of the 353 are *preachers?*" he asked.[22]

The short life of many of the associations, their tendency to unite and to separate, their frequent change of officers, of title, and of areas of interest, as well as the great number of local units or affiliate societies, make it very difficult to establish their number with any degree of accuracy. A list of seventy-nine has been compiled by Julius H. Parmelee, in his study of the aid societies.[23]

Of the societies devoted primarily to the relief of suffering throughout the South, the American Union Commission was the most prominent. It was organized in 1864, and had offices in New York, Boston, Philadelphia, Baltimore, and Chicago. Its purpose was stated thus: "Organized to aid in the restoration of the Union upon the basis of freedom, industry, education, and Christian morality." The motivating impulse which probably led to the establishment of this commission was the destitute con-

---

[20] George Whipple, Richmond, Virginia, to J. W. Alvord, March 14, 1867, B.R.F.A.L. MSS.

[21] George Whipple, New York, to J. W. Alvord, June 22, 1867, B.R.F.A.L. MSS.

[22] D. C. Haynes, New York, to J. W. Alvord, March 16, 1867, B.R.F.A.L. MSS.

[23] Julius H. Parmelee, "Freedmen's Aid Societies, 1861–1871," United States Department of Interior, Office of Education, *Bulletin,* 1916, No. 38, pp. 299–300. The smaller auxiliary societies are not included in this list.

dition of some 3,000 women and children refugees of Union families concentrated at Clarksville, Tennessee. It was a non-denominational organization, recognizing "no distinctions of caste or color," and claimed to be "neither political nor sectional" in its work.[24]

Andrew Johnson approved the relief work of this society, and the War Department aided it in its work. Between 75,000 and 100,000 persons were assisted by the Commission.[25] Among its officers Lyman Abbott, General Secretary, was most prominent. Other officers included Martin Brimmer, Christopher R. Robert, Major General George G. Meade, and Professor D. C. Gilman. E. A. Ware, later of Atlanta University, and C. Thurston Chase, Superintendent of Education for Florida, were among the agents of this Commission.

The American Missionary Association was probably the most important representative of the sectarian associations engaged in missionary and educational work. The group of which "the A.M.A." was one of the leaders also engaged in relief activity, as did the American Union Commission and others, but the religious, moral, social, and political uplift of the freedmen was the chief aim of the American Missionary Association.

The American Missionary Association was an outgrowth of the Amistad Committee, which was organized by S. S. Jocelyn, Joshua Leavitt, and Lewis Tappan in 1839, for the defense of a group of slaves who had killed the master of a "slaver," the *Amistad,* upon which they were being held captive, and who had been taken into custody by Federal officials off Long Island. After the liberation of the Negroes by order of the United States Supreme Court, the Amistad Committee engaged in African missions and anti-slavery agitation. In 1846, at Syracuse, New York, the American Missionary Association was organized, with William Jackson, of Massachusetts, president, George Whipple, of

---

[24] *The American Union Commission: its Origin, Operation and Purposes* (New York, 1865), 3–4.

[25] It is interesting to note that the American Union Commission maintained a special office in New York City for those who wished to emigrate to the South, in which might be found maps, Southern newspapers, and "detailed information as to business openings, prices and character of lands, etc." *Ibid.,* 2.

Ohio, corresponding secretary, and Lewis Tappan, of New York, treasurer.[26]

From 1846 the American Missionary Association engaged in foreign and domestic missions. The home mission work in the West was "conducted with special purpose to bear decided testimony against slavery and the sin of caste," and that in the South was directed toward the abolition of slavery, even though the association was condemned in the North as a "disturber of the peace of the churches."[27] The position of the A.M.A. in 1850 was stated thus:

> Resolved, that we believe the Christianity of the nation is about to be tested, in view of the late act of Congress for recovery of fugitive slaves, which appears equally at variance with the principles of the Association, the Constitution of the country, and the law of God, and that as Christians we do solemnly covenant with each other and our colored brethren that we cannot obey it, nor any law that contravenes the higher law of our Maker, whatever persecution or penalty we may be called to suffer.[28]

The A.M.A. schools "followed the army," and by 1866 there were 353 teachers in the field, while an expenditure of $377,027.78 in cash and supplies was reported.[29] In 1868 there were 532 teachers, and in the preceding year the Association expended $334,500 in cash, and distributed clothing valued at $90,000.[30]

Among the prominent schools established by the A.M.A. are Hampton, Hampton, Virginia; Fisk, Nashville, Tennessee; Avery, Charleston, South Carolina; Ballard, Macon, Georgia; Talladega, Talladega, Alabama; Atlanta, Atlanta, Georgia; Straight, New Orleans, Louisiana; Le-Moyne Normal, Memphis, Tennessee; and Tougaloo, Tougaloo, Mississippi.

The A.M.A. was avowedly nonsectarian, but many of its leaders were prominent Congregationalists, and in 1865 the Congregational National Council recommended that the Association be accepted by the Congregational churches of the nation as their

[26] See Augustus F. Beard, *A Crusade of Brotherhood, A History of the American Missionary Association* (Boston, 1909).
[27] *Ibid.*, 97–107.
[28] *Ibid.*, 109–110.
[29] *American Freedman*, I, 10 (January, 1867), 146.
[30] Parmelee, "Freedmen's Aid Societies," 275.

agent for work among the freedmen.[31]   The Free-Will Baptist, the Wesleyan Methodist, and the Reformed Dutch churches also selected the A.M.A. as their agent for this work.[32]

One of the strongest of the strictly denominational societies was the Freedmen's Aid Society of the Methodist Episcopal Church. This society was organized in Cincinnati, August 7, 1866. Those who called the organization meeting did so in view of the fact that the other denominations were, as the call stated, manifesting "a strong tendency toward denominational movements."[33]   It also felt that the Methodist Church must cease its co-operation with the American Freedmen's Union Commission, and establish its own work on a more secure basis. The Friends and the United Presbyterians had organized aid societies in 1862, the Baptists in 1863, the Old School Presbyterians and the United Brethren in 1864, and the Congregational Church had adopted the American Missionary Association as its agent in 1865. In that year the Protestant Episcopal Church had organized a society, so that the Methodist Episcopal Church and the New School Presbyterian Church were the only denominations "of any size" in co-operation with the nonsectarian commissions.[34]

One of the principal points at issue was financial in character. A large proportion of the funds collected in the West—about $100,000 in 1865—had been contributed by Methodists. The Methodist schools and missions were thus deprived of badly needed support. As one minister said, "Methodist hands should have handled Methodist funds, and been appropriated to pay Methodist teachers, to found Methodist schools, and carry on a work for which the denomination should have its due credit."[35]

After much discussion, an organization was effected. Bishop D. W. Clark was chosen president, Clinton B. Fisk, Grant Good-

[31] Beard, *Crusade,* 133.   Also letter of George Whipple to J. W. Alvord, September 5, 1865, B.R.F.A.L. MSS.

[32] Parmelee, "Freedmen's Aid Societies," 275–276.

[33] "Call to the Convention," Freedmen's Aid Society of the Methodist Episcopal Church, *Reports, 1866–1875* (Cincinnati, 1893), First Report, 3.

[34] *Ibid.,* 6, and letter of R. S. Rust to J. W. Alvord, January 15, 1868, B.R.F.A.L. MSS. See also, David H. Moore, *John Morgan Walden . . .* (New York, 1915). Among those present at the organization meeting were Adam Poe, R. S. Rust, Grant Goodrich, and J. M. Walden. Walden had been secretary of the Western Freedmen's Aid Commission.

[35] *Reports,* First Report, 6, 11.

rich, and I. W. Wiley, vice-presidents, and R. S. Rust general field superintendent.

In the first two years of its work this society established fifty-nine schools, sent out 124 teachers, and expended more than $60,000.[36]   By 1869 its receipts had reached $98,513.50, and ten years later the Society had received $790,218.95 for use in the education of the freedmen.[37]   In 1878 the Society claimed to have had in its schools in the preceding twelve years 60,000 pupils, who, in turn, had taught at least 500,000.   J. Braden, President of Central Tennessee College, reported that 2,700 different students had attended the college in the fifteen years prior to 1879.   He declared that the teachers who had gone out from the school had made a great contribution to education throughout the South, but had received very low salaries for their work.[38]

The Friends were very active in the work among the freedmen, both in denominational societies and in nonsectarian associations. The Friends' Association of Philadelphia and its Vicinity for the Relief of the Colored Freedmen was organized in 1863.[39]   Between November, 1863, and March, 1864, this group raised $53,800, and by 1867 the total amount raised had reached $210,500.[40]   The work of this Society was done mainly in North Carolina and Virginia.[41]   Among the officers were Richard Cadbury, Thomas Scattergood, Benjamin Coates, and Charles Rhoads.   The Philadelphia Friends also organized the Friends' Association for the Aid and Elevation of the Freedmen.   In 1869 this society was supporting nine schools in Virginia, four in South Carolina, and one in Mississippi.   The cash expenditures of the society were not very large, the total for the period 1864 to 1869 amounting to only $57,-200.   This sum, however, does not include the value of the large

[36] *Reports,* Second Report, 10, 13.

[37] R. S. Rust, Cincinnati, Ohio, to J. W. Alvord, September 12, 1870, B.R.F.A.L. MSS. R. S. Rust, *The Freedmen's Aid Society of the Methodist Episcopal Church* (Society Series No. 6, New York, 1880).

[38] From $7.00 to $55.00 per month.   Freedmen's Aid Society of the Methodist Episcopal Church, *Twelfth Annual Report,* 1879 (Cincinnati, 1880), 12.

[39] Parmelee, "Freedmen's Aid Societies," 277.

[40] Friends' Association of Philadelphia and its Vicinity for the Relief of Colored Freedmen, *Report of the Executive Board* (Philadelphia, 1864), 4; Alvord, *Report,* July 1, 1868, pp. 67–68.

[41] M. E. Shearman, Philadelphia, Pennsylvania, to J. W. Alvord, September 24, 1870, B.R.F.A.L. MSS.

quantity of food and supplies sent out by the group.[42] The Indiana Friends were supporting about twenty teachers as early as 1864, and in that year collected $23,000 for the relief of freedmen.[43] The New England Yearly Meeting opened stores in Washington in 1864, and established an industrial school there.[44]

The work of the Baptist Church was carried out through its Home Mission Society. By 1870 this Society had established such schools as Shaw and Benedict, and had under instruction 3,720 students.[45]

The New England Freedmen's Aid Society, nonsectarian in character, was the first of the many Freedmen's Aid Societies, Unions, and Commissions to be organized. This society was the outgrowth of the Boston Educational Commission, which came into existence as the result of the work of E. L. Pierce, special agent of the Treasury Department. Pierce was sent by Secretary Chase to Port Royal to supervise the plantations there, and to investigate the possibility of securing supplies of cotton.

Pierce went to the Sea Islands in January, 1862, and upon his return he and Chase agreed upon a plan for using confiscated cotton as a basis for payment of school expenses. He then talked to several members of Congress, but "they seemed either to dread the magnitude of the social question, or to feel that it was not one with which they as legislators were called upon immediately to deal."

Of the cabinet members, only Chase was interested. He and F. L. Olmsted, who was connected with the United States Sanitary Commission, "alone seemed . . . to see the necessity of immediate action."

Pierce interviewed Lincoln on the subject. The President was not very enthusiastic, but finally gave Pierce a card bearing the words:

[42] Jacob M. Ellis, Philadelphia, Pennsylvania, to J. C. Cook, Chief Clerk, Educational Department, B.R.F.A.L., April 23, 1869, B.R.F.A.L. MSS.

[43] Report of Joseph Dickinson, of the Indiana Yearly Meeting of Friends, *Minutes of the Convention of Freedmen's Commissions Held at Indianapolis, Indiana, July 19 and 20, 1864* (Cincinnati, 1864), 14.

[44] Alvord, *Report*, July 1, 1868, pp. 67–74.

[45] Dwight O. W. Holmes, *The Evolution of the Negro College* (New York, 1934), Teachers College, Columbia University, *Contributions to Education* 609, pp. 122–123.

I shall be obliged if the Sec. of the Treasury will in his discretion give Mr. Pierce such instructions in regard to Port Royal contrabands as may seem judicious.

A. Lincoln

Feb. 15, 1862.[46]

While still at Port Royal Pierce had written the Rev. J. M. Manning and Samuel Cabot, Jr., of Boston, "setting forth the condition of the negroes within [Federal] lines, their disorganized state, their destitution and their exposure by contact with the army to injurious influences,"[47] and asking for clothing, money, and teachers.

In response to this request a meeting was held at the home of the Rev. Manning on February 4, 1862, and at the Young Men's Christian Union on February 7. At the latter meeting the Boston Educational Commission was organized. Soon afterward a great meeting was held in the Old South Church, and Governor John A. Andrew was elected president of the Commission.

On March 3, 1862, the first group of teachers to be sent out left New York for Port Royal. The party consisted of thirty-one teachers and superintendents, who had been chosen by the Commission and accepted by Pierce. Transportation, sustenance, and quarters were furnished by the Treasury Department. Seventy-two teachers were sent to Port Royal the first year, and the Committee on Clothing and Supplies spent $5,306.93 for clothing, blankets, seeds, and, in addition, sent clothing valued in excess of $20,000, all goods being carried at Government expense.

The subscriptions were at first purely voluntary, but soon branch or auxiliary societies were organized, each branch adopting a teacher who promised to write frequently "and thus keep alive the interest in the work."[48] In January, 1865, there were twenty-two such societies, and about July 1, 1868, there were seventy such groups supporting teachers, and a total of two hundred auxiliary

[46] Edward L. Pierce, "The Freedmen at Port Royal," *Atlantic Monthly,* XII (September, 1863), 296–297.
[47] Brief History of the New England Branch of the American Freedmen's Union Commission, by J. H. Chapin, B.R.F.A.L. MSS. See, also, the Port Royal Correspondence, The National Archives, Washington, D.C.
[48] Chapin, History, B.R.F.A.L. MSS.

societies.[49] Each teacher cost the supporting society about $500 per year.[50]

The aim of the New England Branch was expressed by Secretary Chapin as follows: "The aim of the Society is to pave the way for a good free school system at the South, open alike to all races and colors, and supported by all for the good of all. The New England district school has been their model,—with such modifications as the very different circumstances imperatively demands [*sic*]." [51]

That the members and friends of the Society earnestly supported the work among the freedmen is shown by the fact that the Society spent $240,420.83 between May, 1863, and July 1, 1868, and contributed supplies valued at almost $200,000.

The New York friends of the freedmen organized the National Freedmen's Relief Association of New York in February, 1862. Among the prominent citizens present at the organization meeting at Cooper Institute were the Rev. S. H. Tyng, Frances Shaw, William Cullen Bryant, Edgar Ketchum, and George Cabot Ward.[52] In 1866 this society, then a branch of the American Freedmen's Union Commission, supported 125 schools and 222 teachers.[53]

The Pennsylvania Freedmen's Relief Association, or Pennsylvania Branch of the American Freedmen's Union Commission, was the successor of the Port Royal Relief Association. This organization was the result of a "Jubilee Meeting" held in Philadelphia on March 5, 1862, in response to appeals from General Sherman and Admiral Dupont on behalf of the freedmen of the islands of Georgia and South Carolina. At the very outset, the Port Royal Association spent $1,000 for a supply of fish, bacon, and molasses, and sent it to the Sea Islands, where it was distributed by Reuben Tomlinson, John Heacock, Laura M. Towne, and Ellen Murray. These, and other goods, were "gratuitously

[49] Alvord, *Report*, July 1, 1868, p. 69.
[50] *National Freedman*, I, 7 (August 15, 1865), 241; statement of O. B. Frothingham, *American Freedman*, I, 2 (May, 1866), 30.
[51] Chapin, History, B.R.F.A.L. MSS.
[52] New York *Times*, February 23, 1862.
[53] Alvord, *Report*, July 1, 1868, pp. 67–74.

distributed when it was necessary, but sold to those who were able to pay for the price of transportation." The society sent J. Miller McKim on a tour of inspection of the Sea Islands, and one result of his report was the establishment of a store, under the direction of John Hunn, in order to prevent the exploitation of the Negroes by the army.[54] This society supported from sixty to sixty-five teachers each year from 1864 to 1868, and spent from $3,500 to $4,000 a month in support of its schools and for relief.[55]

The Pennsylvania Association supported an asylum at Nashville, Tennessee, and a school for "poor whites" at Stevenson, Alabama. The latter place was called "the roughest of all our stations." "The country there," said one of the officials of the association, "reminds one of the country through which Dickens' Jo guided the lady of Bleak House." The natives were considered "the most abject beings in all creation, not excepting the blacks." [56]

In May, 1865, delegates from the aid societies of New England, New York, Pennsylvania, and Maryland met in New York City and organized the American Freedmen's Aid Union. Later in the same year the Pittsburgh, Cincinnati, and Chicago societies joined this Union, and the new group took the name "American Freedmen's Aid Commission." In December, 1865, this new Commission united with the American Union Commission, "a society also laboring in the South but supporting schools for whites as well as for freedmen." [57] Thus was formed the Freedmen's Aid Union Commission.

Much debate arose over a clause in the proposed constitution of the new union "providing that the schools and supply depots should be open without distinction of race or color," but it was finally passed, and the new society thus accepted the practice of the American Missionary Association and the American Union Commission. The teachers were now instructed to admit pupils of both races into the schools, but little change took place, since

[54] MS. history, The Pennsylvania Branch of the American Freedmen's Union Commission, "written by the lady secretary of our Women's Branch," sent to J. W. Alvord by Robert R. Corson, February 24, 1868, B.R.F.A.L. MSS.

[55] Alvord, *Report*, July 1, 1868, pp. 67–74.

[56] William F. Mitchell, *Pennsylvania Freedman's Bulletin*, I, 1 (February, 1865), 14–18.

[57] Chapin, History, B.R.F.A.L. MSS.; *Independent*, November 2, 1865.

prejudice still kept the "poor white" away from schools to which colored children were admitted.[58]

In May, 1866, all the nonsectarian societies united in the American Freedmen's Union Commission. The American Missionary Association did not join. It was a religious as well as an educational organization, and, therefore, could not join any union of societies to which nonsectarian groups might belong.[59]

Although the societies usually co-operated to a marked degree in the Southern work, there were two points upon which there was rather bitter disagreement. The earliest and most obvious point of conflict was the question of segregation of races in schools and at supply depots. The majority of the associations forbade segregation. The case against segregation was stated in an editorial entitled "Equal Rights," in the *American Freedman,* the organ of the American Freedmen's Union Commission.

> The wisest and best friends of the freedmen do not aver that the African race is equal to the Anglo-Saxon. Neither do they admit any race inferiority. They simply assert that the negro must be accorded an opportunity for development before his capacity for development can be known. They simply insist . . . that both races shall enjoy the same rights, immunities and opportunities; and that, until this is accorded to them, the white man's claim to superiority rests upon a very shadowy foundation. . . . Our Commission is pledged to the maintenance of the doctrine of equal rights. . . . We proclaim as the motto of our movement: 'No distinction of race, caste or color in the Republic.' . . .
>
> It took America three quarters of a century of agitation and four years of war to learn the meaning of the word 'liberty.' God grant to teach us by easier lessons the meaning of the words 'equal rights.' [60]

In answer to an inquiry on the matter from an agent who suggested segregation in the schools, Lyman Abbott, Secretary of the Commission, declared that the question of segregation had been fully discussed, and that the officers realized that the adoption of the practice of non-segregation would arouse opposition in the South. Nevertheless, the principle had been adopted, "not only as a common principle, but as a right platform." The exclusion of any child from a school because of his color was "inherently

[58] Chapin, History, B.R.F.A.L. MSS.; *Nation,* December 21, 1865, p. 769.
[59] George Whipple, New York, to J. W. Alvord, September 5, 1865, B.R.F.A.L. MSS.
[60] *American Freedman,* I, 1 (April, 1866), 1–3.

wrong," and must, therefore, be condemned by the Commission. He had been inclined to "move gradually" in the matter, but further thought had convinced him that separate schools once begun would not be easily abandoned. Therefore there must be no distinction whatever.[61]

The second question was one of procedure. Should schools simply educate the freedmen, or should they be used to convert the freedmen? The controversy over this point was even more bitter than over that of segregation. For example, the Contraband Relief Commission of Cincinnati was organized for relief purposes, but on January 19, 1863, eight members, led by Levi Coffin, J. M. Walden, and C. B. Boynton, withdrew from the Contraband Association and formed the Western Freedmen's Aid Commission. The eight had introduced a resolution which stated that "while the present physical wants of the Freedmen" should be relieved, this should not delay "the far more important work of providing for their general welfare." The freedmen must be fitted "for their new condition," which would be "most effectively done, not by bringing them North, but by locating them on Southern soil, and organizing their labor there." [62]   J. M. Walden said that the "religious element" entered so largely into the organization of the Western Aid Commission that it was believed necessary to "send missionaries to evangelize as well as teachers to instruct the freedmen." [63]   The W.F.A.C. united with the A.M.A. in the fall of 1866. The Commission retained its identity, but united with the A.M.A. in the actual work and in its support.[64]

In the early months of 1867 the Cincinnati and Cleveland Societies withdrew from the American Freedmen's Union Commission and joined the American Missionary Association, because of a disagreement over the question of purely educational versus parochial schools.[65]

[61] *Ibid.*, 5–6.

[62] *American Missionary*, VIII, 3 (March, 1863), 59.

[63] Statement of J. M. Walden, Corresponding Secretary of the Western Freedmen's Aid Commission, *Minutes of the Convention of Freedmen's Commissions*, 23–24. See Moore, *Walden*.

[64] Thomas Kennedy, Ohio Medical College, Cincinnati, to J. W. Alvord, February 7, 1868, B.R.F.A.L. MSS.

[65] *American Freedman*, II, 1 (April, 1867), 194.

The work done by the numerous societies and associations was quite extensive. In 1866 the American Freedmen's Union Commission reported 359 schools supported by the Commission and its branches, in every Southern state except Texas.[66] In the years 1862 to 1874 sixteen of the Freedmen's Aid Societies received, in cash and supplies, $3,933,278. In 1865 twelve of the societies contributed $328,670.08 in cash, and were supporting 307 schools, with 773 teachers.[67] Lyman Abbott estimated in 1867 that $5,500,-000 had already been contributed.[68]

There was great interest in Europe in the work of the societies. Many of the societies sent agents to Europe, and freedmen's aid societies were organized there.[69] Meetings were held in 1865 at Bloomsbury, Derby, Sheffield, and other English towns, at which Levi Coffin and Crammond Kennedy spoke. William Lloyd Garrison estimated that the English had contributed in money and goods about $800,000 by March, 1866.[70] The "English Fund," originated by Arthur Albright of Birmingham, had given more than "[$?] 500,000" by July, 1869. Thirty-eight schools with 1,054 pupils were supported by this fund, which was administered by W. F. Mitchell, of Columbus, Georgia. The schools were located in eleven Southern states.[71]

An example of the interest of Englishmen in the work of the societies is seen in the following letter:

> The British Workman Office
> No. 2 Paternoster Row
> London, Aug. 25, 1868
>
> Dear Sir:
> Can you oblige me with copies of the 'reports' which have been issued of the 'Schools for freedmen?' I have taken a lively interest in the welfare of the poor freedmen and shall be glad to receive *any* documents relative to their past or present condition. If you can aid me in the collection of a few interesting cases of freedmen who by their own diligence and industry have already become possessed of *their own little cottages* or plots of land I shall feel particularly obliged. . . .

[66] American Freedmen's Union Commission, *First Annual Report*, 1866 (New York, 1866).
[67] *American Freedman*, I, 1 (April, 1866), 9, table 2.
[68] Parmelee, "Freedmen's Aid Societies," 296.
[69] *National Freedman*, I, 3 (April, 1865), 95, 96, 108.
[70] *National Freedman*, III, 6 (April, 1869), 3.
[71] Alvord, *Report*, July 1, 1869, p. 81.

P. S. The 'British Workman' for Sept. gives the fact of a *navy* with *one* leg erecting his cabin. A somewhat similar fact of a Freedman would be acceptable if you can kindly put me in the right track for attaining such cases.[72]

Nor was the work of the societies confined to England. C. C. Leigh, agent of the National Freedmen's Relief Association, held a meeting in Paris in 1865.[73] In December, 1865, the Ladies' Auxiliary of the Paris Aid Society sent 10,400 francs, in addition to previous gifts.[74] In Holland, Leigh received, in December, 1865, 8,186 florins from groups at Amsterdam, Leyden, The Hague, and other cities. The Swiss of Lausanne contributed $3,000 in the spring of 1865. Societies were also organized at Bremen, Hamburg, Berlin, Frankfort, Utrecht, Geneva, Neufchatel, Bale, Zurich, Tessen, Heidelberg, and Mannheim.[75]

[72] J. O. Smithies to O. O. Howard, B.R.F.A.L. MSS.
[73] *Nation,* November 3, 1865, p. 677.
[74] *National Freedman,* I, 11 (December 15, 1865), 371.
[75] *Ibid.,* I, 8 (September 15, 1865), 273; I, 11 (December 15, 1865), 374.

Chapter II

THE OFFICERS OF THE ASSOCIATIONS: MOTIVES AND RELATIONSHIPS

PROPER evaluation of the "Yankee teacher" requires an investigation not only of the teachers, but also of the organizations and individuals who were responsible for their selection and support. As has been stated, the teachers were selected and supported by aid societies and educational associations. They reported to the central office of the organization by which they were accredited and, in many cases, to auxiliary societies as well. It is obvious that the officers of the societies and associations would select teachers whose ideals and attitudes were in harmony with those of the majority of the officers. Certainly, too, this philosophy would be carried into the classroom. Hence, a proper understanding of the philosophy of the teachers necessitates a study of the attitudes, beliefs, and background of the officers of the associations.

For the purpose of studying the interests and activities of the officers a list of over three hundred individuals was compiled and brief sketches of the lives of the 135 most active and most widely known were prepared.[1] These studies reveal definite occupational patterns among the officers. They also reveal significant trends of association and relationship which suggest the presence of common motivating factors.

The occupational interests of the officers of the associations fall into two broad groups.[2] In one group, which may be called the in-

[1] See Appendix.
[2] Table showing occupational distribution among 135 officers of freedmen's aid societies and educational associations

Financier	26	Minister	55
Railroad executive	20	Educator	34
Merchant	17	Editor	28
Manufacturer—chiefly textiles and		Politician	28
heavy machinery	14	Author	25
		Lawyer	14
		Physician	7
Total	77		191

23

dustrial-commercial, are to be found the manufacturers, merchants, financiers, and railroad executives. The second group includes those individuals whose occupations are generally accepted as professions, such as lawyers, editors, and ministers. In the industrial-commercial group five principal vocations are represented seventy-seven times, and in the second group seven professions are represented 191 times. Obviously some individuals are included in more than one vocational classification within each group. The varied interests of the men necessitated such duplication. This duplication is especially noticeable in the professional group, where many individuals, such as Lyman Abbott, minister and editor, O. B. Frothingham, minister and editor, and William Cullen Bryant, author and editor, fall in two vocations. It is less apparent in the industrial-commercial group but even here there are occasional instances. Stephen Colwell, for example, was both an iron manufacturer and a railroad executive.

Among the prominent individuals who may be given as examples of the industrial-commercial group are Edward Atkinson, M. W. Baldwin, C. G. Hussey, J. P. Crozer, J. V. Farwell, and James W. White. Edward Atkinson was, perhaps, the outstanding textile manufacturer of his day. He was an active member of the New England Cotton Manufacturers Association. His pamphlets on economic and political questions, usually published under the signature, "E. A.," were widely circulated. M. W. Baldwin is best known as the inventor and manufacturer of the Baldwin locomotive. C. G. Hussey was one of the leaders in the development of the brass and copper industry in the United States and was also interested in iron and steel manufacturing. J. P. Crozer was a textile manufacturer, John V. Farwell the head of a large mercantile house, and James W. White the head of the world's largest dental supply house.

Some of the most influential Americans of the period 1830–1890 are included in the professional group. Many of these men held positions of political power and influence. This is, of course, especially true of John A. Andrew and William Claflin, each of whom, as Governor of Massachusetts, lent prestige and strong support to the New England Freedmen's Aid Society. It is equally true of Salmon P. Chase, who enthusiastically supported the educational associations from the very beginning of the movement, and of Schuyler Colfax, who preceded Chase as president of the American Freedmen's Union Commission. Many lesser political figures, such as Hugh L. Bond, of Baltimore, and Morton McMichael, of Philadelphia, were also officers of the associations.

It is not surprising that many prominent ministers participated in the work among the freedmen. Lyman Abbott, Congregationalist minister; Henry Ward Beecher, "America's Great Preacher"; Phillips Brooks, minister, orator, and poet; O. B. Frothingham and James Freeman Clarke, Unitarian leaders; and Matthew Simpson, "War Bishop" of the Methodist Church, were among the clergymen active in the movement for freedmen's aid and education.

Among the twenty-five authors and twenty-eight editors who supported the movement are to be found such well-known figures as John Greenleaf Whittier, William Cullen Bryant, Edward Everett Hale, William Lloyd Garrison, and Thomas Wentworth Higginson. Also of importance are the thirty-four college and university professors and administrators, many of them of national reputation and influence. For example, Daniel Coit Gilman was a member of the education committee of the American Union Commission. Between 1854 and 1892 Robert Allyn, one of the managers of the Methodist Freedmen's Aid Society, was, successively, Commissioner of Schools of Rhode Island, teacher at Ohio University and at Wesleyan Female Academy, Cincinnati, and president of McKendree College and of Southern Illinois State Normal University. J. C. Burroughs, member of the advisory board of the American Freedmen's Union Commission was president of Chicago University from 1857 to 1873. For many years he was assistant superintendent of schools in Chicago. Jonathan Blanchard, of the American Missionary Association and the American Freedmen's Union Commission, was president of Knox College. Francis J. Child, professor of English at Harvard University, was an officer of the Boston Educational Commission and of the New England Freedmen's Aid Society. William Nast, one of the Managers of the Freedmen's Aid Society of the Methodist Episcopal

Church taught at the United States Military Academy and at Kenyon College. As leaders of the press, the pulpit, and the classroom, these men occupied positions which inevitably lent weight to their words and power to their example.

The determination of motive is a difficult task in any case, and especially so when the act which follows the impulse is of a highly controversial nature or when the evidence is not easily available. Both of these conditions are present in a study of the motives which underlay the actions of the officers of the associations in organizing the aid societies, establishing schools, and sending out teachers. Some of the men were motivated by abolitionist zeal. Others were moved by pity for the helpless freedmen. Some saw the necessity of educating the Negro if he was to be made a citizen of the republic. Others, perhaps, realized the economic implications of their actions, or it may be that they merely regarded the anticipated profits as the just reward of the righteous. Others may have recognized several or all of these factors. However varied and complex the motives of each individual officer may have been, it is clear that the group, as a whole, was actuated by a combination of impulses. Without such a community of interest these individuals and groups could never have co-operated in the work among the freedmen.

The outstanding characteristic common to the majority of the officers was a profound interest in various humanitarian movements and social experiments. The most aggressive of all the social movements of the nineteenth century was abolitionism. In this movement many of the officers had been active for decades. Their interest in the education of the Negro was merely the continuation of a pre-war activity which had been the dominant force in the life of the individual. Of the entire group of 135, sixty-six were sufficiently prominent in the abolition movement to merit notice in the standard biographical dictionaries as leading abolitionists. The available evidence suggests that a much greater number were abolitionists, even though not sufficiently active to bring them national recognition as such. Representing, as many of them did, the most vocal social groups, the impact of their influence would have been great even if they had served a less emotional cause. Since they supported that most violently emotional of all American movements, and since they were "filled with the faith that moves mountains" and "clad in the armour of righteousness," their influence was even greater than their number would indicate.

Many of these men had devoted their lives to abolitionism. This is especially true of such well known men as William Lloyd Garrison, who was vice-president of the New England Freedmen's Aid Society, an officer of the American Freedmen's Aid Commission and of the American Freedmen's Commission, and a member of the executive board of the American Freedmen's Union Commission; and of Levi Coffin, "reputed president of the Underground Railroad," who was general agent of the Western Freedmen's Aid Society and an officer of the American Freedmen's Union Commission. Certainly Thomas Wentworth Higginson, underground railroad operator, advisor and supporter of John Brown, commander of a regiment of Negroes, and vice-president of the New England Freedmen's Aid Society, was no stranger to work among the Negroes. Many other officers, such as John A. Andrew, J. W. Alvord, Salmon P. Chase, R. S. Rust, and George Whipple, had been abolitionists since youth. Before the war these men had fought for the abolition of slavery with the fervor of crusaders. Now that the institution which they so bitterly hated had been purged from the land by four years of bloody war they felt that the freedmen must be educated, converted, and safeguarded in the possession of their hard-won rights. The battle was not yet over, the victory not yet won. Schools must be established, the freedmen organized. The "fruits of victory" must be gathered by those who had so long labored in the vineyard.

These conclusions are supported by a statement made by the Superintendent of Education for the American Missionary Association in 1884. In an address entitled "The Supplementing of the War," the Superintendent said, "Those very men, extremists, enthusiasts, 'fanatics,' who had formed the backbone of the abolition movement, veritable John the Baptists of the era which has now opened upon us, became the dauntless leaders of an educational movement which was the natural sequel and supplement of their first crusade." He admired these men, in spite of their partial blindness, he said. The leaders of "great renovating movements" need to be zealous, and these men were zealots. Their zeal was not always "tempered with wisdom," but in this instance prudence would have meant failure, declared the Superintendent.[3]

This continuation of interest, so clearly stated by an official of one of the leading associations, was certainly one of the most powerful forces in the entire movement. To what extent did the "renovating" zeal of the leaders extend beyond the simple education of the Negro? Were they the sympathetic followers of the Radical reconstructionists, or did the Radicals take their cue from the "renovators"? These questions must remain unanswered in the absence of complete insight into the motives of the officers and of the Radical leaders. It does seem probable, however, that the Radical reconstructionists recognized the dynamic power inherent in such a continuation of the abolitionist crusade and that they directed it to the support of the Radical political program. In short, the Radical group in Congress, consciously or unconsciously, manipulated the educational efforts of the abolitionist-supported associations for the furtherance of their own political ends. It is obvious that in many cases individuals were members of both the Radical-politician and the abolitionist-humanitarian groups. To suggest that one group may have exerted great pressure upon the other is not to neglect the fact that the two groups cannot be completely separated.

It should be noted, too, that these men were interested not only in abolitionism but in many other types of philanthropy and social reform as well. Some of them were not only opposed to slavery, but to war, to tobacco, and to the use of intoxicating beverages. They were advocates of woman suffrage, penal reform, the Sunday School, the Y.M.C.A., and socialistic communities. They organized societies for the prevention of cruelty to animals, for the education of the blind and the deaf and dumb, for the liberalization of divorce, for the elevation of "fallen Magdalens," for the protection of women and children in industry. They established

[3] Albert Salisbury, in National Education Association, *Journal of the Proceedings and Addresses of the Annual Meeting,* Madison, Wisconsin, 1884 (Boston, 1885), 97.

homes for unfortunates of all types—prostitutes, orphans, news-boys, working girls, the aged and infirm. They were the earnest supporters of home and foreign missions, and they established or endowed numerous schools, colleges, and universities.

For example, William Claflin, president of the New England Freedmen's Aid Society and an officer in the American Missionary Association, was the first governor of Massachusetts to advocate woman suffrage. During his term as governor much progressive legislation was enacted, such as acts broadening the legal rights of women, protecting destitute children, and regulating the work of women and children in industry. He was an active prohibitionist. He and his father, Lee Claflin, endowed Claflin University, a school for Negroes at Orangeburg, South Carolina. Lee Claflin, Isaac Rich, and Jacob Sleeper, vice-president of the Boston Educational Commission and of the New England Freedmen's Aid Society, established Boston University. Christopher R. Robert, New York financier and member of the American Union Commission, established Robert College, Constantinople, and a school for "mountain whites" at Chattanooga, Tennessee. He also contributed heavily to Hamilton College, to Beloit College, and to Auburn Theological Seminary. C. G. Hussey, of the American Freedmen's Commission, established the School of Design for Women at Pittsburgh, was one of the founders of Allegheny Observatory, and was a trustee of Pittsburgh University. He was also an abolitionist and an advocate of peace, temperance, and feminism. G. S. Griffiths, president of the Baltimore branch of the American Union Commission, was a pioneer in penal reform, temperance, and Y.M.C.A. work. He organized the first prison Sunday School in the United States. The work of the Tappan brothers, Lewis and Arthur, in the American Sunday School Union, the American Bible Society, the American Tract Society, the American Home Mission Society, the American Education Society, the American Missionary Association, the American Anti-Slavery Society, and the New York Magdalen Society is too well known to require discussion here.

There is no doubt that opposition to tobacco, temperance sentiment, and advocacy of similar reform movements was stronger among the officers as a group than is evident from the available data. Such attitudes are not found singly. They spring from a frame of mind, from a psychology peculiar to the reformer. Not only does he refrain from evil and abstain from self-indulgence, but he is not content until the forbidden pleasures have been denied all men. He feels that upon him is laid the burden of the sins of others, and he cannot rest. Clad in "the armour of righteousness," and armed with the sword of the Scripture, he is happiest when in the thick of the fray. Thus it is only natural that the abolitionist should have been opposed to liquor and to tobacco, and that he should have supported feminism, missions, and every other movement for social reform.

Despite the inadequacy of the available information it is possible to point to several individuals whose activities illustrate still further this combination of interests. J. W. Alvord was secretary of the Lincoln National Temperance Association, an organization which encouraged sobriety among the freedmen. Alvord asked the officials of the Freedmen's Bank (of which he was president) to use their influence in behalf of the Association. In the temperance pledge circulated by the Lincoln Association and by the Vanguard of Freedom, a similar organization, tobacco was included, to the disgust of many freedmen.[4] In this campaign Alvord received the hearty support of George Whipple, Secretary of the American Missionary Association.

Alvord and Whipple were by no means alone in their opposition to alcohol and tobacco. J. B. Walker, of the New England Freedmen's Aid Society, was a fiery abolitionist of the Weld school. In 1849 he established a religious newspaper devoted to abolition, temperance, and kindred doctrines. Two years later he became the pastor of a Congregational church "composed chiefly of abolitionists and temperance reformers."[5] J. M. Walden, one of the most influential men in the Methodist Church, as well as in several freedmen's aid societies, also published a paper in opposition to liquor and, incidentally, to squatter sovereignty. Jacob Sleeper, vice-president of the New England Freedmen's Aid Society, was

---

[4] B.R.F.A.L. MSS.; Alvord, *Report,* July 1, 1868, p. 77; July 1, 1869, p. 17.
[5] *Dictionary of American Biography,* XIX, 347.

president of the Massachusetts Temperance Association. E. N. Kirk, president of the American Missionary Association, was a strong abolitionist as early as 1819, and was noted for his uncompromising attitude on temperance and missions. James Freeman Clarke, officer in the New England Freedmen's Aid Society, was active in abolitionism, temperance, and woman suffrage.

The moving spirits in the abolition and temperance movements were also the leaders in the agitation for woman suffrage and "equal rights for all." Before and during the war the advocates of woman suffrage were among the most bitter advocates of immediate emancipation. The first Woman's Rights Convention held after the war met in New York in May, 1866. As "the same persons were identified with the Anti-slavery and Woman's Rights Societies," it was suggested that the cause of suffrage for the Negro and for women be united in one movement, and that all petitions, appeals, and bills, include "both classes of disfranchised citizens." [6] As a result of this sentiment the American Equal Rights Association was formed, its objective being equal suffrage for all, irrespective of race, color, or sex.

Among the officers of the freedmen's aid societies who were associated with the movement for woman suffrage were Henry Ward Beecher, William Claflin, James Freeman Clarke, Robert Collyer, O. B. Frothingham, William Lloyd Garrison, R. P. Hallowell, James E. Yeatman, S. H. Tyng, and T. W. Higginson.

Even though many of the officers who are listed in the industrial-commercial group were abolitionists by conviction and experience, and were interested in a variety of humanitarian and reform movements, the fact that railroads, heavy industry, and finance are represented seventy-seven times in a group of 135 suggests that there might have been economic motivation in the movement.

It might be said that these men were chosen as officers of the associations because of their position and their wealth. This was doubtless true of many of the individuals in the group. It is to be assumed that at times a society might have selected a prominent businessman as vice-president or advisor merely in the belief that such an appointment would add to the prestige of the society, or,

[6] Stanton, Anthony, and Gage, *History of Woman Suffrage*, II, 152–153.

perhaps, in the hope that such an appointment would result in financial contributions. This, however, was certainly not true in the case of such men as Arthur and Lewis Tappan, M. W. Baldwin, William Claflin, Harvey B. Spelman, and Christopher R. Robert. These men, and many other officers in this group, had been abolitionists since youth. Their interest in the Negro was not feigned; they were not new converts to the struggle.

Only by the most careful and painstaking examination of the correspondence of a large number of the officers would it be possible to determine whether they were conscious of any economic significance in the movement to which they contributed so much of their time and money. It is clear, however, that some of them recognized this factor and believed it to be the most important reason for educating the Negro. It is also evident that the general public was aware of the economic implications of the movement and that at least a portion of that public approved.

For example, in discussing the National Freedmen's Relief Association of New York, the *Herald* noted that the officers of the new society were "men of prominence." Business men, said the *Herald,* "take business views of all movements, and there is a commercial as well as a humanitarian aspect to this work." The free, educated Negro would be a better citizen and a "better consumer of Northern manufactures" than the slave. It would "pay the North to teach him, and the South to encourage him to be taught."[7] Northern businessmen should "be awake" to the fact that the emancipation of four million slaves would give great "impetus to Northern manufactures" and to trade in furniture, cutlery, cloth, yarn, rope, sewing machines, stoves, shoes, kettles, dry goods, and "all sorts of Yankee notions."[8] At the cost of a "light brigade of school-mistresses" the North might organize a "colony" which would be worth more than any English possession, and a huge new market might be developed, the profits of which

[7] New York *Herald,* no date, quoted in National Freedman, II, 2 (February 15, 1865), 48–49.

The "men of prominence" who organized the N.F.R.A. included Francis G. Shaw, William Allen Butler, Charles Collins, John Jay, Eleazar Parmly, O. B. Frothingham, and others. See Appendix.

[8] "E. A." [Edward Atkinson], New York *Evening Post,* July 27, 1864, as given in *Freedmen's Record,* I, 5 (May, 1865), 85; *National Freedman,* I, 4 (May 1, 1865), 131–134; *Independent,* November 8, 1865.

would be insured to the North by hastening "the work of education" among the freedmen.[9] Such a market would "set all the
mills and workshops astir" and would solve the industrial problems of the North.[10] The problem of emancipation was thus "re-
duced to a simple one in the 'Rule of Three,'" wrote one periodical. If the few Negroes freed by Federal occupation of Southern
territory proved to be "such valuable customers" for "Northern
products and Northern merchandise" what would be the result of
the liberation of four million? "Answer: 'Godliness hath the
promise of the life that now is as well as that which is to come!'"[11]
To this pious epigram the *Independent* added the sequel: "Verily
Godliness has the promise of the life that now is, as well as that
which is to come; and verily this promise is often redeemed in
federal currency."[12] In fact, from the business and commercial
viewpoint, said a New York newspaper, "the rebellion was only a
miserable means to a most happy end."[13]

It should also be noted that Edward Atkinson, William Endicott, Jr., John A. Andrew, E. S. Philbrick, John Murray Forbes,
and other officers were interested in cotton planting and land
speculation in the South, and that the profits from these ventures
were sometimes enormous. It is also significant that the phrase,
"he was interested in Western [or Southern] railroads," recurs
with much frequency in the biographies of the officers, and that
their letters give numerous illustrations of their interest in such
enterprises.

This deep interest in the economic possibilities of the work
among the freedmen appears frequently in the letters of the teachers, in the reports of the associations, and in other literature on the
subject. In the conflict between the industrial and the agrarian
sections industry had triumphed, and the freedmen's school was
to be one of the means by which the economic and political "fruits

[9] *Independent*, November 8, 1865.
[10] E. L. Pierce, "Freedmen at Port Royal," *Atlantic Monthly*, XII (September, 1863),
311.
[11] *Pennsylvania Freedman's Bulletin*, I, 1 (February, 1865), 11.
[12] *Independent*, November 8, 1866.
[13] New York *Evening Post*, in *National Freedman*, I, 4 (May 1, 1865), 131–134. In
the October issue the *Freedman* contained the following brief item: "In the West Indies,
it was a familiar remark that the instant a slave was freed, he began by buying a pair
of shoes." October 15, 1865, p. 286.

of victory" were now to be harvested. While the evidence available does not justify any categorical statement concerning the importance of economic interest as a motivating factor, it does not seem unjust to conclude that the interest of many of the individuals connected with the work was not purely humanitarian.

To assert that some of the officers of the associations were not moved solely by humanitarian impulses is not to impugn the sincerity of all the men who were interested in the education of the freedmen. Undoubtedly many of the officers were sincere in their humanitarian interest. They earnestly desired that the Negro might be uplifted, civilized, and educated, and they were willing to give both time and money in supporting the Northern teacher in the hope that these aims might be realized.

CHAPTER III

THE YANKEE TEACHER: MOTIVES AND ATTITUDES

IN 1869 there were 9,503 teachers in freedmen's schools in the South, of whom possibly 5,000 were natives of the Northern states. Who were these people who so eagerly left their homes, families, and friends in order to "teach young nigs"? What forces impelled them to engage in the work among the freedmen? Complete answers to these questions could be given only after long and exhaustive study of the character, background, and experiences of a large number of the teachers.[1] Many of them were relatively obscure individuals, and extensive, detailed, and accurate knowledge concerning them is not easily located. Sufficient material has been examined, however, to justify certain statements. It is evident that there was a pattern in the reasons which impelled the teachers to go South.

Probably the outstanding motivating factor was religious and humanitarian interest. Many of the teachers had been abolitionists; practically all were profoundly religious. In fact, the outstanding characteristic of the Yankee teacher seems to have been

[1] Some comment on the Northern teacher will be found in the following works: Walter L. Fleming, *Civil War and Reconstruction in Alabama* (New York, 1905); James W. Garner, *Reconstruction in Mississippi* (New York, 1901); Francis B. Simkins and Robert H. Woody, *South Carolina During Reconstruction* (Chapel Hill, 1932); William W. Davis, *Civil War and Reconstruction in Florida* (New York, 1913), *Columbia University Studies in History, Economics and Public Law*, Vol. LIII; J. G. DeRoulhac Hamilton, *Reconstruction in North Carolina* (New York, 1914), *Columbia University Studies in History, Economics and Public Law*, Vol. LVIII; Thomas S. Staples, *Reconstruction in Arkansas, 1862–1874* (New York, 1923), *Columbia University Studies in History, Economics and Public Law*, Vol. CIX; C. Mildred Thompson, *Reconstruction in Georgia, Economic, Social, Political, 1865–1872* (New York, 1915), *Columbia University Studies in History, Economics and Public Law*, Vol. LXIV; James Ford Rhodes, *History of the United States from the Compromise of 1850* (New York, 1920); W. E. Burghardt Du-Bois, *Black Reconstruction. . .* (New York, 1935); Laura J. Webster, "The Operation of the Freedmen's Bureau in South Carolina," *Smith College Studies in History*, edited by J. S. Bassett and S. B. Fay, Vol. I, No. 2 and No. 3, October, 1915–July, 1916; L. P. Jackson, "The Educational Efforts of the Freedmen's Bureau and Freedmen's Aid Societies in South Carolina, 1862–1872," *Journal of Negro History*, VIII (January, 1923), 1–40; Oliver S. Heckman, The Penetration of Northern Churches into the South, 1860–1880. Unpublished Ph. D. dissertation, Duke University, [1938?]; Bell I. Wiley, *Southern Negroes, 1861–1865* (New Haven, 1938).

piety. Many of the teachers were also ministers, and practically all were religious to the point of fanaticism. The American Missionary Association specified that its teachers must be fired with missionary zeal. They must be men of "fervent piety."[2] The missionary need not go to Africa, it was said. There he would find "a lethargic and almost effete race, speaking an unwritten language, requiring years of toil to catch its fugitive words and bind them with arbitrary signs, slaves of superstition . . . where years must be spent without a single convert." The missionary should remain at home where was to be found "near at hand, within a day or two's journey a people speaking our own language, with a wonderful reverence for the Bible, and stimulated, as no ignorant, degraded and vicious people ever were before, with 'a wild desire to know.'" Surely there were victories to be won for Peace, surely "the Church militant" had "heroes to give, to what, in the esteem of many, is but a continuation" of the previous conflict.[3] The war was over, but "the work of Christianity was just commencing," said an official of the American Missionary Association. "We might withdraw our swords, but we should send spelling books and Bibles to the front. The military might be disbanded, but the missionaries should organize."[4]

Another officer frankly declared that the South must be "renovated by Northern principles." "There must be," he said, "an infusion of Northern element throughout the South." The war had already "done much to infuse this element into the South," but now that peace had come, other steps must be taken. "Schools and education were the means which now must be relied upon. Education must be given the blacks."[5]

This view was typical of that held by the other denominational societies. The attitude of C. B. Boynton and Levi Coffin in establishing the Western Freedmen's Aid Society, and of R. S. Rust,

[2] *American Missionary*, X, 7 (July, 1866), 152–153; VIII, 3 (March, 1863), 58.
[3] *Ibid.*, X, 7 (July, 1866), 153.
[4] Statement of Reverend E. B. Webb, at the Anniversary meeting of the American Missionary Association, Boston, May 30, 1866. *American Missionary*, X, 7 (July, 1866), 145–146. In 1869 the American Missionary Association still felt that "the war with bullet and bayonet" was over, but "the invasion of light and love" was not. *Ibid.*, XIII, 5 (May, 1869), 98.
[5] Statement of Reverend Horace James, *ibid.* James was A.M.A. Superintendent of Education of North Carolina.

J. M. Walden, and other Methodist leaders in organizing the Freedmen's Aid Society of the Methodist Church has been noted. The fact that practically all the denominations ceased their support of the nonsectarian associations and either established their own societies or adopted those already in existence (as in the case of the Congregational Church and the American Missionary Association), is, in itself, a demonstration of the influence of the missionary motive. On the other hand, the teachers of the American Freedmen's Union Commission were told that they were not "missionaries, nor preachers, nor exhorters"; they must have nothing to do with "churches, creeds or sacraments," and were "not to inculcate doctrinal opinions or take part in sectarian propagandism of any kind." They were to be teachers and friends of the Negroes, and must confine their work to the schools. "Speculative and ceremonial religion belong to the missionary alone, and may be, should be, kept wholly distinct from mental instruction," they were told by the Rev. O. B. Frothingham. The separation of church and education has been won after a long struggle. Catholic influence over schools had long been an object of criticism, but why should such opposition be confined to "the Romanist? Why not suspect every *religionist* as such?" he asked. Rationalists and Unitarians, whose religion was chiefly ethical, whose interests were "intellectual culture, domestic virtue, social kindness, the priceless worth of the simply human relations," might well "mingle such religion as they have with education," he said, but "evangelical men" whose chief interest was "the salvation of souls" would compromise both the secular and the sacred, should they secure control of the schools.[6]

In August, Lyman Abbott, General Secretary of the American Union Commission, Francis R. Cope, of the Pennsylvania Freedmen's Relief Association, and Nathan Bishop, of the Executive Committee of the American Freedmen's Union Commission, issued a statement in which they strongly supported Frothingham's position and, by inference, criticized that of the American Missionary Association, the Methodist Freedmen's Aid Society,

---

[6] Statement of O. B. Frothingham, *Independent*, July 12, 1866. See, also, *American Missionary*, X, 9 (September, 1866), 194, and X, 10 (October, 1866), 226–228.

and the other "evangelical" educational groups. "The school-house without the church produces China," they declared, "the church without the school-house, Italy; the church *and* the school-house, Republican America." They bitterly condemned the parochial school, and cited numerous examples to demonstrate the pernicious effects of such a system. They declared that the American Freedmen's Union Commission represented all denominations, that it was Christian but undenominational, and that its nonsectarian character was "jealously maintained." Its teachers possessed "true religion," and had been led to engage in this work not because of a desire to promulgate any particular doctrinal tenets, not "by curiosity, or love of adventure, or its compensation," but because they loved their fellow-man.[7]

Much strong feeling was engendered by this controversy. Bishop Matthew Simpson, of the Methodist Church, and the Rev. Joseph P. Thompson, prominent Congregationalist, resigned their positions with the American Freedmen's Union Commission because their views were at variance with those of Frothingham and others. Thompson advised his English friends to support the American Missionary Association rather than the American Freedmen's Union Commission, since the American Missionary Association was evangelical in spirit.[8]

The Boston *Recorder* was bitter in its denunciation of the dangerous doctrines of the American Freedmen's Union Commission, and enthusiastic in praise of the American Missionary Association. The teachers of the American Missionary Association, said the *Recorder,* were spreading education, industry, morality, and civilization based upon religion, not "civilization *without* religion." The highest degree of civilization can be attained only where the people are "imbued with the principles of evangelical religion," it declared.[9]

The American Missionary Association believed that "history, reason, and the peculiar character" of the freedmen required that their education be based upon religion. Man lives in the cold "torpor of death" of depravity, and there is hope for him only if

[7] *Independent,* August 23, 1866.
[8] *American Missionary,* X, 9 (September, 1866), 194.
[9] *Ibid.*

he be brought nearer the "spring-like warmth of the Divine Spirit." The schools of the American Missionary Association were based on this philosophy, and were "pervaded by religious influences." [10]

In reply to this editorial Frothingham declared that the time had come for the separation of religious and secular education in the South, and that the American Freedmen's Union Commission would devote itself to the promotion of popular secular education there. [11]

The American Missionary Association felt, however, that even the teacher of sewing and knitting should take every opportunity to win the pupil to Christ. If there was any conflict between the two classes of learning, "the teaching of divinity and the Word of God" must take precedence over "letters and the wisdom of man." [12] Its officers wished to select as teachers only those who loved "to point souls to the Lamb of God." They believed "that philanthropy without faith in the Redeemer" was inadequate, and should be discouraged. The great task of the teacher was to enlighten and Christianize the people of the South. [13] The chief ground for hope for the elevation of the Negro was to be found in "the religious element" in his character, and this element must be "cultivated" in a school which was under "thoroughly religious influence." "Genuine piety" was thought to be the best soil in which to plant schools. [14]

The quarrel between these two philosophies was, perhaps, evidence of a deeper schism. The evangelical churches condemned the American Freedmen's Union Commission because it was headed by Universalists, Unitarians, and Rationalists. Frothingham, chief advocate of secular education, was one of the leaders of Unitarianism and was extreme in his belief, being even more liberal than the majority of the Unitarians. [15] The opposition of the evangelical churches was, therefore, based on a difference of

---

[10] Editorial, "Education and Religion," *ibid.*, 202–204.
[11] *Ibid.*, X, 10 (October, 1866), 225.
[12] *Ibid.*, X, 9 (September, 1866), 194. See, also, X, 10 (October, 1866), 226–228.
[13] W. T. Richardson, Beaufort, South Carolina, August 25, 1864, *American Missionary*, VIII, 11 (November, 1864), 262.
[14] M. E. Strieby, *Independent*, September 24, 1868.
[15] *Dictionary of American Biography*, VII, 44.

opinion greater than a mere dispute over pedagogical method.

The New England Society, even though it became a branch of the American Freedmen's Union Commission, emphasized religious instruction in its schools. "We do not undertake that our teachers shall be instructors in theology," said the secretary of the Committee on Teachers of that Society, but it was hoped that the teachers would "lead aright and apply to daily life the religious sentiment, which is so emotionally strong in the negro race; following thus the plan which has made our New-England schools the backbone of the nation, as the war proved."[16]

Many of the teachers, then, were selected because of their "fervent piety" and religious enthusiasm. The "missionary spirit" is reflected in their correspondence. For example, one of the teachers wrote, in great joy:

> The only important news I wish to communicate is this:
> Five of my day scholars have become Christians, and I have every reason to believe that their hearts have been changed.
> I am so happy. Sixteen are seeking the Saviour, and there seems much good feeling in my school.
> The Lord is certainly here. There is some interest in my night-class. I pray that it may increase.
> Oh! for more faith and earnest prayer.[17]

"I am happy to say that some religious interest appears among my pupils," wrote another. "One of them today expressed the hope that his sins are forgiven, a boy of sixteen, who could not read two years ago, but is now studying elementary algebra and Latin lessons. . . . It is easy to talk and pray in school. I feel that this is a precious opportunity."[18] Another Georgia teacher reported that three of her pupils had "found Jesus to be precious," while still another was so filled with "GLAD TIDINGS" that she simply could not "hold it."[19]

Many of the teachers were eloquent in their expressions of

[16] Hannah E. Stevenson, Boston, October 18, 1866, *Freedmen's Record,* II, 11 (November, 1866), 195–196.

[17] Mary E. F. Smith, Macon, Georgia, May 18, 1868, *American Missionary,* XII, 8 (August, 1868) 179.

[18] Caroline Merrick, Augusta, Georgia, December 11, 1867, *ibid.,* XII, 2 (February, 1868), 29.

[19] *Ibid.,* XII, 8 (August, 1868), 179, 180.

thankfulness that they had been allowed to serve among the freedmen. A teacher stationed in South Carolina wrote:

O what a privilege to be among them, when their morning dawns; to see them personally, coming forth from the land of Egypt and the house of bondage. . . . It is a joy and glory for which there are not words. Never before have I realized so much the grandeur of that passage. . . . 'Behold I create new heavens and a new earth!' Truly the heavens and earth are clothed in a new light, consecrated to freedom.[20]

A Georgia teacher declared that she was more thankful for the privilege of teaching the freedmen than for any other blessing of her life. The work demanded all the strength, sympathy, and love of which the teachers were capable, and should be considered the greatest opportunity of a lifetime.[21]

The first day among the freedmen was one to be "treasured in memory's casket." The field of labor grew larger day by day, and the teachers felt themselves highly privileged to be sowers of the seed, although "perchance some other hand [would] gather in the ripened sheaves." [22]

"Praise the Lord Jesus for the work in our Eden," wrote another. "Both white and colored feel the shower from the skies. I wish you could have heard the songs of praise echo through the pines last Sabbath evening." [23]

Numerous similar illustrations of this feeling might be given. One of the most enthusiastic teachers was Miss Susan B. Clark, of Meadville, Pennsylvania, whose letter may be given as an example of the height of religious ecstasy experienced by some of the teachers.[24]

We are having a precious season. At least fifty here found a hope in the Saviour, and fifty or more are anxious and inquiring the way. . . . All

[20] Martha L. Kellogg, Hilton Head, South Carolina, January 3, 1863, *ibid.*, VII, 3 (March, 1863), 64–65.

[21] Mrs. William Conkling, Augusta, Georgia, November 4, 1867, *ibid.*, XI, 12 (December, 1867), 269; Elizabeth James, Roanoke Island, North Carolina, May 20, 1864, *ibid.*, VIII, 7 (July, 1864), 177.

[22] Mrs. Nickerson, Roanoke Island, North Carolina, January 9, 1864, *ibid.*, IX, 4 (April, 1865), 75; Miss C. A. Drake, Savannah, Georgia, *ibid.*, X, 3 (March, 1866), 55.

[23] Unnamed teachers, *ibid.*, IX, 9 (September, 1865), 194.

[24] Miss Clark was the daughter of William F. Clark of Meadville, Pennsylvania, and was stationed at Mill Creek, Virginia. She and her assistant, Miss Sarah Pew, of Mercer, Pennsylvania, opened a school in the basement of the home of a "rebel." *Ibid.*, IX, 8 (August, 1865), 187–188.

seem in deep earnestness. Oh, if you could see our little ones, with pensive faces, and many with tears in their eyes, listening as we try to tell them how to do better it is a scene that would touch your heart, and arouse every Christian grace. We can hear many of them say that Jesus is precious. . . . Precious lambs of the flock! our prayers are being answered in their behalf. . . . Every day one or more will come to tell us that the Lord is precious. Their exclamations are: 'Thank you, Jesus, thank you, Jesus.' It is very touching. . . . They need so much instruction. They are told that they must not eat or sleep until they find relief, and they sometimes lie out all night, and go out to the graveyard to stay. . . . Nearly all Sarah's school are either christians or are seeking to be such. They are scholars that we have had under our care for two sessions; and many who have left for the other school are serious too.

Many of the teachers were constantly "in a state of *almost* perfect happiness." [25] They felt great sympathy for the "untutored minds of the South," and wished to "labor in amelioration" of their lot.[26]

It is probable that many of the teachers would have agreed with the teacher who said, "our work is just as much a missionary work as if we were in India or China." [27] Another felt that the task was "more than Herculean." Important as the foreign missionary work of the churches was, the "Southern field" presented "a far more important and inviting theatre of Christian and benevolent operations than all foreign nations together. The greatness of the task could not be overestimated." [28]

Many of the teachers had been missionaries before the War. S. J. Whiton found the present field to compare unfavorably with "the dear mission work in Africa." [29] E. J. Adams, teacher at Beaufort, South Carolina, had been stationed at Mindi mission,

[25] Mrs. H. C. Foote, Augusta, Georgia, February 11, 1866, *ibid.,* X, 3 (March, 1866), 56.

[26] George L. German, Baltimore, Maryland, to O. O. Howard, June 3, 1867, B.R.F.A.L. MSS.

One young man observed, with Puritanical horror, that some of the women wore "nothing but an outside dress, and that full of holes." "I do not see how our civilization can bear the shocking sight," he said. John Oliver, Newport News, Virginia, July 6, 1862, *American Missionary,* VI, 8 (August, 1862), 185.

[27] Unnamed teacher, Beaufort, South Carolina, *ibid.,* VI, 6 (June, 1862), 137.

[28] H. H. Moore, Chaplain, and Superintendent of Education, State of Florida, to F. G. Shaw, President of the National Freedmen's Relief Association, January 1, 1866, *National Freedman,* II, 1 (January 15, 1866), 3–5.

[29] Fortress Monroe, Virginia, December 1, 1865, *American Missionary,* X, 1 (January, 1866), 5–6.

one of the leading American Missionary posts in Africa.[30] One of the most prominent men engaged in the work among the freedmen was Samuel C. Armstrong, founder of Hampton. He was the son of Richard Armstrong, Hawaiian missionary who had been sent out by the American Board of Missions.[31] J. P. Green and his sister, Mary E., who taught in a freedmen's school in Virginia, were the children of J. S. Green, veteran Hawaiian missionary.[32] Frederic Ayer, American Missionary Association teacher at Atlanta, Georgia, had served as a missionary among the Indians of the Northwest from 1843 until 1863. He maintained an Indian school at Ripley, Minnesota, until 1863.[33]

The teachers were, then, to use the words of a Freedmen's Bureau inspector, "a band of missionaries who have come from the Christian homes of the land—following the example of their Divine Master—going about doing good." [34] The editor of the *Congregationalist* praised them as missionaries "in the highest sense of the word." They braved great danger, "slander and vituperation" in order that they might initiate the Negro "into the mysteries of knowledge." [35] When the Boston teachers returned home in 1867 they were compared to the original Seventy whom Jesus sent out as missionaries, and their safe return from the great dangers and severe hardships of their work in the South was considered a direct fulfillment of the promise of Christ to the chosen few.[36]

The letters of the teachers make evident the fact that they were, with few exceptions, deeply religious individuals. Those accredited by the evangelical societies were possibly more vocal in the expression of their piety, but many of those sent out by other societies were also very devout. Many of these men and women were sincere, kindly individuals. Frequently, however, the teacher

---

[30] *Ibid.,* IX, 8 (August, 1865), 175.

[31] *Dictionary of American Biography,* I, 359–360.

[32] J. P. Green thought the Negroes as "much heathen as the Sandwich Islanders." Statement to Annual Meeting, American Missionary Association, Hopkinton, Massachusetts, October 21–22, 1863, *American Missionary,* VIII, 12 (December, 1863), 269, 273.

[33] *Ibid.,* XI, 11 (November, 1867), 257–258.

[34] John Bradshaw, Washington, D.C., to O. O. Howard, November 20, 1866, B.R.F.A.L. MSS.

[35] *Congregationalist,* April 9, 1868.

[36] *Independent,* July 25, 1867.

felt such deep sympathy for the Negro that he became a fanatical zealot, eager to become a martyr in a sacred cause. His sincerity and zeal were often so strong that he disregarded even the most fundamental rights of the Southern white people.

There were those, however, whose interests went beyond the purely religious into the field of what may be called, for lack of a better term, humanitarian effort. How many of the teachers should be placed in this category is, of course, a moot question. The assignment of the proper motive for an action is not an easy task, but the work of some of the teachers was patently of a different calibre from that of many of their fellows. For example, Laura M. Towne, Ellen Murray, Rachel Crane Mather, and Martha D. Schofield spent from thirty-eight to forty-five years among the Negroes, and E. A. Ware spent the last twenty years of his life in the work. They were interested in the physical, social, and cultural development of the Negro. They felt that religion in itself was not enough.

Miss Towne, famous as the founder of Penn School, St. Helena Island, South Carolina, was a native of Pennsylvania. Although she became "an ardent abolitionist" under the influence of the Rev. William Henry Furness [37] she seems to have been as deeply interested in the physical welfare of the Negro as in his moral development. She was a physician, and was particularly interested in the prevention and treatment of disease among the freedmen of the Sea Islands.

Miss Towne also attempted to protect the financial interests of the freedmen. She was secretary to E. L. Pierce, upon whom she evidently had great influence. She was a keen observer and noted that the basic reason for the criticism of those who directed the "Port Royal Experiment" was that they had been determined to "make the negroes show" what they could do "in the way of cotton, unwhipped." She felt great sympathy for the Negroes, who begged Pierce to let them plant corn and not cotton.[38]

Miss Towne and her associate, Ellen Murray, were sent to the

[37] Laura M. Towne, *Letters and Diary . . . Written from the Sea Islands of South Carolina, 1862–1884*, edited by R. S. Holland (Cambridge, 1912), x.

[38] *Ibid.*, 15, 18, 21, 55.

Sea Islands by the Pennsylvania Freedmen's Relief Association. Here they established the school known today as "Penn School." [39]

Rachel Crane Mather, of Boston, established a school at Beaufort, South Carolina, in 1868, in which she worked for thirty-six years. Mather School still serves the people in whom its founder was so deeply interested.[40] About 1848, at the time of her marriage, Mrs. Mather was a member of the South Boston Church, of which J. W. Alvord was pastor. After the death of her husband Mrs. Mather taught in the Bigelow School, Boston, until 1867, when she became an American Missionary Association teacher. She was deeply distressed over the poverty-stricken condition of the freedmen at Beaufort. Many were famishing. Scores, sometimes hundreds, came to her every day, begging food. She and her Northern friends gave as liberally as they could, but hundreds were faced with starvation. She used her salary in purchasing food, since she could not, she said, "send away these pitiful cadaverous looking people without giving them a few qts. or pints, of grits." [41]

Another teacher whose interests extended beyond the purely religious was Edmund Asa Ware, president of Atlanta University. Ware began his career in the South as agent of the American Union Commission at Nashville, Tennessee, where he went in 1865, two years after his graduation from Yale University.[42] He was principal of a high school at Nashville, where he met Clinton B. Fisk, and became interested in the education of the freedmen.[43] In 1866 Ware went to Atlanta as an agent of the American Mis-

[39] It is interesting to note that Francis R. Cope, Philadelphia merchant and insurance agent, member of the American Freedmen's Commission, the American Freedmen's Union Commission, and the Pennsylvania Freedmen's Relief Association, was financial agent for the Penn School. [*Letters and Diary*, 242, note.] Francis R. Cope, of Dimock, Pennsylvania, was, in 1936, Chairman of the Board of Trust of Penn School. [Penn Normal, Industrial and Agricultural School, *Annual Report, Seventy-Sixth Year, 1938* (St. Helena Island, South Carolina, 1938).] The editor of the *Letters and Diary* acknowledges his indebtedness to Francis R. Cope, Jr., and to C. Yarnall Abbott. Ellis Yarnall, of Germantown, Pennsylvania, was active in the early work among the freedmen, and the secretary of the Pennsylvania Abolition Society in 1938 was Florence P. Yarnall, of West Philadelphia, Pennsylvania. [Private correspondence.]

[40] Mather School, *Bulletin*, 1937, Mather School, Beaufort, South Carolina.

[41] Mrs. R. C. Mather, Beaufort, South Carolina, to J. W. Alvord, March 19, 1868, B.R.F.A.L. MSS.

[42] *American Union Commission: Its Origins* . . . , 9; *Dictionary of American Biography*, XIX, 446, 447.

[43] *National Cyclopaedia of American Biography*, V, 380.

sionary Association. In the same year he became a minister in the Congregational Church.[44] In 1867 he became principal of the Storrs School, the predecessor of Atlanta University. In 1867 he was appointed Superintendent of Schools for Georgia, under the Bureau of Refugees, Freedmen, and Abandoned Lands.[45] Ware became president of the newly incorporated Atlanta University in 1869, a position which he held until his death in 1885. His successor was Horace Bumstead, a classmate of his at Yale.[46]

Miss Towne, Ware, Bumstead, and Armstrong are examples of the highest type of Northern teacher. Highly educated, trained in the classics, philosophy, science, and music at Harvard, Yale, Dartmouth, the University of Michigan, and other schools; devout, sincere, idealistic, such men and women—and there were many of them—brought to the schools with which they were associated the very best of the Northern culture.

A study of the geographical distribution of the teachers reveals several interesting and suggestive facts. The homes of 1,035 teachers have been definitely located. Of this number the New England states contributed 496, or almost fifty per cent, Massachusetts "leading the van" with 260.[47]

In New England, Boston, Worcester, New Haven, Hartford, Nashua, and Providence show the heaviest concentration. Salem, Norwich, Barnet, Leominster, and many other towns and cities also sent teachers.

A close examination of the distribution pattern reveals a very high correlation between those cities from which teachers went to the South and "depots" or posts on the underground railroad. In Vermont, for example, of the eighteen towns from which teach-

---

[44] *Dictionary of American Biography*, XIX, 446, 447.
[45] Dr. R. G. Pope to E. A. Ware, September 2, 1867, B.R.F.A.L. MSS.
[46] *The Atlanta University Bulletin*, Catalog Number, 1937–1938, p. 15.
[47] The leading states are as follows:

Massachusetts	260
New York	183
Ohio	117
Connecticut	89
Pennsylvania	67
Maine	56
New Hampshire	49
Michigan	30
Vermont	29

ers went during the period 1862–1870, eleven were on main or
"trunk" lines of the underground railroad.[48] Of the remaining
seven, at least six are near the main routes and were strong abolitionist and underground centers as early as 1836. Since the routes
of the underground railroad were not absolutely definite it is logi-
cal to suppose that these six were as important as some of the
stations shown on the maps of the railroad.

For example, St. Johnsbury and Barnet, though not on the main
line from New Hampshire, are only a few miles from Lunenburg,
which was the terminus of the route up the Connecticut River. A
third town, Peacham, is about five miles from Barnet. The Barnet abolition society was one of the oldest in the state, being one of
three organized in 1833. A fourth town, Cuttingsville, is only six
miles from Wallingford, a station on the railroad, and East Poult-
ney is five miles from Fair Haven, which was an important station
on the Whitehall, New York-Rutland, Vermont, line. Here, as
early as 1830, fugitive slaves were rescued from officers who sought
to return them to their owners. Bridport is only fifteen miles
from Middlebury, which was "well supplied with abolitionists,"
and which became an important station as early as 1820. In 1837
the local abolition society contained 175 members. Since the
seventh town, Topsham, is only about fifteen miles from the Connecticut River, and on a direct road to Montpelier through Barre,
it is not illogical to assume that its citizens, too, had helped to
speed the fugitives along the North Star route to freedom.

This same pattern is apparent in Massachusetts and Connecticut. The "New England trunk line" of the underground railroad
seems to have been the Connecticut valley route.[49] Fugitives entered Connecticut from New York, via Norwalk and Danbury,
and followed the valley through Massachusetts into Vermont, and
thence to Canada. Abolitionist captains gave passage to fugitives,
who landed at New Haven, New London, New Bedford, Boston,
Salem, Gloucester, or Portland, where they were cared for by
local agents, and spirited away on the northern route. As is
shown on the accompanying map, in every case these routes, es-

[48] Wilbur H. Siebert, *Vermont's Anti-Slavery and Underground Railroad Record* (Columbus, Ohio, 1937).
[49] *Ibid.*

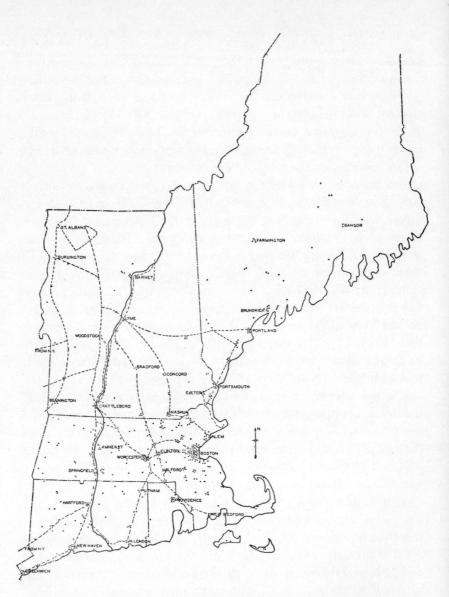

MAP OF NEW ENGLAND SHOWING HOMES OF TEACHERS AND PRINCIPAL UNDER-
GROUND RAILROAD ROUTES

tablished in the opening years of the century, traversed many towns which sent teachers to the South in the decade 1862–72.

It may be assumed, then, that many of those New England individuals who felt the call to service among the freed blacks came from localities in which abolitionist sentiment had been very strong during the period of controversy over the fugitive slave.

The lines of the underground railroad in New York cannot now be determined with great accuracy, but there were two principal routes, one leading up the Hudson and thence to Canada via Lake Champlain or Whitehall and Rutland, the other turning westward at Albany and following the Mohawk Valley to the Finger Lake region. Fugitives then crossed over into Canada at Oswego, Rochester, Parma, and other points. Doubtless there were connections with Binghamton, Elmira, and other towns in the southern part of the state and thus with stations in northern Pennsylvania.[50]

Although a map showing the location of teachers' homes in New York does not reveal the high correlation observed in New England, the heaviest concentration is in the vicinity of New York City, along the Hudson River, and westward through the Mohawk Valley to the Finger Lake region. Albany, Troy, Saratoga, Richfield, Utica, Syracuse, Auburn, Rochester, Ithaca, and many other towns sent teachers to work among the freedmen. All these cities and towns lie in the general region traversed by the New York lines of the underground railroad.

A much more interesting and significant condition is revealed, however, when this map of New York is compared with one showing New England settlement in the state. By 1820 the population of Central New York included many natives of New England. New England settlements extended in a wide belt across the center of the state from Troy to Rochester and Buffalo, with heavy concentration in north central and northwestern Pennsylvania.[51]

---

[50] See W. H. Siebert, *The Underground Railroad from Slavery to Freedom* (New York, 1899).

[51] Lois K. Mathews, *The Expansion of New England, the Spread of New England Settlement and Institutions to the Mississippi River, 1620–1865* (Boston, 1909), Chapter VI. See map, p. 168.

Practically all the towns which sent out teachers in the period 1862 to 1870 are located in the area of heavy New England settlement. From this area Charles Grandison Finney and Theodore Weld extended their influence over New York and the Middle West, here Gerrit Smith and John Brown planned their expedition for the release of the slaves, and from this area came strong supporters of feminism, socialism, temperance, and other movements for social reform. The residence in this area of the majority of the 183 teachers located in New York state conforms to a well established tradition.

This fact becomes even more interesting when the state of Ohio is examined. Ohio was so thoroughly covered by a network of underground railroad routes that it is impossible to trace all of them. Nor have all the teachers from Ohio been located. Of the 117 who have been located, however, seventy-eight were from towns in the Western Reserve, and fifteen from other centers of New England settlement. Thus, a total of ninety-three of 117 teachers from Ohio came from centers of heavy New England settlement. Among the towns sending teachers were Oberlin, Cleveland, Kent, Medina, Ashland, New Lyme, Kinsman, Sheffield, and Elyria.[52]

These facts suggest a pattern. In the first place, the majority of the teachers who have been located were natives of New England. Of a total of 1,035, New England supplied 496. Of this 496, Massachusetts and Connecticut account for 349. If, to the total for New England, are added the ninety-three who went out from New England settlements in Ohio, and the very large portion of the New York group of 183 (approximately 115), who were natives of the section settled by New England, it is seen that 704 of the total of 1,035 teachers now located were either from New England or from sections under the influence of the New England spirit. How many of the remaining 331 should be placed in this category cannot now be stated with certainty.

Also, it seems probable that the teachers who went South during the period 1862–1870 were simply carrying out a tradition of long standing, since they were, in most cases, natives of towns or

[52] See map in Mathews, *Expansion of New England,* 210.

regions in which the public sentiment was sufficiently abolitionist to support the operation of the underground railroad as early as the decade 1830–1840.

The abolitionist note is frequently struck in the letters of the teachers. "From a child I have heard my father pray for days like the present," wrote one teacher. No doubt it could have been said of many, as it was of two martyrs to the cause, that they were "descended from parents who warmly espoused the cause of the slave, even when most unpopular," and were the product of "early anti-slavery training." [53]

Occasionally a definite plea was made for teachers who were abolitionist in conviction and practice. In 1864 a correspondent from Louisiana plead with the American Missionary Association for teachers who had the courage of their abolitionist convictions.

We need teachers, men of the 'right stamp,' actuated by pure philanthropic motives—*working men*—men who *hate* slavery—ABOLITIONISTS! dyed with the pure dye—men who dare face this *miserable, wheedling conservatism,* and *do* something to merit at least the prevalent epithet '*nigger on the brain*'—men who can feel that they are in this work elevating in the scale of being and manhood those who, like themselves, were created in the likeness of God, *free* and EQUAL—men who can see in the *slave,* blinded with ignorance, . . . the future intelligent Christian *citizen.* . . . [54]

No doubt the sentiment of many teachers was expressed by Phillips Brooks when, in an address to a rally of the American Freedmen's Union Commission, at West Chester, Pennsylvania, he said that the members of the association had always considered slavery a "fearful wrong." Indeed, he said, they had been abolitionists since the cradle. They must now devote themselves to the task of "freeing those who, though personally free," were "yet slaves." [55]

Among the many prominent teachers with abolitionist background were Laura Smith Haviland, Susan Walker, Martha Schofield, and James Redpath. Miss Haviland was a member of the first anti-slavery society to be organized in the state of New

[53] *American Missionary,* IX, 8 (August, 1865), 175; *Freedmen's Record,* II, 9 (September, 1866), 161–162; *ibid.,* III, 5 (May, 1867), 71.
[54] Captain H. R. Pease, Port Hudson, Louisiana, *American Missionary,* VIII, 6 (June, 1864), 150. Pease later became Superintendent of Education for Mississippi.
[55] *Pennsylvania Freedman's Bulletin,* May, 1867, p. 3.

York.[56] She was an intimate friend of Levi and Catherine Coffin and of Josephine Griffing. Her home was a station on the underground railroad. During the war she was a nurse in the Federal army in the West. She assisted in the organization of the Freedmen's Relief Association of Detroit, and in 1864 became one of its agents. In this capacity she visited schools throughout the South. In 1866 she became a teacher for the American Missionary Association and was sent to Atlanta. E. M. Cravath, district superintendent for the A.M.A., sent her to Memphis, where she was placed in charge of the mission home. General Howard sent her to Charleston, but she soon returned to Adrian, Michigan, where she was associated with J. R. Shipherd and George Whipple, of the American Missionary Association, in the establishment of an orphan asylum.

Susan Walker, of Philadelphia, was sent to the Sea Islands by Secretary Chase. She was "a fervent abolitionist," well known "as an influential partisan, and an associate of Sumner, Andrew, Phillips, Garrison, and Greeley." [57]

Martha Schofield, one of the outstanding teachers of South Carolina, was also a native of Philadelphia. She had been "exposed to the exhortations of William Lloyd Garrison and his doctrines and had succumbed heart and soul" to abolitionism. Her last act before leaving New York for the South was to attend Plymouth Church where she heard an "excellent sermon" by Henry Ward Beecher.[58]

James Redpath was a native of Scotland who came to America in 1850. He was a "fiery abolitionist" and an energetic reformer. During the Kansas controversy he made several tours of the Territory and of the South, and in 1859 he published two works, *The Roving Editor, or Talks with Slaves in the Southern States,* and *Handbook to Kansas Territory.* He was also the author of

56 Laura S. Haviland, *A Woman's Life-work, Labors and Experiences of Laura S. Haviland* (Chicago, 1887), 32.

57 Susan Walker, "Journal of Miss Susan Walker, March 3–June 6, 1862," edited by H. N. Sherwood, *Quarterly Publications of the Historical and Philosophical Society of Ohio,* VII (January–March, 1912), introductory note, 4.

58 Katherine Smedley, The Northern Teacher on the South Carolina Sea Islands (unpublished M.A. thesis, University of North Carolina, 1932), 31.

The Public Life of Captain John Brown and *Echoes of Harper's Ferry*.

In 1859 Redpath became Haitian commissioner of immigration in the United States. He established the Haitian Emigrant Bureau, with offices in Boston and New York, and was instrumental in the migration of several thousand Negroes from the United States to Haiti.[59] At the close of the war Redpath became Superintendent of Education in Charleston, South Carolina. Here he established a home for Negro orphans, the "Col. Shaw Orphan House" at the home of "Mr. Ross, fugitive slaveholder." Redpath was assisted by his son, D. C. Redpath, Dr. Hawks, Reuben Tomlinson, and Gilbert Pillsbury.[60]

Many of the teachers went South for their health. They believed that the warmer climate of the South would prove beneficial, and so sought positions in the freedmen's schools. Obviously no definite statement can be made as to the number of teachers who actually went South for this reason, but the American Missionary Association received so many applications from such people that it was necessary to publish a warning: "This is not a hygienic association, to help invalids try a change of air, or travel at others' expense." [61]

J. W. Alvord frequently received applications from those who wished to "try a change of air." One young woman, whose parents had died of tuberculosis, desired to go to the deep South. She believed her health would be aided by the Southern climate. "My physicians," she said, "have thought *me* disposed to a scrofulous habit, yet now I seem to be dropsical." [62] Another applicant wrote, "I care not how far South I might be sent for my constitution is not of the strongest, and a warmer climate would be bene-

[59] *Dictionary of American Biography*, XV, 443–444.

[60] *National Freedman*, I, 7 (August 15, 1865), 211–213. Redpath was the founder of the famous Redpath's Chautauqua or Lyceum Bureau. Among his clients were Emerson, Greeley, Thoreau, Sumner, Phillips, Julia Ward Howe, and Henry Ward Beecher. [*Dictionary of American Biography*, XV, 443–444.] Beecher was an intimate friend. During the Beecher-Tilton scandal Redpath telegraphed Beecher in Latin, for secrecy. He paid Beecher at the rate of $1,000 per lecture. Paxton Hibben, *Henry Ward Beecher, an American Portrait* (New York, 1927), 309, 325.

[61] *American Missionary*, X, 7 (July, 1866), 152–153.

[62] Mary L. Humaston, Windsor, New York, to J. W. Alvord, August 10, 1867, B.R.F.A.L. MSS.

ficial." [63]   A Pennsylvania applicant simply did not like the climate of that state. He had been teaching in Pennsylvania for twenty-five years, and now desired a position in a Negro school.[64]

Instead of health, many of the teachers found death in the South, some from malaria, some from tuberculosis, some from accident, others from a variety of diseases. William S. Clark, Boston teacher at Port Royal, died of tuberculosis. Francis E. Barnard, St. Helena Island, died in 1862, of malaria or sun stroke. Samuel D. Phillips and Daniel Bowe also died in service.[65] Bowe's fiancée went to South Carolina after his death and took charge of his school. Mrs. N. C. Dennett, daughter of Secretary S. S. Jocelyn of the A.M.A., taught in Florida from 1863 until her marriage, in 1866, to the cashier of the Freedmen's Savings Bank of Jacksonville. She died February 1, 1868, after childbirth.[66] Numerous additional instances might be given.

Some teachers came South for financial reasons. The salary of a teacher, while not extremely high, was attractive, especially to any individual who had not been very successful in the ordinary channels of business. In the first years of the work salaries varied, but in 1866 the various societies fixed the minimum salary at thirty-five dollars per month. The New England Society paid some of its teachers as high as one thousand dollars per year.[67] Many teachers organized "pay schools" charging from twenty-five cents to one dollar per month per pupil. Thus a school of fifty to one hundred and fifty pupils might be quite profitable.

Superintendent Alvord constantly received applications from individuals who desired to recoup their fortunes by teaching in Negro schools. For example, when John Waldo, of Boston, was dismissed by the Mission House, of Boston, in which he had been employed for ten years, he applied to Alvord. He had tried to secure a position in a bank but had failed.[68] H. Clay Smith, em-

[63] Hattie E. Hatch, Woodstock, Vermont, June 19, 1866, to "National Freedmen's Bureau," B.R.F.A.L. MSS.
[64] William Job, Wernersville, Pennsylvania, to J. W. Alvord, December, 1867, B.R.F.A.L. MSS.
[65] Pierce, "The Freedmen at Port Royal," *Atlantic Monthly,* XII (September, 1863), 299, 300.
[66] *American Missionary,* XII, 3 (March, 1868), 63.
[67] Chapin, History, B.R.F.A.L. MSS.
[68] John Waldo to J. W. Alvord, February 12, 1867, B.R.F.A.L. MSS.

ployee of the United States Sanitary Commission, had a sister who desired a place in the freedmen's schools.[69] Miss Arabella Merrill, well educated spinster of forty years, had no other means of earning a livelihood and must have a position in a freedmen's school.[70] Miss Mary Hatch, of Washington, was the sole support of a sister and a widowed mother. A position in the freedmen's schools would enable her to support them.[71]

That such applications were not confined to the office of Superintendent Alvord is adequately demonstrated by the admonition of the American Missionary Association that no teachers need apply who wished to go South because they had been unsuccessful in business in the North.[72]

Many of the teachers had been soldiers, chaplains, doctors, and nurses, during the war. Some had entered the army because of their abolitionist convictions. Further service in behalf of the Negro was to them a golden opportunity. Others saw in this work a means of support, now that their military service was at an end. For example, S. C. Armstrong, founder of Hampton, was Colonel of the Ninth Regiment, U.S.C.T. Horace Bumstead was a major in the Forty-third Massachusetts Regiment, U.S.C.T. J. Milton Hawks was a surgeon in the Twenty-first Regiment, U.S.C.T. His wife, Esther H. Hawks, was also a physician, and a nurse. Hawks became an agent of the Freedmen's Bureau, and Mrs. Hawks taught in freedmen's schools in South Carolina and Florida.[73] Walter McDonald, a disabled Federal soldier, a native of Maine, remained in Georgia after the war, married a Southern woman, and supported himself by teaching white children, then Negro children, under the Freedmen's Bureau and the American Missionary Association.[74] O. L. Andrews, a New York veteran

[69] W. F. Bascom, U. S. Sanitary Commission, to O. O. Howard, March 11, 1867, B.R.F.A.L. MSS.

[70] N. P. Kemp, American Tract Society, Boston, to J. W. Alvord, July 7, 1869, B.R.F.A.L. MSS.

[71] J. R. Evans [?] to O. O. Howard, June 13, 1867, B.R.F.A.L. MSS.

[72] *American Missionary*, X, 7 (July, 1866), 152–153.

[73] Hawks MSS., Library of Congress. Mrs. Hawks was an advocate of woman suffrage, a member of the executive committee of the American Woman Suffrage Association, vice-president of the Equal Rights Association of Florida, and a member of the Women's Loyal National League. See Stanton, *History of Woman Suffrage*, II, 381, 765.

[74] W. L. Clarke to E. A. Ware, September 14, 1868, B.R.F.A.L. MSS.

who lost a leg in the war, taught at Cleveland, Tennessee, at a salary of twenty-five dollars per month.[75] E. M. Cravath, field secretary of the American Missionary Association and one of the founders of Fisk University, was a chaplain in the 101st Regiment, Ohio Volunteers.[76] The teacher who opened the first school at Edisto Island, South Carolina, was a nurse, the wife of Surgeon Wright of the Thirty-second Regiment, U.S.C.T.[77] The principal of the Freedmen's Institute, Jackson, Mississippi, had been a soldier in the Federal army.[78]

It is probable that many of the teachers were moved by a love of adventure, a desire to visit strange and new places. Others may have been moved by curiosity. At least one lady went South in order to collect material for a book.[79]

The forces which impelled the Yankee teachers to go South were, then, religious and humanitarian interest and abolitionist experience, desire for improvement of financial status, search for health, previous vocational connections, and love of adventure.

The correspondence of the Yankee teachers indicates that the majority went South with little knowledge of the social order which had existed there. Their knowledge seems to have been derived from abolition literature. Further, they believed that the people of the South had sinned, both in holding to that abominable institution, slavery, and in rebelling against the Union. The slaves had been freed and the Union saved by the Christian valor and fortitude of "the army of blue-coated heroes." The people of the South were not only sinners, but defeated sinners, who refused to be properly humble and abject, and who, worst of all, refused to repent of the error of their ways. Many of the teachers felt that everything which was, or had been, was wrong and must be uprooted and discarded. The Southern people, defeated and recalcitrant rebels, had forfeited all claim to individual or group consideration. The humanitarianism and love of individual rights

---

[75] *American Freedman*, I, 10 (January, 1867), 147.
[76] *Dictionary of American Biography*, IV, 516.
[77] *National Freedman*, I, 2 (March 1, 1865), 49.
[78] *Ibid.*, I, 9 (October 15, 1865), 266.
[79] Towne, *Letters and Diary*, 15. Mrs. A. M. French, whose book was published under the title, *Slavery in South Carolina and the Ex-Slaves, or the Port Royal Mission* (New York, 1862).

of the teacher did not extend to the Southerner. Many of the teachers seem to have been completely detached from the world in which the white Southerner lived. They looked upon the Southerners as some peculiar species to be examined, questioned, or disregarded.

This attitude was, of course, almost inevitable. Psychologically, the average teacher was incapable of calm consideration or of restraint. Highly emotional, he saw only two colors—white and black. He represented the forces of God, the Southerner the minions of Satan. His strongly religious mentality, stirred to its depths by the abolition crusade and the intense excitement of a long and bitter war, which had been waged for a purpose which he held most dear, rejoiced in the fact that the hosts of Satan had been confounded. It would have been too much to expect of human nature that the teachers should have gone into the South with any other attitude. Fanatics, zealots, they were; their fanaticism was the flower of tradition, long training, psychological conditioning, and sectional bitterness and misunderstanding.

The teachers considered themselves the spiritual followers of the armies of Grant and Sherman. "The army of blue-coated heroes who had marched down to battle with so lofty a courage," wrote one of the teachers, "was succeeded by the army of 'Yankee school mams,' armed with the Bible and spelling-book, who invaded the South in as genuine a spirit of heroism as the grand army of pioneers who had led the way. . . ." [80] What the sword had conquered the school must now make secure. The work of the teachers was the culmination, the climax, of a long struggle between the forces of light and of darkness. The nation was passing through a crisis which "began with the attack on Sumter, culminated in the surrender of Lee, and [would] close with the complete reconstruction, social and civil," of the Southern states. The education of the freedmen was considered to be the first essential of the new regime. [81] The "second stage" of the "great conflict" which had torn the nation for seventy-five years, the conflict between "Civilization and Barbarism," had now been reached.

[80] Linda Warfel Slaughter, *The Freedmen of the South* (Cincinnati, 1869), 110.
[81] *Independent,* November 1, 1866.

There must be no flagging of determination. Many years of work were yet necessary before "complete moral, as well as political, reconstruction [could] be effected." The South must be free for the travel and settlement of "the reddest Republican" or "the blackest Abolitionist," and "the political rights of the blackest man" must be "put on a level with the whitest." If loyal citizens carried out their duties, they would live to see "the face of Southern society gradually change." Barbarism would "gradually disappear," and "one common civilization" would "cover the land as the waters cover the sea." [82]

Where the loyal soldier had planted the bayonet, the loyal teacher now planted the institutions of the Union, and where he had waved the sword, the teacher now waved the primer. [83] Only through the school could the North "hope to redeem and regenerate the South." There must be a " 'Yankee school' in every Southern county," so that the people of the South would, in the future, "march arm in arm with Massachusetts," declared a Massachusetts newspaper. [84] By means of schools the New England leaven was now to transform "the whole lump of Southern ignorance and prejudice." [85] Although slavery had been overthrown, the great problem was as yet unsolved. The Negro must be taught the "intelligent use of the ballot," declared an official of the A.M.A. [86] In *"no other way"* could so much good be done "for reconstruction and freedom" as by supporting the societies who were sending "thorough, Christian, Yankee teachers" to the South. [87] In this way the "power that had its germ in the Mayflower" would go to work on Southern soil, and "learning and religion" would walk "arm in arm about the land" spreading "light and salvation." [88]

At a meeting of the National Teachers Association, at Harrisburg, Pennsylvania, in 1865, the President of the Association de-

[82] Editorial, *Independent,* October 22, 1868.
[83] See speech of T. W. Higginson in introducing Governor Hawley, of Connecticut. *Independent,* June 21, 1866.
[84] Boston *Advertiser,* in *Freedmen's Record,* II, 9 (September, 1866), 159.
[85] B. F. Whittemore, Assistant Superintendent of Education, South Carolina, *Freedmen's Record,* III, 4 (April, 1867), 61.
[86] M. E. Strieby, *Independent,* September 24, 1868.
[87] "Zed," in *Congregationalist,* November 28, 1867.
[88] L. C. Lockwood, Macon, Georgia, April 15, 1868, *Congregationalist,* April 30, 1868.

clared that the teachers of the nation were now given a glorious opportunity. The people of the South must be educated, he said.

Let us buckle on the armor, and meet the new exigency of our times. Before the war no Northern teacher dared to discuss the whole truth at the South. In morals there must be one code for the North and another for the South. There could be no free discussions in all our political contests. Southern men could come before a Northern audience and speak their sentiments freely, even vilify with impunity our ways and institutions, but the instant a Northern man attempted at the South to utter sentiments at all condemnatory of Southern institutions or Southern life, he was forced to leave the country. . . . *I pray God, that martial law may prevail in every Southern State* till Northern men may discuss educational, political, social, moral, and religious topics in every part of the South as freely as in Faneuil Hall.[89]

At another meeting President C. G. Finney, of Oberlin College, from which many teachers came, said: "The efforts of the humane should never cease, until the emancipated are rewarded for their toil by being put in possession of so much of the soil of the South, for ages moistened by their blood and tears, as would be necessary for their support." [90]

It was to be expected that the teachers would find fault with the South, that everything should have been wrong. The fact that they held such opinions is, in itself, not important. Their attitude becomes important only when it is considered in relation to their work. By their attitudes they, at the outset, destroyed any possibility of securing co-operation, or even acquiescence, from the Southern whites. As they pushed into the interior of the South, and as their influence among the Negroes became increasingly evident, and the ends toward which their educational program was directed became clear, they forfeited even the toleration with which they had been met, and the Southerners turned to social ostracism, persecution, and open violence.

There were, no doubt, teachers who did not hold such opinions, but many were in agreement. For example, E. S. Philbrick, as he approached the shore of South Carolina, wrote his wife that while even "Egypt was sufficiently enterprising to line its coast

[89] *Nation*, August 24, 1865, p. 225. Italics in original.
[90] "Jubilee meeting at Oberlin," *American Missionary*, VII, 2 (February, 1863), 35.

with windmills," South Carolina had "not yet arrived at a state of civilization sufficiently advanced to provide" them.[91] Yet, four days later, he was writing:

Our quarters are in a very fine house in the east end of town, bordering on the river. . . . There is something very sad about these fine deserted homes. Ours has Egyptian marble mantels, gilt cornice and center-piece in parlor, and bath-room, with several wash-bowls set in different rooms. The force-pump is broken and all the bowls and their marble slabs smashed to get out the plated cocks. . . . The officers saved a good many pianos and other furniture and stored it in the jail, for safe-keeping. But we kindle our fires with chips of polished mahogany, and I am writing on my knees with a piece of flower-stand across them for a table, sitting on my camp bed-stead.[92]

From Norfolk the wife of a prominent school official wrote that she and her family had moved into the home of a rebel who had run the blockade to Richmond, leaving his furniture. "It is impossible," she said "to describe the anger of the secesh neighbors to think that 'these detestable nigger-teachers' should occupy the house of their friend . . . and walk on her tapestry carpets, and drink out of her China cups. . . . But we dwell securely in the midst of our enemies." [93]

In similar vein, another teacher wrote:

Mrs. —— and family occupy a part of this house (their former home) with us. They are as rank rebels at heart as ever, as indeed nearly all who return are. The idea of having 'Nigger' schools and meetings in their own house, is terrible to them, and nothing but fear of the authorities keeps them from violence. I did waste some sympathy upon them when they came back so destitute and apparently humbled, and I thought of their great fall from wealth and splendor to poverty, but since I have seen more of their hearts, and their deadly hatred of our Government, that is all gone, and I now think the Government cannot deal too severely with them.[94]

The attitude of many of the teachers is well expressed in a letter from a Virginia teacher to the *Independent*. When she went South in 1865 she was "disposed to be generous to the Southern

[91] March 6, 1862. Elizabeth Ware Pearson, *Letters from Port Royal, Written at the Time of the Civil War* (Boston, 1906), 5.

[92] *Ibid.*, 7–8.

[93] Mrs. J. M. Coan, Norfolk, Virginia, November 28, 1863, *American Missionary*, VIII, 1 (January, 1864).

[94] *Ibid.*, IX, 9 (September, 1865), 197–198.

people," she said. Her heart was "full of forgiving pity and yearning sympathy." She was prepared to do everything for them that she could do "without violating conscience." She soon learned, however, that the Southern people "would accept no sympathy that was not founded on the acknowledgement that right was, and always had been, on their side." Not finding the people properly humble, she soon realized that "the nigger teacher must take her place, in Southern estimation, by the side of the 'nigger.' " [95]

Even the "carelessness and neglect" apparent in the Southern villages "grated harshly" upon "New England ideas of order and thrift." [96] Everything was disorderly and dirty. "Dilapidated fences, tumble-down outbuildings, untrimmed trees with lots of dead branches, weedy walks and gardens and a general appearance of *un*thrift" were characteristics of even the best of Southern towns, according to one teacher.[97] "It is a peculiarity of this region," wrote another, "a part of its former institutions, nothing can ever be provided before it is absolutely needed in order that patience may have its perfect work perhaps." There were no locks or bars on the doors, and no place but the chimney corner for wood. " 'The barbarism of Slavery everywhere,' trumpet tongued, proclaims against every form of progress, and hugs the chains that limit it," was her rather bombastic observation.[98] There were many things to be done, things which had been neglected by "these folks" who did not know how to "work our way." [99] The houses must be scrubbed, polished, painted, "for the 'chivalry' look not to *corners* and *cupboards*," wrote another teacher. "They leave this to the poor despised 'mudsie' of the north. Such a kitchen as supplied the luxurious tables would nowhere else be suffered. Bah! *what* filth—years only could have *so matured* it." [100] The people of the South were "deluded," a "century behind the times." Great effort would be necessary if they were to be correctly taught.[101]

---

[95] *Independent*, April 16, 1868, p. 5.
[96] New York *Daily Tribune*, February 3, 1866.
[97] Pearson, *Letters*, 7.
[98] Susan Walker, "Journal," 25.
[99] Smedley, The Northern Teacher, 42, citing Schofield, Diary, March 4, 1865.
[100] Susan Walker, "Journal," 14–15.
[101] S. K. Whiting, *National Freedman*, I, 11 (December 15, 1865), 349–350.

"The chivalry," wrote a North Carolina teacher, "stand at the corner of the streets in blissful idleness from morning till night. Of the ladies of the town we see very little. They spend the greater portion of their time in listless seclusion, mourning over the hopeless state which has overthrown their pet institution and substituted for the slave mart and its attendant honors our peaceful school for the freedmen." [102]

Of Yorktown another teacher wrote: "How strangely old-fashioned everything appears there. It seems as if the place had been fossilized at the surrender of Cornwallis. Were it situated in the North, there would be a towering monument of that crowning event in our Revolutionary history, now the spot where the sword was delivered up is altogether a matter of supposition." [103]

At Norfolk, Virginia, the teachers established a school on the farm of Governor Wise. Each Negro man was given a house and eight acres of land, and was "drilled in the use of arms," that he might "hold as well as till the soil." "We have organized an interesting school in the dining-room of Gov. Wise's house!" wrote one of the teachers. "Here, where treason was talked over and toasts drunk to the success of the traitors, we every day hear sung the famous John Brown song. We lack one thing; the young folks want very much to see the likeness of the old hero. Can't some kind friend send us one to be *hung* on the wall of our school-room?" [104]   At a later date, he wrote, "On one of the panes of glass in this mansion . . . cut, I suppose, with a diamond, is 'J. S. Wise, April, 1861,' on another 'Jeff Davis,' and on another a profile, with the words near it 'Jeff Davis.' So you see what sort of people formerly occupied these rooms." [105]

A school was also established at the summer home of John Tyler. "His once outraged victims now live securely on his premises, and learn to read the word of God while his proud mansion is

[102] New York *Daily Tribune,* February 3, 1866.
[103] L. C. Lockwood, Tyler House, Fortress Monroe, Virginia, October 27, 1862, *American Missionary,* VI, 12 (December, 1862), 277.
[104] W. S. Bell, December 7, 1863, *ibid.,* VIII, 2 (February, 1864), 37.
[105] December 20, 1863, *ibid.*

the home of missionaries and teachers for the freedmen," commented one observer.[106]

One of the leading teachers of Tennessee declared "THE REBELS look upon us with jealous eyes, and still aver that these 'Niggers' 'can't learn.' But it is not beyond even the probabilities, in my opinion, that *their children,* if taught at all, will be taught by colored teachers before ten years has elapsed." [107]

The teachers were horrified by the poverty of the South. "It is startling to measure the real *poverty* of the South," said one. "We have nothing like it in the North; we never have had anything like it. . . . The planters have literally nothing left, save the bare land. But the people are not more poor than they are rebellious." [108] A Georgia teacher wrote her sister that she should be thankful that she was

not a poor *secesh* lady, going about peddling your old 'before the war' clothes, as I often see them doing here, and trying to get plain sewing of the 'Yankee' ladies. Alas! for the poor F.F.G's. What a *glorious* fall they have had—while the 'unbleached American Nobility' are on the topmost round of Fortune's ladder! I am just at this time feeling as if it would be pleasant, had I the power, and an *iron heel* strong enough, to grind every one of the Secessionists deep into the earth. I am feeling more than usually *ugly* toward them as I have just received a visit from an 'Aunty' who has been telling me how our Union prisoners were treated. . . . Tell my friends I am a four-fold Abolitionist. I have seen the effect of slavery in all its forms.[109]

Some of the teachers were especially bitter. One diatribe reveals a strong undercurrent of personal animosity:

What a magnificent revenge Massachusetts has now an opportunity to have upon South Carolina, and especially Boston upon Charleston, for all the sneers and insults heaped upon them by this Southern State and city, —for the expulsion of Judge Hoar, for the betrayal of Daniel Webster, for the beating of Charles Sumner, and for the numberless indignities which the oligarchs of Carolina have delighted to cast upon the sons of the old Bay State.

Oh for one hour of the wizard's cunning, to evolve the spirit of Calhoun

[106] S. S. Jocelyn, *ibid.,* VII, 9 (September, 1863), 202–205.
[107] John Ogden, Fisk University, February 29, 1868, *ibid.,* XII, 5 (May, 1868), 103.
[108] Mobile, Alabama, January 15, 1868, *ibid.,* XII, 3 (March, 1868), 60.
[109] Savannah, Georgia, April 12, 1865, *ibid.,* IX, 6 (June, 1865), 123.

from the trance of death, and show him the thronging thousands of the people he despised as brutes, crowding around the school-house doors. . . .

And then to show him the stores of goods sent down from the friendly hands busied around countless firesides at the North, proving that love is the inspiration of liberty, and *brotherhood* the basis of Christian civilization.

And then to tell him that these things come from the New England which he hated; from Boston, which he reviled; and from the abolitionists whom he detested; and that this is the answer Massachusetts makes to South Carolina.

Would this punishment be too severe even for his crimes? Not greater at any rate than that which his *misguided disciples* are suffering here every day. . . .[110]

Not all the teachers looked upon the South with such a completely disapproving eye. One South Carolina teacher was charmed with the South, particularly the picturesque beauty of the pines, Spanish moss, and luxuriant flowers. The Negroes she also found interesting. "The negroes," she wrote, "sang to us in their wild way as they rowed us across—I cannot give you the least idea of it. Indeed, I can't give you the least idea of anything, and you must not expect it." [111]

There were others to whom the strangeness and beauty of the Southern landscape appealed. One teacher extravagantly praised Roanoke Island:

I wish I could transmit to you, even the faintest conception of the beauty of our island in its 'living green.' I can but wonder how any could ever call it desolate. The air is heavy with the fragrance of magnolias, azaleas, and the wisteria; the forests are one vast conservatory where towering mounds of snowy dogwood—the yellow jasmine and scarlet honeysuckle neighbor with or festoon the sturdy oak or sombre pine.

The velvet carpeting of the marshes almost rivals the rainbow with its mosaic of saracenia, lillies [*sic*] and the emblematic Fleur-de-lis.[112]

A very remarkable attitude toward the South was expressed in a statement of the Rev. Crammond Kennedy, corresponding secretary of the New York Branch of the American Freedmen's Commission. Kennedy's statement follows.

[110] James P. Blake, Charleston, South Carolina, March 29, 1865, *Freedmen's Record*, I, 5 (May, 1865), 76.

[111] Pearson, *Letters*, 19.

[112] Ella Roper, Roanoke Island, April 20, 1865, *American Missionary*, IX, 7 (July, 1865), 157–158.

Before we can appreciate the Southern estimate of our work, we must consider the state of Southern society; the South, as far as her male population, is the disbanded remains of a defeated army; and her women have scarcely ceased nursing their wounded. . . . The effects of an enthusiasm made devotion by unparalleled sufferings . . . and of four years experience of 'Federals' with rifles and torches cannot be counteracted in a day. Bereavement is universal. It seemed to me that all the females of every congregation with whom I worshipped were in mourning. . . .

Many of my own friends, who were rolling in luxury before the war, have no carpets on their floors, scarcely bedding enough to keep them warm. . . .

The freed people never believed in their freedom until they had packed up their rags and swarmed from the old plantation into the adjacent villages, towns, and cities.

All these things . . . should be considered in order to account for the hatred of everything Northern which burns in many. . . . It is very easy for us to philosophize, victorious as we are, and especially as our houses are standing, our children comfortable and at school . . . and only a fourth cousin or so, among the missing.

Lastly, and by no means least, *they are suspicious of Yankees;* and I must confess that their experience of some poor specimens, both lay and clerical . . . who enriched themselves as a war measure with everything portable, was not calculated to give a better impression. All the professed Christians with whom I conversed on the subject of negro education, indorsed our attempt, and believed it of the most valuable assistance to themselves, but I am sorry to say that few of them treat our teachers with anything but studious avoidance. I met with some good-hearted men, of no church connections, who were desirous of schools in their neighborhood, or on their plantations, and would welcome the teachers.

Those of the more intelligent of the Southerners who are not thoroughly disheartened . . . are at least *tolerant* of our work. Some of them will speak warmly of it. . . . After a tour through Virginia, North Carolina, South Carolina, three of the Sea Islands, Georgia and Tennessee, I am prepared to say, *all things considered* the attitude of the South to our work is as favorable as we could expect. It is incorrect . . . that no Southern white woman will teach negro children. There are such to my certain knowledge . . . in the Normal School in Charleston, South Carolina, and the Baptist Sabbath School in Raleigh, North Carolina. None speak more contemptuously of 'the nigger' and his 'school-ma'am' than too many of the Northern merchants and speculators in the South.[113]

[113] Crammond Kennedy, *National Freedman,* I, 10 (November 15, 1865), 237–238. Kennedy was a native of Scotland, a famous preacher of New York, and chaplain of the Seventy-ninth New York,—"The Highlanders." Appleton's *Cyclopaedia of American Biography* (8 vols., New York, 1887–1918), III, 516.

The attitude of the teacher toward the Negro was a continuation of the traditional abolitionist, equalitarian, individualist philosophy. A man was an individual, and his color or race must not be considered. Every trace of racial distinction must be eradicated. The terms "freedman" and "Negro" must be dropped from the national vocabulary. Individuals must be considered simply as individuals, as component units of society, as brothers in the great family, not as members of races, classes, or groups. The humanitarian and educational work of the various societies must deal simply with *"men,* as fellow creatures, fellow citizens, or fellow members of the household of faith." The teacher must "educate not whites nor blacks specifically, but all men equally as members of the same great commonwealth." [114]

This attitude had neither its origin nor its termination in the mind of the Northern teacher. The controversy between the advocates of "racial distinction," or "racial discrimination," and those who bitterly oppose either distinction or discrimination has remained to trouble the relations of the Negro and his white neighbors.

Practically all the teachers seem to have agreed that the Negro was very intelligent and that he learned very quickly. One declared that his "sable friends" journeyed up "the hill difficulty . . . quite as rapidly as our *white* boys and girls." [115] Another declared that if there was any difference in intellect between the Negroes and the whites of Virginia, "the advantage is on the side of the colored people." [116] A third said that the Negroes of Virginia were far more intelligent than the whites. [117] The general opinion seems to have been that the Negro children compared favorably with white children of the North, the older pupils learning even more rapidly than white children because they put forth more effort. [118]

---

[114] Joseph P. Thompson, *Congregationalist,* February 27, 1868.

[115] H. R. Smith, Norfolk, Virginia, November 5, 1864, *Freedmen's Journal (Record),* I, 1 (January, 1865), 5.

[116] J. B. Lowry, Yorktown, May 19, 1863, *American Missionary,* VII, 7 (July, 1863), 160.

[117] S. K. Whiting, *National Freedman,* I, 11 (December 15, 1865), 349–350.

[118] Clara B. Kimball, Beaufort, South Carolina, *American Missionary,* IX, 8 (August, 1865), 175; Mary T. Root, Beaufort, South Carolina, *ibid.,* VII, 4 (April, 1863), 90; W. R. Smith, Portsmouth, Virginia, *ibid.,* VII, 6 (June, 1863), 137.

There were some teachers whose enthusiasm led them to make statements so extreme as to raise doubt as to the value of their letters as evidence. One said that in twenty years experience in the schools of Massachusetts and New York he had never seen such "rapid advances made in reading and spelling" as had been made in his school. "The blessing of God seems to be again descending upon the people here," he said.[119] Another asserted that "no class of human beings" had ever developed faster, "in every desireable [*sic*] sense," than the freedmen. "No children learn faster, and but few so fast as these poor plantation children," he wrote.[120] Such statements as these were common:

After several years spent in teaching in *white* schools at the North, I feel no hesitation in saying that these children learn the alphabet, the figures and rudiments of arithmetic, more readily than the whites.[121]

In seven years of teaching at the North, I have not seen a parallel to their appetite for learning, and their active progress.[122]

I have taught white pupils for the last twelve years . . . and never did I see more rapid progress in any school.[123]

In some ten year's experience in the schools of my native state I have never seen greater advancement in the same time. I have never known children commit to memory more readily.[124]

One teacher, who evidently had come into contact with a skilled trader, assured her friends in the North that the "African brethren" were quite capable of caring for themselves. "They are exceedingly keen in their financial calculations. A Wall street broker would scarcely get ahead of some of them," she said.[125] The Negro studied arithmetic in order to avoid being cheated in business and to learn to detect counterfeit money, said another.[126] One admitted that the Negro might be lazy and grasping, but

[119] H. S. Beals, Portsmouth, Virginia, November 30, 1863, *ibid.,* VIII, 1 (January, 1864), 15.

[120] George Candee, St. Louis, Missouri, *ibid.,* VIII, 1 (January, 1864), 17.

[121] Mrs. M. W. Wheeler, Harper's Ferry, Virginia, May 31, 1864, *ibid.,* VIII, 7 (July, 1864), 175.

[122] Miss Root, Andersonville, Georgia, *ibid.,* XI, 3 (March, 1867), 52–53.

[123] Emily Stuart, Vaughan Farm, Virginia, December 2, 1864, *ibid.,* IX, 2 (February, 1865), 37.

[124] Joseph Beardsly, Baton Rouge, Louisiana, February 15, 1865, *ibid.,* IX, 4 (April, 1865), 75–76.

[125] Miss S. Drummond, Portsmouth, Virginia, June 1, 1863, *ibid.,* VII, 7 (July, 1863), 159.

[126] L. C. Lockwood, *Independent,* February 5, 1863.

asserted that the white man was not less so. The tendency toward greed and aggressiveness should be encouraged, as an evidence of the ability of the Negro to take care of himself. Now that he was "relieved from the necessity of supporting [his] master's family" he should be given an opportunity to show what he could do.[127] Their real ability was not understood, even at the North. In fact, they were the equals, if not the superiors, of even the Northern whites, so great was their mental capacity and energy.[128]

Contact with them was stimulating in the extreme. The work was "wholly absorbing," yet even that phrase was inadequate to express the intensity with which mind and soul engaged in the work. Every day revealed some new development of character, some new flash of nobility in the Negro. The Negro had attained a higher moral and spiritual level, a "purer and more vital" nature, than the white. He was unspoiled by civilization. God had richly endowed him, and his nature would expand to a wondrous beauty under "a tender and general culture." The teacher was conscious of a strong "sense of obligation to devote every mental and physical power" to teaching the Negro, and many were determined to "consecrate the brief years of a lifetime" to this work.[129]

These were the expressions of theoretical abolitionists, whose contact with the Negro had been either entirely vicarious, or had been confined to aiding some fugitive in his effort to escape. An awakening was inevitable. No group, whatever its merits, powers, or potentialities, could have realized the expectations of the radical abolitionists. No large group of white people, North or South, could have measured up to the standard which they set. Certainly it was not to be expected that the Negro, who had lived only a few generations in America, could have reached that standard.

Gradually, as continued contact forced upon them the realization that they had overestimated the Negro, the teachers began

---

[127] Susan Walker, "Journal," 30. Miss Walker added, "We need have no fear that they will not more than support themselves. Of course Government will not expect to *make anything out of them* this year." Italics in the "Journal."

[128] James A. McCrea, Beaufort, South Carolina, January 1, 1863, *American Missionary*, VII, 4 (April, 1863), 87.

[129] Mary C. Fletcher, Norfolk, Virginia, *Freedmen's Journal*, I, 1 (January, 1865), 5–6; Storrow Higginson, *ibid.*, 11; Sara G. Stanley, Norfolk, Virginia, *American Missionary*, IX, 2 (February, 1865), 36–37.

reluctantly to admit their error. By 1865 some of the most enthusiastic friends of the Negro admitted that it would "take many
years to make an economical and thrifty man" of the freedman.
There was even doubt whether the educational work of the societies need be carried on any longer. It was a "laudable and a
noble work," but could not be sustained "after the novelty" was
over. By this time there was "a lethargy" among the Northern
people, a general agreement that the Negro "must make the most
of his chances and pick up his a, b, c's as he can." "Of course,"
said E. S. Philbrick, "there is not much enthusiasm about sending
teachers South to teach the poor whites, so the negro suffers from
the magnitude of the undertaking, from his remoteness from
view, and the general disposition among mankind to let every-
body hoe their own weeds so long as they don't shade one's own
garden." [130]
Less philosophical and even more definite opinions were expressed by other teachers and agents. In discussing a group of 120
laborers a superintendent declared that the satisfaction derived
from the honesty of thirty was insufficient to atone for the anxiety
caused by the remaining ninety "who lie by habit and steal on the
least provocation." "From them," he declared, "all the artifices
of a lawyer cannot draw a fair statement of fact, even when it is
obviously for their own interest to tell the whole truth. 'Where-
fore he is called the everlasting Niggah.'" Their dishonesty was
most discouraging. They were, he declared, "almost incorri-
gible." [131] During the winter of 1865 and 1866 the Sea Island
Negroes were "stealing cotton at a fearful rate," and the superintendents felt "such rascality" to be "more discouraging than cater-
pillars and drought." [132] The "untrustworthiness" of the Negroes
was a source of great annoyance to their Northern friends. "Their
skill in lying, their great reticence, their habit of shielding one
another (generally by silence), their invariable habit of taking a
rod when you, after much persuasion, have been induced to grant
an inch . . . joined with an amazing impudence in making

[130] E. S. Philbrick, Boston, to W. C. Gannett, October 15, 1865, Pearson, *Letters,*
317–318.
[131] C. P. W., October 24, 1863, *ibid.,* 227–228.
[132] R. Soule, Jr., to C. P. W., December 17, 1865, *ibid.,* 322–323.

claims—these are the traits which try us continually," wrote an agent.[133]

One disillusioned abolitionist and teacher published a very critical article. Contrary to his expectations, he said, he had never seen parents "more apathetic." "Certainly the expression of affection is rare to any children who are old enough to get out of the way." The children were frequently whipped, but the whippings were evidently less painful than "the usual New England chastisement." After careful consideration of the subject, this writer doubted that the slaves, "as a class," had suffered as much, "body and mind together," as did the laboring classes in "our Northern cities," who suffered from "want, anxiety and responsibility." [134]

On the whole, it is possible that a statement of Brigadier General John Tarbell, lately of the Federal army, was finally accepted by many as a true picture. He believed that many people in the North tended to "greatly overrate the present character and capacity of the plantation negro, as well as his capacity for future improvement." The ardent friends of the Negro would eventually be disappointed, he thought.[135]

Insofar as a generalization is possible, it may be said that the freedmen, as a group, were enthusiastic in their reception of the teachers and their schools. The literature on the subject is replete with illustrations of the fervor with which the Negro embraced his educational opportunities. Their enthusiasm was not for revenge or for pillage, said Harriet Beecher Stowe, but for education. "They rushed not to the grog-shop but to the schoolroom—they cried for the spelling-book as for bread, and pleaded for teachers as a necessary of life." [136] Freedmen of all ages, colors, and conditions crowded the schools when they were first opened. Old women, bent over "walking sticks," grandfathers leading grandchildren, mothers with their babies, all appeared at the school house door.

[133] C. P. W., November 19, 1865, *ibid.*, 287.

[134] [W. C. Gannett], "The Freedmen at Port Royal," *North American Review*, CI (July, 1865), 5–7. See Pearson, *Letters*, 312.

[135] Testimony of Brevet Brigadier General John Tarbell, March 4, 1866, *Report of the Joint Committee on Reconstruction at the first session Thirty-ninth Congress* (Washington, 1866), Part III, 157. Hereinafter referred to as *Reconstruction Committee*.

[136] "The Education of the Freedmen," *North American Review*, CXXVIII (June, 1879), 613.

Such is the conventional picture. A careful examination of the situation in Georgia leads to the tentative conclusion that in one state, at least, the initial flush of enthusiasm was followed by a period of controversy and flagging interest.

In the early years of the period the freedmen of the state clamored for schools. The "hands" in the rice fields of the Savannah region begged for a chance to exchange their labor for a school.[137] The people at Brunswick were "ripe for the work." They held "but one opinion" on the subject of education. They were unanimous in their desire for schools. "The most unbounded enthusiasm" prevailed among them.[138] At Calhoun the freedmen owned a house which could be used as a school and had raised money for the salary of a teacher.[139] At Sandersville an old church was made available, and the freedmen offered to support a teacher. "All the parents" were anxious for the school to open. There was "universal desire for education." [140] The Negroes at Lexington, Columbus, Albany, Ellijay, Athens, and a dozen other towns and hamlets anxiously awaited the arrival of the first contingent of teachers. They, like the freedmen at Lawrenceville, Virginia, were more than anxious for education—"crazy to learn." They thought "their very salvation" depended on their learning to read.[141]

This haste and eagerness obviously had a psychological as well as a social basis. The freed Negro felt that the explanation of the social prestige, the economic position, and the political power of the white lay in his superior education. If the Negro could acquire the necessary education, he would immediately become the equal of the white in all these fields. From missionaries, preachers, teachers, agents of the Freedmen's Bureau, Union League organizers, and officers and men of the Federal army he heard new and exhilarating theories. They depicted to him a new day,

[137] Woodward Samuell, Savannah, to W. H. Seward, August 11, 1862, B.R.F.A.L. MSS.

[138] D. G. Risley, Agent, B.R.F.A.L., Brunswick, Georgia, to Brigadier General C. C. Sibley, August 31, 1867, B.R.F.A.L. MSS.

[139] A. A. Buck, Calhoun, Georgia, to G. S. Eberhart, September 16, 1867, B.R.F.A.L. MSS.

[140] James R. Smith, Sandersville, Georgia, to O. O. Howard, August 22, 1867, B.R.F.A.L. MSS.

[141] S. K. Whiting, Lawrenceville, Virginia, *National Freedman*, I, 11 (December 15, 1865), 349–350.

entrance to which might be attained by education and the ballot. The school had all the glamor of the new and the strange, and the printed word that peculiar attraction which is characteristic of all forbidden fruit.

This fact was recognized by many officers of the associations. As the editor of the *Freedmen's Record* wrote, "The guard around the tree of knowledge has given them almost an exaggerated idea of its wonderful power; and the spelling-book and primer seem to them Alladdin's [*sic*] lamp, which will command all the riches and glory of the world."[142]   J. W. Alvord declared that the "thirst for knowledge" among the freedmen could hardly be overestimated. He attributed it to that natural desire for knowledge which is common to all men; to the fact that they attributed the power and influence of the whites to superior learning; and to strong curiosity as to the "mysteries of literature." To the freedman the school-house was the "most attractive" and most dearly beloved of all places, he said.[143]

The general situation is, perhaps, well summarized in the observation of one of the many migratory journalists of the period. The Negro, he said, felt that an education was a "sort of talisman" which could "protect its possessor from the curse of Adam, and insure a life of dignified ease and gentility." It was "the white man's fetich," to which he owed his wealth and power.[144]

In 1884 the Superintendent of Education for the American Missionary Association explained that the Negro had "looked upon education as the secret of the white man's power"; hence, "learning to read" became the "main business" of "old and young." But the old people "found the acquisition of knowledge attended by unexpected difficulties, subjective and objective, and largely abandoned the pursuit," he said.[145]

Whatever the reason for the general, even universal, enthusiasm among the freedmen in the early years, there was a very definite

[142] "What Ought We to Expect," *Freedmen's Record*, I, 8 (August, 1865), 122.
[143] *Senate Executive Documents*, 39 Cong., 1 Sess., no. 27 (Serial 1238), 107.   J. W. Alvord, Report to O. O. Howard.
[144] *Harper's New Monthly Magazine*, XLIX (September, 1874), 466.
[145] Albert Salisbury, in National Educational Association, *Journal of the Proceedings and Addresses of the Annual Meeting*, 1884, Madison, Wisconsin, 99. The Negroes, said Salisbury, mark time by "when freedom came in," and "when the Yankee teachers went away."

decline of interest by the close of the period. The strong opposition of the whites, the ruthless suppression of political activity among the Negroes and their Radical friends, and the inevitable reaction from the high plane of abolitionist idealism, were causative factors.

It is quite evident that there was a very definite decline of interest among the freedmen of Georgia by 1870. In many cases the Negroes were "not fully up to their interest." They ungraciously accepted the "charity" which the Northern people were "so graciously bestowing" as "a matter to be expected." They received schools "not as a gift, but *as a due.*" This was particularly true at Savannah, where enthusiasm had reached a great height in the early days of the movement.[146] At Greensboro, Georgia, the pastor of the Negro church "positively forbad" any member of his congregation to attend a meeting called to further co-operation with the Northern teacher.[147] In Columbus, where the Boston teachers had been welcomed in 1866, five teachers sent by the New England Society in the fall of 1868 could find neither home nor school among the Negroes.[148] By 1869 the situation at Columbus had become so grave that the Bureau took official cognizance of the "trouble." The Negroes were warned that unless the schools were "supported well and kept full" the teachers would be withdrawn by the Association, which would be "an irreparable calamity to the colored people of Columbus."[149]

In 1869 there was such "bickering" among the freedmen at Americus that the teacher resigned, and in 1870 the teacher at Hamilton declared that the freedmen had become so "careless about educating their children" that the school should be abandoned.[150] Despite the construction of a good building at Madison, and "very material assistance" every year, the freedmen there had, by 1870, lost all interest in the school. "They have made

[146] E. B. Adams, Agent of the A.F.U.C., to Lyman Abbott, April 21, 1866, *American Freedman*, I, 3 (June, 1866), 45. See, also, James Porter, Savannah, Georgia, to J. W. Alvord, June 28, 1867, B.R.F.A.L. MSS.

[147] J. H. Sullivant, Agent, B.R.F.A.L., Greensboro, Georgia, to E. A. Ware, October 12, 1868, B.R.F.A.L. MSS.

[148] C. W. Chapman, Agent, B.R.F.A.L., Columbus, Georgia, to E. A. Ware, October 21, 1868, B.R.F.A.L. MSS.

[149] J. R. Lewis to J. G. Mitchell, November 23, 1869, B.R.F.A.L. MSS.

[150] William Steward, Americus, Georgia, to J. R. Lewis, May 8, 1869; J. W. Brown, Hamilton, Georgia, to J. R. Lewis, May 18, 1870, B.R.F.A.L. MSS.

very poor returns for all this kindness," said the Superintendent of Schools, "and I think it will serve them right to leave them alone in their wilful ignorance for a time. . . . It is impossible to procure teachers except through the charitable Societies, and they will only go where the people will take a proper interest in the work and do their portion."[151]

If the attitude of the Negroes of Georgia is typical of those of other states, it would seem that the flagging interest of the freedmen themselves was a large factor in causing a general exodus of teachers after 1869–70. A more positive statement will be possible only after a careful examination of the records of the Freedmen's Bureau for other states.

Quite naturally, the teachers were deeply interested in the religion and music of the Negro. The teachers frequently attended "shouts" at the "praise-houses." "They do not enjoy a prayer meeting as we conduct it, but they want to sing and shout till midnight, else they have not had a meeting," wrote one teacher, adding that the old people would not attend Sunday School because it was too quiet.[152]

The teachers attempted to show the Negroes "the difference between sense and sound," although they did not wish to stifle the sincerity and earnestness and love of prayer which they saw in the Negro. One teacher had never seen "exhibitions of sorrowing so deep, so sincere," although he had been in many revivals. "I have seen their tears fall like rain drops," he said, "and sometimes, their sobs almost break my heart."[153] Another teacher sorrowfully declared that the Negro religion was merely "effervescence of emotional feeling, with very little understanding of even the first elementary principles of the Gospel." He had been unable to find a single Negro preacher who had "an intelligent notion of the atonement." The removal of the "mass of religious rubbish" would necessitate much patience and untiring labor.[154] Nevertheless, at some of the schools there was preaching every evening,

---

[151] J. R. Lewis to E. Heyser, November 10, 1869, B.R.F.A.L. MSS.

[152] E. B. Evaleth, Magnolia, Florida, May, 1869, *American Missionary,* XII, 8 (August, 1868), 182–183.

[153] H. S. Beals, Portsmouth, Virginia, April 28, 1863, *ibid.,* VII, 6 (June, 1863).

[154] W. G. Kephart, Decatur, Alabama, May 9, 1864, *ibid.,* VIII, 7 (July, 1864), 179.

and "the inquiring" were "called forward." Those upon the mourners' bench were "conversed with," while the congregation sang and prayed, "singing and praying continuing for some time." The scene when a sinner "got through" was described as "awful." "The excitement," wrote one of the teachers, "is beyond description. Their sense of sin sometimes seems indescribably fearful, and when the burden is lifted, the joy is correspondingly great." [155] At these meetings the Negroes "rubbed their hands in glee," "laughed outright," "leaped up in the air or twisted themselves into grotesque attitudes, as if their joy was too intense to be entertained at a staid perpendicular." [156] One of the teachers questioned a "praise leader" concerning "the shouts." "Why do you make so much noise in your meetings?" she asked. "Why, didn't ye ever read in your Bible, that hollered be Thy name?" was the reply. [157]

The behavior of the Negroes seemed so strange that rumors of queer sects were circulated, coming finally to Superintendent Alvord. In 1867 he asked Superintendent Manly, of Virginia, to give him information concerning the existence of a sect which professed to believe that God was dead. Manly had not heard of such a group among the freedmen, but admitted that he saw "traces of ancestrial heathenism in their style of worship." [158]

The teachers were shocked by the freedom with which the Negroes exchanged marital companions. In some cases they prepared "marriage vows" for the use of those who had been married, or who wished to be. The Negroes were highly pleased, and "took the oath" in droves. One chaplain married seventy-five couples in one day. On August 6, 1863, forty couples took the following marriage oath at Camp Fiske, Tennessee:

You Africa Bailey, you Wilson Polk . . . here in the presence of God and all these witnesses, do each take the woman whose right hand you hold, to be your *only,* your lawful wedded wife. You promise to love and cherish her; to maintain her honorably, by a manly industry and energy;

[155] H. Eddy, Macon, Georgia, April 4, 1866, *ibid.,* X, 5 (May, 1866), 113–114.
[156] New York *Tribune,* April 13, 1862, in *American Missionary,* VI, 5 (May, 1862), 145.
[157] Mary C. Fletcher, Norfolk, Virginia, March 5, 1865, *Freedmen's Record,* I, 5 (May, 1865), 76.
[158] R. M. Manly to J. W. Alvord, February 22, 1867, B.R.F.A.L. MSS.

to nurse her in sickness, to bear with her faults; to be true to the thought of her in all the separations through which Providence may lead you, carefully avoiding improper intimacy with any other, till God shall separate you by death. Do you thus solemnly promise?

You, Emma Turner, you Martha Woods . . . do, on your part, each take the man whose right hand you hold, to be your *only* and lawful husband. You promise to love and care for him; to aid him, diligently, in gaining an honorable livelihood; to be true to him in prosperity or adversity, in sickness or in health, whether you be together, or by Providence separated, avoiding all improper intimacy with any other, till God shall separate you by death. Do you thus solemnly promise?

Each couple was given a marriage certificate "neatly printed, bearing a picture of the old flag." [159]

[159] *American Missionary,* VII, 10 (October, 1863), 235. See, also, VII, 5 (May, 1863), 115, and VII, 4 (April, 1863), 88. Italics in original.

CHAPTER IV

THE YANKEE TEACHER AT WORK

IN THEIR work among the freedmen the Yankee teachers met conditions which would have daunted less determined souls. No hardship was too great, no inconvenience too irritating, no region too remote for these consecrated missionaries. They did not hesitate to go into the back country, far from their fellows. Two young ladies, sent by the American Missionary Association to Arkansas, rode 175 miles by wagon, through the wildest portions of that frontier region, to their post in the southwestern part of the state.[1] Their living quarters were often of the crudest type. The teachers at Wilmington, North Carolina, used an army goods-box for a washstand, wardrobe, and table. Their bed was of pine straw, and they had not even a single chair.[2] In one large party of teachers, labor superintendents, and officers, there were "three or four plates and as many knives and forks."[3] Another party had knives and forks, but not enough spoons.[4] One group had neither bed, chair, nor table. Only a missionary could appreciate the many uses of a tin plate, wrote a member of this party. "A long one answers for a plate for two persons; one corner can be partitioned off for salt, another for sauce, another for bread, and a potato in the middle. This same tin plate will make an excellent mirror."[5]

One very fastidious teacher found herself compelled to choose between no bath at all or such a bath as could be had in a basin. Since "the good Wesley" had said that "cleanliness is next to godliness," she used the basin.[6] Having neither pillow case nor sheet, she "split open a white peticoat [*sic*]" and used the pieces for

[1] Alvord, *Report,* July 1, 1868, p. 44.
[2] L. S. Haskell, Wilmington, North Carolina, January 12, 1866, *American Missionary,* X, 3 (March, 1866), 53.
[3] J. Milton Hawks to Mrs. Hawks, March 30, 1862, Hawks MSS.
[4] Susan Walker, "Journal," 16.
[5] *American Missionary,* XII, 3 (March, 1868), 56–57.
[6] Susan Walker, "Journal," 13.

sheets. In the morning she wrote in her diary, "Friends have sometimes called me *fastidious,* am I so?" [7]   Another teacher had no sheets during her first seven weeks in the South, and her pillow was "contrived out of the sawdust" in which her jars of fruit had been packed.[8]

The teachers cordially disliked Southern insects, which, like everything else Southern, differed from those "at the North." One young man declared that the mosquitoes were a "great annoyance." "They introduce themselves under the netting at night in a very mysterious way," he wrote, "and wake us up early with their singing and stinging. My theory is that those that can lick the others get themselves boosted through the apertures; the animal is smaller than ours at the North. . . . Slapping, if not fatal, only excites their curiosity." [9]   Three young ladies slept "three-deep" on "a very thin mattress of straw," which was also occupied by "a variety of creatures or insects." [10]   Although this was only a temporary arrangement, one of the three had to be content with a "frame of rough boards" and a narrow straw-stuffed mattress. Her table was a packing box, her candlestick a potato, her only chair a wooden bench. Her room contained "a single piece of furniture—a *marble-top mahogany wash-stand. . . .*" [11]

Some of the teachers went about their work with a sense of humor which must have been a very valuable asset. One young man reported that when he asked his pupils to name the three things most necessary for a successful school one solemnly replied, "Father, Son, and Holy Ghost." [12]   A young woman (sister of the gentleman whose mosquitoes entered the net through co-operative effort) noted that she allowed her pupils to use slates every day, in the hope that they would eventually learn not to use the pencil "like a hoe." In some of the slates there were furrows "made by their digging in which you might plant benny-seed, if not cotton!" [13]   Her brother "amused himself" by coaxing several of her

[7] *Ibid.,* 15.
[8] Smedley, The Northern Teacher, 43, citing Schofield, Diary, October 31, 1865.
[9] Pearson, *Letters,* 73.
[10] Susan Walker, "Journal," 14.
[11] *Ibid.,* 15.
[12] Pearson, *Letters,* 32.
[13] *Ibid.,* 149. The "benny-seed" evidently refers to benne, or sesame.

pupils to "read to him upside down, which they did as readily as the right way." The same teacher reported that during the small-pox epidemic at Port Royal the Negroes called it "de Govement lump." Those who had it were "Union," those who did not were "Secesh," and the accompanying fever was "de Horse Cavalry." [14]

The schools were held in barracks, barns, basements, court-houses, churches, and in the open air. In one case, at least, classes were held in the room in which two teachers slept, cooked, and ate. [15] An A.M.A. teacher at Savannah "held school" under an awning stretched on a framework of pine poles, a "very rude, though cool and pleasant" arrangement. [16] At Newton, Georgia, the school was begun in a kitchen. [17] At Wilmington, North Caro-lina, the school was held in a sadly dilapidated church. The roof leaked to such an extent that water often "stood on the floor in large puddles," and the stove smoked so vigorously that both teacher and pupils gasped for breath and were often unable to see across the room. There were no desks, no blackboards, no maps or charts. [18] Another teacher taught in what had been the poultry house of a plantation. "Had the comfort of the feathered tribe been more thought of in its erection, *mine* would have been better secured at present," she wrote. "The crevices are numerous, and the keen winds easily find them. On the most exposed side, I have nailed up an army blanket, and if I could only get more to *tapestry* the rest of the building it might make the hens sigh for their old quarters." [19] In Virginia a teacher met her pupils in the smoky, damp basement of a church until they became too nu-merous for the small room. The Negro pastor refused to allow her to use the auditorium, and for two weeks during January a class of fifty met in the open air, until a dirty, dilapidated kitchen was secured. [20] At Richmond the school supported by the Ameri-can Union Commission met in the Confederate naval arsenal. Shell boxes were used for seats, ammunition cases for study tables,

---

[14] *Ibid.*, 180, 252.
[15] *American Missionary*, IX, 2 (February, 1865), 38.
[16] *Ibid.*, IX, 8 (August, 1865), 177.
[17] *Ibid.*, XII, 6 (June, 1868), 127–128.
[18] *National Freedman*, II, 1 (January 15, 1866), 14.
[19] *American Missionary*, XIII, 2 (February, 1869), 38.
[20] *Ibid.*, XIII, 6 (June, 1869), 135–136.

and "the stained pine desks used by the Confederate Senators" were put to service by "the future rulers" of the state.[21]

Many of the schools were wholly without supplies. One resourceful lady, in her attempt to make the best of a bad situation, adopted object lessons and anything else she could think of which might "awaken thought." The little Negroes did not understand oral instruction, however, considering it merely a plan to "keep their ivory on exhibition." Finding that oral instruction was unsuccessful, the teacher hung on the wall "a 'silent comforter' which consists of several sheets of paper fastened together, on which are printed in large type, choice passages of scripture." She then arranged her pupils in semicircles around the post upon which the "comforter" was nailed, and taught the alphabet from the scriptural passages. Her pointer, she said, was "a rod which had formerly striped the back of my best pupil. 'Not much did I tink,' said he, 'dis yere rod would eber point out to me, de words of 'ternal life.' " [22]

The typical freedmen's school opened with prayer, scripture reading, and the singing of hymns and patriotic airs, such as "The Battle Hymn of the Republic" and "John Brown." The school was usually in session from four to six hours, divided equally between morning and afternoon. Many schools also held night classes. Some schools kept the children only four hours, devoting most of the time to singing. In some cases the morning session included a "regular sermon," and the afternoon was spent in visiting the homes of the pupils, and there teaching the entire family.

One teacher described her school thus:

We have school from eight to twelve o'clock, in the forenoon. . . . We open school by reading in concert a portion of scripture; I read, and all repeat. I then make a few remarks, with such application as seems best suited. After a short prayer, all unite in repeating the Lord's prayer. We then spend until nine o'clock in singing, and you will find few Sabbath Schools that sing better. We then separate to the different school rooms . . . and spend the time until noon in much such exercises as may be seen in the primary and secondary departments of any well conducted Northern school. The proficiency of many is remarkable.[23]

[21] "Pilgrim," *Independent,* January 18, 1866.
[22] *American Missionary,* VII, 5 (May, 1863), 115–116.
[23] G. N. Caruthers, Corinth, Mississippi, June 12, 1863, *ibid.,* VII, 8 (August, 1863),

In another school the order was good, the discipline "mild but firm." The children moved from their seats to the blackboard, or marched out for recess, to the "tap of a bell," exactly as did the pupils of a Northern school.[24]

In general the curriculum included geography, physical and political; spelling, with definitions; oral and written arithmetic; and singing.[25] The texts were those used by the schools throughout the North: "The National Series," Smith's *Arithmetic and Grammar,* Mitchell's *Geography,* Webster's *Speller,* Monteith's *Geography,* Davis and Hutton's *Arithmetic,* Quackenbois' *Primary Arithmetic* and *Primary Grammar.*[26] The famous McGuffey readers and the Hilliard series were also used. Higher texts included Martindale's *United States History,* Tate's *First Book in Philosophy* and *Natural Philosophy,* and Rolfe and Gillet's *Philosophy.*[27]

The Superintendent of Education for Florida recommended that a "carefully compiled History of the late war" be made available for use in the Southern schools. The duty of the teachers would not be done unless they took definite steps to counteract the prejudice which was being "instilled into the minds of the community," he said. That such texts were necessary was shown by the attitude of the Southern press, which demanded that all books sent from the North "for use in Public Schools be carefully examined, that no sentiment offencive [*sic*] to the South [should] find its way into the hands of the pupils."[28]

Many of the schools, however, did not limit themselves to such

---

185. See, also, Mrs. F. S. Williams, St. Helena, South Carolina, January 8, 1863, *ibid.,* VII, 3 (March, 1863), 66–67; Emily Stuart, Vaughan Farm, Virginia, December 2, 1864, *ibid.,* IX, 2 (February, 1865), 37.

[24] George Newcomb, Elizabeth City, North Carolina, January 2, 1866, *National Freedman,* II, 1 (January 15, 1866), 11.

[25] *Nation,* December 14, 1865, p. 746.

[26] F. J. Gould, Thomasville, Georgia, to E. A. Ware, September 10, 1867, B.R.F.A.L. MSS; John A. Rockwell to John R. Lewis, May 30, 1867, B.R.F.A.L. MSS.

[27] J. R. Lewis to Edmund Arnold, Cave Spring, Georgia, October 12, 1870, B.R.F.A.L. MSS.; J. R. Lewis to George Ormond, Perry, Georgia, [?], 1870, B.R.F.A.L. MSS. These texts ranged in price from twenty cents to $1.25 each. One writer states that there were "several series of 'Freedmen's Readers' and 'Freedmen's Histories,'" and asserts that "for ten or fifteen years northern histories were taught in white schools and had a decided effect on the readers." See W. L. Fleming, *Civil War and Reconstruction in Alabama,* 623–624.

[28] George W. Gile to Brigadier General E. Whittlesey, December 31, 1867, B.R.F.A.L. MSS.

elementary concepts as the "three R's," geography, and spelling. Greek, Latin, and dialectic were offered. In brief, the entire classical curriculum was lifted bodily from New England and carried to the South. According to one writer, "Especial stress was laid on classics and liberal culture." [29]

Many of the teachers believed that the interests of the Negroes would be better served by a more practical type of instruction. They were convinced, said one, that "the most effectual part" of the education of the Negroes was not to be derived from books, but from "examples and precepts of thrift, industry, and decency in the common acts of life." [30]   Another believed it desirable to "combine industry with other teachings." Others were "trying to teach cleanliness as well as reading and spelling," but found it a "tough job." [31]   The teachers taught the Negro women to knit, to sew, and to sweep and clean their cabins. They needed "kind lectures" on cleanliness. [32]   At Atlanta Mrs. Rufus Saxton, Mrs. J. R. Lewis, and other Northern women taught Negro girls to sew and knit. [33]   Imitation was strong in the Negro, the teachers thought, and perhaps continued preaching of "industry and cleanliness," accompanied by repeated scrubbings and whitewashings, might be of some use. [34]

With all their emphasis upon the three R's, and upon practical skills, the Yankee teachers never lost sight of the true aim of the entire movement—the "proper education of the freedman." In other words, the Negro must be taught to recognize his friends, to support with his ballot the party of his friends, and to assume his place as the social and political equal of the Southern white

[29] Dr. J. L. M. Curry, at the Montgomery Conference on Race Problems, quoted by W. L. Fleming, *Civil War and Reconstruction*, 631. I have seen Greek copybooks in which ten and twelve year old students had inscribed, with painstaking care, the Greek letters above and the English translation below. These children, it was said, could not read and write in 1866, but were translating Greek in 1870!

[30] James R. Blake, Beaufort, South Carolina, January 7, 1865, *Freedmen's Record (Journal)*, I, 2 (February, 1865), 2.

[31] Mary Ames, *From a New England Woman's Diary in Dixie in 1865* (Norwood, Massachusetts, 1906), 25.

[32] E. S. Williams, St. Helena, South Carolina, December 18, 1862, *American Missionary*, VII, 2 (February, 1863), 39; Mansfield French, Beaufort, South Carolina, April 2, 1862, *ibid.*, VI, 5 (May, 1862), 108–109.

[33] *Ibid.*, XII, 11 (November, 1868), 243.

[34] Walker, "Journal," 20.

man. "The Freedmen's Aid Societies have never been in the hands of people who supposed that they were going to save this nation or redeem an eighth part of its people from barbarism by primers and spelling books," wrote one observer. "The instructions given to their agents in the field, and the diligent work of those agents, have been founded on the understanding that their work was the construction of civil society on a true basis. . . ." [35]

Lyman Abbott, General Secretary of the American Union Commission and Executive Secretary of the American Freedmen's Aid Commission, declared, in 1866, that the South needed industrial reorganization, political reconstruction, and pure religion. Education was essential to each. Nothing could be done to safeguard the Negro in his freedom unless he could exercise his power at the polls, however, and the "shortest road to the ballot-box" was through the schoolroom. To give the Negro the suffrage without properly educating him would "only increase the power of Southern demagogues," while education and the ballot would "destroy the power of both demagogue and aristocrat." [36]

Some of the officers of the Associations were even more outspoken in their opinions on the political nature of the schools. As the election of 1867 approached the editors of the *Pennsylvania Freedman's Bulletin* and the *Freedmen's Record* warned the members of their associations that they must act quickly and with determination if they hoped to avert disaster. The freedmen would soon "become a power in the land," said the *Pennsylvania Freedman's Bulletin*. The use to which they would put their new power depended largely upon their teachers. "Woe betide us" if they are not properly taught, warned the editor. One hundred teachers must be put into the field at once, before the fall elections. "Imagine the amount of good that could be done by 100 good teachers" before the elections, he wrote. [37]

With equal frankness, the editor of the *Freedmen's Record* declared:

[35] *North American Review,* CI (October, 1865), 529.
[36] November 23, 1866, in an address at Philadelphia. *American Freedman,* I, 9 (December, 1866), 133.
[37] Editorial, "Work for the Summer," *Pennsylvania Freedman's Bulletin,* May, 1867, p. 1.

In the coming struggle with the spirit of rebellion and slavery . . . we must have the freedman on our side. As we stand by him, so may we expect him to stand by us. Every teacher you send to the field is a pledge to the freedman of your determination to see justice done him; it is a pledge to the disloyal rebel that you will not yield to him in the future. A teacher costs less than a soldier. . . . We shall not pretend to predict the political future, but this much we know—*now* we can work for the freedmen; we have a Bureau to back us up; we have a Congress which is not afraid to do its duty by him, in spite of the President, and we have peace and prosperity in our own borders.[38]

The *Independent* felt that since the North had not withheld the armies when they were needed it must not now refuse to send teachers, who were the best leaders of the freedmen, as "schools and the Gospel" were their "munitions of war," [39] and the *Congregationalist* saw in the teachers a more effective agency for correct reconstruction than "Congressmen, President, Supreme Court, or U.S. Army." The teachers were shaping the politics, customs, and constitutions of the nation "for all coming time." They were building "as God does, for the ages," and none were more worthy of support.[40]

A prominent student of the Negro says that the "political tenor of the instruction" was very noticeable. "No little allusion was made to 'Old Jeff Davis' and 'The Rebels!' " "John Brown" and "Marching Through Georgia" were frequently sung, and the Fourth of July and first of January were "carefully observed as holidays." [41] At Andersonville, Georgia, site of the famous prison camp, the closing exercises of the 1869 term consisted of a debate by the Young Men's Debating Society on the question "Whether the Legislature of Georgia had a right to expel its Colored Members." [42] In at least one case, the Christmas celebration consisted of the reading of Wendell Phillips' speech to the Philadelphia Convention.[43] In another school the girls worked samplers with

[38] Editorial, *Freedmen's Record*, II, 6 (September, 1866), 158.

[39] M. E. Strieby, *Independent*, September 24, 1868.

[40] Editorial, *Congregationalist*, April 9, 1868.

[41] L. P. Jackson, "The Educational Efforts of the Freedmen's Bureau and the Freedmen's Aid Societies in South Carolina, 1862–1872," *Journal of Negro History*, VIII, 1 (January, 1923), 30.

[42] Laura A. Palmer, April 30, 1869, *American Missionary*, XIII (July, 1869), 147.

[43] Mrs. E. H. Hawks, Port Orange, Florida, December, 1866, *Freedmen's Record*, III, 2 (February, 1867), 22.

the words "Lloyd William Garrison [*sic*] has been a friend to the colored man for many years." [44]

Irritating as such exercises might have been, they were not important enough to arouse any severe feeling among the white people of the South. It was the realization that the underlying purpose of the schools was nothing less than the establishment of the political and social dominance of the Negro race which caused ill feeling among Southerners. They distrusted such statements as that of Superintendent Tomlinson of South Carolina, who said, "In the present state of society in the south, any tuition which does not include some information upon the character and condition of our whole country will fail of producing what is most needed, an intelligent and loyal population. But the statement that politics, in a partisan sense, are taught in the schools, is without foundation in fact." [45]

The attitude of the Southerners is well shown in a correspondence between Miss Anna Gardner, teacher at Charlottesville, Virginia, and James C. Southall, editor of the Charlottesville *Chronicle*. Miss Gardner requested diplomas for the graduating class of her school. In reply, Southall declared that he was interested in the welfare of the Negro, that he was "anxious" to see the Negro educated. The impression among the white people, however, was that the instruction given in Miss Gardner's school "contemplated" more than the teaching of the ordinary branches of study. "The idea prevails," he said, "that you instruct them in politics and sociology; that you come among us not merely as an ordinary school teacher, but as a political missionary; that you communicate to the colored people ideas of social equality with the whites." He approved the education of the Negroes, but regarded such teaching of "politics and sociology" as "mischievous" and likely to "disturb the good feeling between the two races." Even though she might not teach such ideas in the classroom, she might "by precept and example, inculcate ideas of social equality with the whites."

[44] Smedley, The Northern Teacher, 31, citing Dorcas Pringle to Mary Pierce, February 17, 1866. Frequently schools were named for prominent political figures, such as Lincoln, Grant, Garrison, and Phillips.
[45] Alvord, *Report*, July 1, 1867, p. 23.

Miss Gardner somewhat tartly replied, "I teach *in school and out,* so far as my influence extends, the fundamental principles of 'Politics' and 'sociology' viz:—'Whatsoever ye would that men should do to you, do you even so unto them.' Yours in behalf of truth and justice." [46]

Undoubtedly, many of the teachers were deeply interested in the political development of their charges and sponsored political organizations. For example, a teacher in Virginia reported, in 1867, that the freedmen were holding numerous political meetings. The meetings were always opened with prayer. It was a "heart throbbing sight" to see such a meeting, he said. The Negroes were "unanimously in favor of the republican party." [47] The Negroes of Charleston, South Carolina, as a sign of their "patriotic feeling" organized a Union League, "for the purpose of increasing and extending the feeling of devotion to the Union, and of fostering the spirit of nationality." "It was not to be supposed," wrote an observer, "that they initiated and prosecuted these undertakings without assistance from their white friends. Mr. Redpath has been ever at hand with his suggestions and practical wisdom." [48] When the freedmen of North Carolina held a convention at Raleigh the principal speakers were F. A. Fiske, Superintendent of Education for North Carolina, and E. Whittlesey, Commissioner of the Freedmen's Bureau for the state. [49] In 1866 the "loyal colored citizens" of Gallatin, Tennessee, met at the schoolhouse and drew up resolutions strongly endorsing "Parson" Brownlow. [50] The Negroes of Macon County, Alabama, realizing the opposition of the whites to political organization among the Negroes, requested their Radical leaders not to hold political meetings in their churches or schools. When meetings were held in schools before the election of November, 1870, three buildings were burned. [51]

[46] *Freedmen's Record,* III, 4 (April, 1867), 54.

[47] Unnamed teacher, Carsville, Virginia, *American Missionary,* XI, 8 (August, 1867), 172.

[48] *National Freedman,* I, 4 (March 1, 1865), 134. "Mr. Redpath" was James Redpath.

[49] *Ibid.,* I, 9 (October 15, 1865), 289.

[50] Nashville (Tennessee), *Daily Press and Times,* April 9, 1867.

[51] Testimony of William Dougherty before the Committee on Affairs in the Insurrectionary States, October 18, 1871. U.S. Congress, *Report of the Joint Select Commit-*

A Kentucky teacher thought that the Negroes must be given "more correct views of government."[52]   At New Bern, North Carolina, the cashier of the Freedmen's Bank was lecturer at the local school. He endeavored "to instruct the colored people in the meaning and use of suffrage," gave lectures on the constitution, and urged the Negroes to exercise their new rights. His actions brought down upon him "a storm of hatred and malice," he said, but he was determined to use every means in his power to "instruct the colored men in political affairs."   There need be no anxiety concerning the freedmen of New Bern and vicinity—they would be "orderly, loyal, Republican."[53]   In this hope he was in accord with the sentiment expressed by the cashier of the bank at Tallahassee, Florida, who said that the Negroes of his state looked upon the entire school organization as simply "an auxiliary of Republicanism."[54]

The teacher at St. Mary's, Georgia, hoped to make his school not only the center "of educational influence," for the county, but the "center of correct political influence as well."[55]   One of the leading teachers of the American Missionary Association in Georgia said that it was politically necessary to educate the "poor white" as well as the Negro. "There is a religious, and what is synonomous, a political necessity for approaching this class," he said. "The freedmen are loyal—they can be depended upon to vote with good men and for the good measures, of the country. It will be a long time before what is called the 'intelligent' portion of the whites will sustain anything that is good. But the poor whites, by reasonable and well directed effort in their behalf, can be made good republican Americans. . . . Of the present generation there can be made an army of loyalists."[56]

A Freedmen's Bureau agent at Albany, Georgia, admitted that

---

tee Appointed to Inquire into the Condition of Affairs in the Late Insurrectionary States . . . (Washington, 1872), IX, Alabama II, 1026. Hereinafter cited as *K.K.K.*

[52] S. G. Wright, Columbus, Kentucky, *American Missionary,* VII, 4 (April, 1863), 81.

[53] H. A. Ellsworth, Freedmen's Savings and Trust Company, New Bern, North Carolina, to J. W. Alvord, April 10, 1867, B.R.F.A.L. MSS. Ellsworth was a native of Maine.

[54] Wm. Steuard, Tallahassee, Florida, to J. W. Alvord, no date, B.R.F.A.L. MSS.

[55] Virgil Hillyer to E. A. Ware, September 26, 1868, B.R.F.A.L. MSS.

[56] W. L. Clark, Bainbridge, Georgia, April 21, 1869, *American Missionary,* XIII, 8 (August, 1869), 175–176.

it was very well to teach the Negro children to read, but he believed the most important task of the school system to be the "capacitating" of the adult freedmen "for the performance of their duties and the exercise of their rights and privileges as men and citizens." He proposed that a series of textbooks be published, "gotten up with the particular view" of not only "teaching the adults to read, but at the same time [imparting] to their minds in an easy, comprehensible and attractive form that particular information on their duties and rights, and their relation to the white race," which would be "of the most immediate practical value to them in every day life." Such a set would prove "a great auxiliary measure" in the effort to uplift the freedmen as "a mass." They must become "good citizens," and such texts would be of great assistance to them in their effort.[57]

However just and progressive the aims here expressed may have been, they were the very principles which, with the single exception of the advocacy of amalgamation, aroused the bitterest and most spontaneous opposition among native Southerners. Whether the political views of the teachers were correct or incorrect, just or unjust, is not a matter of concern here. The advocacy of such ideas by the teachers was, in itself, sufficient to insure the opposition of the Southern whites.

Many catechisms illustrating the political tone of the schools might be given. A well-known example is that reported by E. L. Pierce. The teacher, a young lady from Kingston, Massachusetts, propounded the questions, and her class responded in chorus:[58]

Question—Where were slaves first brought to this country?
Answer—Virginia.
　　　　When?
　　　　1620.
　　　　Who brought them?
　　　　Dutchmen.
　　　　Who came the same year to Plymouth, Massachusetts?
　　　　Pilgrims.

[57] Agent, B.R.F.A.L., Albany, Georgia, signature illegible, to E. A. Ware, October 5, 1868, B.R.F.A.L. MSS.
[58] E. L. Pierce, "The Freedmen at Port Royal," *Atlantic Monthly,* XII (September, 1863), 306.

Did they bring slaves?
No.

At a meeting of over one thousand Negroes at Richmond, Virginia, the teacher led the following catechism for the benefit of visitors: [59]

Are you glad you are free?
Yes, indeed.
Who gave you your freedom?
God.
Through whom?
Abraham Lincoln.
Is Mr. Lincoln dead?
Yes.
Who is your president?
Johnson.
Are you glad you have schools and teachers?
Yes.
Do you want these friends who are here today to go North and send you more teachers?
Yes, indeed.

A more interesting exchange, surprisingly modern in sentiment, took place in a Louisville school. An officer of one of the Aid Societies led the discussion: [60]

Now children, you don't think white people are any better than you because they have straight hair and white faces?
No, sir.
No, they are no better, but they are different, they possess great power, they formed this great government, they control this vast country. . . . Now what makes them different from you?
MONEY. (Unanimous shout)
Yes, but what enabled them to obtain it?
How did they get money?
Got it off us, stole it off we all!

A song popular in the schools was "We are Free": [61]

[59] *National Freedman,* I, 5 (June 1, 1865), 162.
[60] Miss S. G. Stanley, Louisville, Kentucky, April 3, 1866, *American Missionary,* X, 6 (June, 1866), 139. For another example see W. L. Fleming, *The Sequel of Appomattox* . . . (New Haven, 1919), 219.
[61] Slaughter, *The Freedmen of the South,* 134.

Free! We are free! With a wild and joyous cry
We children in our gladness shouting far and nigh!
Free! We are free! On, let the tidings fly,
We are free to-day!

Glory, glory, Hallelujah, etc.
We are free to-day!
We will think of our President
Who signed the Freedom Bill
We'll think of the Northern hearts who pray for freedom still
We are free to-day!

The spirit of veneration of Lincoln which was common in the schools is well illustrated in the story of the Negro child who stood in the hallway of a school, and gazed with wonder at the portrait of Lincoln. His teacher said, "That is the man who made you free!" "The homely round face was all aglow with the most pathetic wonder, awe and delight, the latter breaking out in as lovely a smile as I ever saw," wrote the teacher. "Is it God?" the child asked. "No," replied the teacher, "it's Lincoln." "The unsophisticated" country lad stood quietly, gazing at the portrait. "It was a perfect triumph of soul over body," a veritable "glory!" [62]

In addition to their influence in the schools, many of the teachers became officers in the "carpetbag" governments. Reuben Tomlinson, an officer of the Pennsylvania Branch of the American Freedmen's Union Commission, was one of the first agents to be sent South by the Port Royal Relief Association. Tomlinson was not a teacher, but he soon became prominent in the educational affairs of South Carolina and one of the most influential members of the "benevolent" group in the state. He was, for two years, a member of the staff of General Rufus Saxton. He represented Charleston in the General Assembly of July, 1868, and during the first session was chosen State Auditor. [63] In 1869 Tomlinson, F. J. Moses, J. K. Jillson, and F. L. Cardozo were elected to the Board of Trust of the state university. [64]

Tomlinson was Commissioner of Education of South Carolina from 1865 to 1868. He resigned in October, 1868, and in 1872 be-

[62] Ellen M. Lee, Columbus, Georgia, *Freedmen's Record*, V, 6 (June, 1869), 12.
[63] J. S. Reynolds, *Reconstruction in South Carolina, 1865–1877* (Columbia, 1905), 107.
[64] *Ibid.*, 123.

came a candidate for the Republican nomination for Governor.[65] The Republican party of the state split on the question of his nomination. One group lauded him as "a pioneer in education, a man whose skirts are clean of any soil or stain," and the other denounced him as "utterly corrupt." Moses was nominated, whereupon the followers of Tomlinson withdrew from the Moses group, held a convention, and nominated Tomlinson. His running mates were three Negroes, James Hayne, Malcolm Allen, and B. L. Roberts, candidates for Lieutenant Governor, Secretary of State, and Superintendent of Education. The Tomlinson ticket carried only ten counties, and Moses was elected.

Tomlinson was connected with the Freedmen's Savings and Trust Company, and with the railroad schemes of "Honest John" Patterson and Niles G. Parker.[66]

Justus K. Jillson, a Massachusetts teacher employed in the freedmen's schools of South Carolina, became one of the most famous figures in the reconstruction government of that state. In 1865 he was a teacher at Camden, South Carolina.[67] He represented Kershaw at the organization of the State Republican party at Columbia in 1867, and at the Constitutional Convention of 1868. He was elected Superintendent of Education on the Scott ticket, and in 1872 was re-elected to that office, this time on the Moses ticket.[68]

B. F. Whittemore, a native of Massachusetts, a Methodist minister and chaplain, was Assistant Superintendent of Education of South Carolina under Reuben Tomlinson. He was Chairman of the Republican Committee for South Carolina, and represented that state in the House of Representatives, from which he was ex-

[65] Alvord, *Report*, January 1, 1869, p. 20; Reynolds, *Reconstruction*, 225.

[66] Tomlinson to J. W. Alvord, September 23, 1865, B.R.F.A.L. MSS; Reynolds, *Reconstruction*, 466–467. Parker was an officer in the Negro regiment commanded by T. W. Higginson, and was "in flight from criminal prosecution in his native State"—Massachusetts. Thomas Wentworth Higginson, *Army Life in a Black Regiment* (Boston, 1870), Appendix; Claude G. Bowers, *The Tragic Era* (Cambridge, 1939), 349.

[67] *Freedmen's Record*, II, 11 (November, 1866), 192.

[68] Reynolds, *Reconstruction*, 60, 77, 87; *Freedmen's Record*, IV, 5 (May, 1868), 1. Jillson was a member of the Board of Trust of the University of South Carolina at the time of the famous Hayne case. Jillson; a Massachusetts soldier, D. H. Chamberlain; a Maryland Negro, Bowley; a New York Negro, Swails; and two South Carolina Negroes, Lee and Jervay, ordered the University opened to both races. The faculty resigned, and the school was closed, remaining closed until 1876.

pelled because of his alleged sale of appointments to West Point and Annapolis.[69]

Northern teachers became administrative officers in the school systems of many Southern states. For example, the Superintendent of Association Schools at Nashville became Superintendent of City Schools. The Superintendent for Hamilton County, Tennessee, was the Rev. E. O. Tade, the A.M.A. teacher and missionary at Chattanooga. In 1868 the A.M.A. schools were part of the city system. In Memphis the A.M.A. schools and those maintained by the Methodist Freedmen's Aid Society were part of the city system, and in 1868 the A.M.A. superintendent was Superintendent of City Schools. The Commissioner of Education for Alabama was a former A.M.A. superintendent, and in North Carolina an A.M.A. teacher at Wilmington was nominated, in 1868, for the joint office of Superintendent of Education and President of the State University. In South Carolina the chairman of the legislative committee in charge of drafting the bill providing for public schools was the A.M.A. Superintendent at Charleston, and in Georgia J. A. Rockwell, A.M.A. agent at Macon, was a member of the legislative committee on education, and of the State Board of Education. He and his associates exerted a "very marked formative influence on the State school system." [70]

It is evident that the Yankee teachers did not confine their activities to instructing their dusky charges in the ABC's, nor even to "the higher branches." Their teaching did, indeed, extend into the controversial fields of "sociology and politics," and in these fields they taught both by precept and by example. Under the circumstances such a condition was almost inevitable. Given a group of zealous abolitionists and missionaries, fired with a desire to educate, convert, and save, and well versed in the propagandist literature of the abolition crusade, stern in their righteous wrath against the people of an enemy section—given, in short, the self-

[69] Mrs. Whittemore was a teacher at Darlington, South Carolina. On the case of Whittemore, see *Freedmen's Record,* IV, 5 (May, 1868), 1, and the very interesting record in the *Congressional Globe,* 41 Cong., 2 Sess., 1469–1472, 1547. Whittemore admitted receipt of money from the parents of cadets, but explained that he had used it for "educational" and "relief" purposes in his district.

[70] George Whipple, Secretary of the A.M.A., *American Missionary,* XII, 4 (April, 1868), 83–84; XI, 9 (September, 1867), 204.

appointed guardians of a nation's conscience—and it was to be expected that even the teaching of spelling and reading would be carried out with an eye to political effect.

Any attempt to evaluate the actual results of the work of the teachers in the pedagogical sense must be based upon an intensive study of many factors, such as the work and influence of the schools and colleges established during this period, and an analysis of trends and developments in Negro education from 1860 to the present. Such a task is obviously beyond the scope of this study, which is limited to the period 1862–1870. The conclusions here presented should not, therefore, be considered pertinent to any later period. The question of immediate concern is the effect of the educational program upon the white people of the South, and the relation of this program to Radical Reconstruction.

CHAPTER V

SOUTHERN REACTION

THE Southern reaction to the presence of the Yankee teacher was definite, decided, and violent. At first the teachers were tolerated, but as they increased in numbers and in influence, the Southern people saw their worst fears realized. The teachers associated with the Negro on terms of social equality, some of them even going so far as to avoid all contact with white people, devoting themselves exclusively to the society of the Negro.[1] They urged the Negro to assert his individuality, to demand that his former master speak to him by "title" instead of by given name.[2] They organized the Negro politically, made him the backbone of the dominant party. In brief, the Yankee teachers promptly identified themselves with the worst enemies of an embittered, angry, and sorely wounded South—the Radical Republicans. As these facts became clear, the toleration with which the Southerners had at first received the teachers turned to scorn, contempt, and social ostracism, and then to active persecution. The teachers became a symbol of victory and of defeat. The Negro soldiers were armed, the agents of the Freedmen's Bureau were surrounded by soldiers and were therefore able to move about at will, but when the teachers dared venture far from the protection of the military, they were met with violence.

Nor was this violence essentially directed against all Northerners, not, it may be said, against Yankees *per se*. The South did not fail to recognize the Northerner as such, but a special condemnation was reserved for the teacher and the agent of the Freedmen's Bureau.

Further, the violent reaction against the Yankee teacher was not the result of a universal condemnation of Negro education. For a

[1] See Haviland, *A Woman's Life-Work*, 384.

[2] For example, one teacher said, "I teach them that an honest, industrious old man should not be called 'Jack' but has a right to keep two names, or name and 'title.'" *American Missionary*, VII, 5 (May, 1863), 109.

time many individuals in various sections of the South gave approval and support to Negro schools. The Southerner did not fear the education of the Negro—he feared Negro education in the hands of the typical "Yankee teacher," under the program of education advanced by the Radical legislatures.

It is, therefore, necessary to study the reaction of the South to the Yankee teacher, the attitude of the South toward other Northerners, and the Southern attitude on the problem of Negro education.[3]

When the teachers first entered the South they found the whites suspicious, cold, but not bitter toward them. There was no active persecution, no physical assault. They were not harmed, but were "entirely passed by, and looked upon with contempt."[4] They were not accepted socially; and they received neither visits nor invitations. At some places even the Unionists refused to associate with them. A teacher at Portsmouth, Virginia, complained that there were "supposed to be some white Unionists" there, but she could not find one who would "shelter a teacher of the 'contrabands.'"[5] As late as 1865 a North Carolina teacher could say: "The whites treat us so-so; the men now and then lift their *hats* while the ladies for variety almost invariably *lift* their *noses*. But we pay little or no attention to either, and 'work goes marching on.'"[6] At Lexington, Virginia, the teachers were the objects of the ribald laughter and taunts of college students and small-town hangers-on. One wrote that on her first visit to town some college students followed her into a store, and then called to their companions to "come take a look at the Yankee, at .25 [*sic*] a look." Corner louts sneered and laughed at her and her companions when they appeared on the street. "From one set of students, whose boarding-house I was compelled constantly to

[3] In this study few statements are made concerning the education of the freedmen of Louisiana. It seems probable that the system of education and labor instituted by the Federal Army in Louisiana constitutes a special case, and that it should therefore be reserved for special investigation.

[4] Testimony of Colonel E. Whittlesey, Assistant Commissioner B.R.F.A.L., Raleigh, North Carolina, February 3, 1866, *Reconstruction Committee*, Part II, 180–183. Whittlesey was Colonel of the Forty-sixth Regiment, U.S.C.T., a native of Maine, a graduate of Yale, and a professor at Bowdoin.

[5] H. Taylor, *American Missionary*, VII, 4 (April, 1863), 87.

[6] Fanny Newcomb, Elizabeth City, North Carolina. *National Freedman*, I, 11 (December 15, 1865), 347.

pass, I habitually received the polite salutation of 'damned Yankee bitch of a nigger teacher,' with the occasional admonition to take up my abode in the infernal regions." More serious than the laughter and curses of the men was the refusal of the women to sell food to the teachers. One woman swore she "would not sell milk to Yankees to save her life, she hated the very ground they trod."[7] A teacher at Sumter, South Carolina, also experienced difficulty in buying food. The grocers raised prices to such exorbitant heights that she could not afford to buy, and it was only after a month of opposition that she could even walk the streets in peace.[8] One teacher dared not purchase food, because the clerks in the stores "perhaps would have been glad of an opportunity to have poisoned us."[9] At Lawrenceville, Virginia, in 1865, the people were so "very hostile" that they received the teachers "very cooly." They took advantage of every opportunity to embarrass them.[10] The teachers at Wilmington, North Carolina, complained that the citizens did not encourage the schools. The teachers were denied "all social privileges." The Wilmington *Dispatch* criticized the teachers, and the editor was arrested by the local agent of the Freedmen's Bureau, but the agent magnanimously refrained from pressing the case.[11]

The worst which could be said by the Florida Superintendent of Education in 1866 was, "In no case have the people shown a willingness to render us any assistance." The people cherished a "deadly hatred to the education and elevation of the freedmen," and would not board the Northern teachers, he said.[12]

The usual methods of ostracizing the teachers were refusal to accept them as roomers, and denial of the courtesy of the local churches. When the teachers first went to Raleigh, North Carolina, not a single private home or boarding house would accept them. "When it was frankly stated to them that these were young

[7] Julia A. Shearman, January 29, 1866, *American Missionary*, X, 3 (March, 1866), 49, 50; Julia A. Shearman, letter to the editor, *Independent*, April 16, 1868.

[8] Etta Payne, *Freedmen's Record*, II, 9 (September, 1866), 164.

[9] Martha N. Lindley, *Indiana History Bulletin*, I, 11–12 (September, 1924), 140–143.

[10] O. K. Whiting, *National Freedman*, I, 11 (December 15, 1865), 349–350.

[11] Testimony of Lieutenant Colonel W. H. Beadle, Agent, B.R.F.A.L., Wilmington, North Carolina, April 4, 1866, *Reconstruction Committee*, Part II, 268. Beadle was a native of Ann Arbor, Michigan.

[12] H. H. Moore to F. G. Shaw, President of the National Freedmen's Relief Association, January 1, 1866, *National Freedman*, II, 1 (January 15, 1866), 3–5.

ladies from the North, who were there for the purpose of teaching colored schools, they turned their backs upon them," said the Raleigh agent of the Freedmen's Bureau.[13] When the teachers succeeded in renting a house they were compelled to pay $1,900 gold or $3,000 currency for a building which, before the war, had rented for $350.[14] A teacher in Virginia, unable to find a boarding house, was forced to take a room in the local hotel. The other roomers were "strong *secesh*" and observed her "with a bitter eye." Only the love of the tavern-keeper for Yankee greenbacks made it possible for her to remain, she said.[15] Often, if a teacher did succeed in renting a room, the owner would refuse to sign a lease, and, without warning, eject the teacher, claiming that he had rented the room at a higher price to another lodger. In Florida, especially in the interior, teachers could not secure boarding places, nor could they rent houses. In this manner the white citizens often prevented the establishment of a school.[16] Every "respectable family" shrank from the idea of boarding Yankee teachers as "from a pestilence." Not one in a thousand had the "moral courage to brook the odium which would be visited upon" him should he "take in" a teacher as "a boarder."[17]

In Georgia the sentiment was such that teachers could not secure homes, and were compelled to manage their own establishments in rented houses of poor quality. The sentiment aroused by the election of 1868 was so strong in southwestern Georgia that it was impossible even to rent a house, and a boarding place was not to be considered. When the five young women teachers sent to Columbus by the Boston branch of the American Freedmen's Union Commission arrived there they could not find a place in which to live or to teach. Nevertheless, with "true Yankee pluck," they arranged temporary quarters, and remained at their post.[18]

[13] Testimony of E. Whittlesey, *Reconstruction Committee,* Part II, 183. See, also, *National Freedman,* I, 8 (September 15, 1865), 276.

[14] *Nation,* November 30, 1865, p. 674.

[15] Sarah E. Foster, Gordonsville, Virginia, June 23, 1866, *Freedmen's Record,* II, 9 (September, 1866), 165.

[16] H. H. Moore to F. G. Shaw, January 1, 1866, *National Freedman,* II, 1 (January 15, 1866), 3–5.

[17] New York *Daily Tribune,* February 3, 1866.

[18] John Leonard, Agent, B.R.F.A.L., to E. A. Ware, September 23, 1868; R. C. Anthony, Agent, B.R.F.A.L., to E. A. Ware, September 11, 1868; W. C. Morrill, Ameri-

When the teachers returned to their station near Macon in the fall of 1868 they were greeted with the salutation: "Here comes Hell," and men were heard to threaten to burn the house which they had rented. Teachers returning to Augusta in 1869 heard one woman say to another, "Here are those mean Yankee school-m'a'ms come back to cheat the niggers!" As they walked up the street another woman shouted such profanity that they "trembled" to hear it "from the lips of a female." On St. Valentine's Day these teachers received cards showing women carrying carpetbags full of gold, and saying, "I cheat every nigger I can get hold of." [19]

The condition is accurately reflected in a letter from an agent of the Freedmen's Bureau to the Superintendent of Education for Georgia. This officer wrote that he

spent two days trying to secure a boarding place for a lady teacher, but utterly failed. There are two Hotels in the place [Greensboro] but neither of them would agree to take them. We applied at six other places three of which were boarding Houses, but none of them would board a 'nigger' teacher. One of them agreed at first to take her, but upon reconsideration declined to do so. . . . There is a colored family with whom board can be had, but it is too far from the school house, being about one mile distant. . . . [I am?] trying to rent a room for her in some private family and arrangements can be made to have her meals carried to her. . . . I have good reason to believe that there is an understanding between the people at Greensboro to keep out Yankee 'nigger' teachers. [20]

Frequently the teachers were insulted when they attended church services. One of the teachers, who was a member of the Society of Friends, attended the Presbyterian church at Lexington, Virginia. She "modestly" took the first vacant seat. Soon after the close of the service the sexton called at her home and delivered a message from the owners of the pew which she had occupied, requesting that she "never again" occupy that seat. [21] Each Sunday the teachers at Bainbridge, Georgia, visited the local "Zion," which was attended by the best citizens of the town, but not once did they receive the slightest sign of recognition. In four months their sole visitor was the pastor of the local Baptist church, a man

cus, Georgia, probably to E. A. Ware, [?], 1868; Sarah D. Lane, Boston, Massachusetts, to E. A. Ware, November 3, 1868, B.R.F.A.L. MSS.
[19] *American Missionary*, XIII, 1 (January, 1869), 15; *ibid.*, XIII, 7 (July, 1869), 149.
[20] W. J. White, Madison, Georgia, to E. A. Ware, November 16, 1868, B.R.F.A.L. MSS.
[21] Julia A. Shearman, *American Missionary*, X, 3 (March, 1866), 29–30.

of Union sympathy. Other white people carefully avoided them.[22] Teachers in North Carolina experienced the same coolness. "Even in the sanctuary the hand of fellowship is not extended to us," wrote a Wilmington teacher. Instead of the cordial handclasp they were greeted with "the scornful curl of the lip, the brushing away of the dress for fear of contamination, the raising of the finger, to touch the *black* ribbon on the hat, thus telegraphing to each other, 'the nigger teachers have come.'"[23]

In fact, there seems to be truth in the oft-repeated assertion that the women of the South were more bitterly "un-reconstructed" than the men. One teacher complained that the ladies had not treated her with "the kindness and respect" which the gentlemen had shown. The women, she said, "shrink from contact with us on the street. . . . It is very obvious that the women of the South are greater rebels than the men."[24]

As the political controversy between President Johnson and the radical Congressmen became more bitter, the tension was reflected in the South. When the victory of the Radicals seemed assured the Yankee teacher was caught in the cross-fire of opposition between local white-conservative and black-and-tan-radical groups. The years 1867 and 1868 saw a decided increase in the activity of the Union League and of the Ku Klux Klan. Rumors of brutality, of murder, and of incendiarism were widespread. Many teachers left their schools, some were beaten, others coated with tar and cotton. No accurate statement can be made concerning the amount of violence which took place during the period.

The newspapers of the North were filled with stories of "Southern atrocities," "Southern barbarianism," and "outrages upon Northern men." The Radical group in Congress seized upon this as a means of furthering their program. Congressmen pointed to the "anarchy" of the South, where "persecution, exile, murder" were "the order of the day." The exiled Union men found refuge in the North, where they were to be seen, "melancholy, depressed,

---

[22] W. L. Clark, *ibid.*, XII, 6 (June, 1868), 126–127.

[23] *Congregationalist*, April 9, 1868. The "drawing away" of the skirt for fear of "contamination" was quite usual, it seems, even in the face of ministerial insistence on the folly of "a rebellious spirit." See *Nation*, August 31, 1865, p. 270. Private interviews also support this statement.

[24] Unnamed teacher, quoted in Slaughter, *The Freedmen of the South*, 119.

haggard, like the ghosts of the unknown dead on this side of the river Styx." The Southern breezes bore the "dying groans" of countless thousands of murdered victims.[25] The North had spent 350,000 men and four billions in cash, only to see 1,500 loyal men, citizens, voters, "massacred in cold blood" within the short space of two years.[26]

Some of the Senators, however, questioned the sincerity of the Radicals, whose hearts bled so copiously for the loyal citizens of the South. For example, Senator Cowan, of Pennsylvania, declared that the Radicals were attempting to "fright the country" by tales of the cruelty of the Southern people, who "kill and murder for pastime, just as a naughty boy would kill flies." Senator Wilson could give the "exact dimensions of crime in the South," asserted Cowan. He could tell "how high it soars, how deep it dives, its superficial measure, or its cubic quantity to a hair's breadth"; he could do anything except prove that "the whole" was not "cooked up and exaggerated expressly for the occasion." Who brought the stories of the Southern atrocities? Agents of the Freedmen's Bureau, cotton thieves, and other "interested" individuals. "These fellows, male and female," said Cowan, "have found the woes of the negro such an easy and profitable way to fame and consideration that . . . to hear and see them we would think the world was exceedingly wicked, wholly on account of the negro, and for no other reason." The "false and foolish notion of equality" which had been "put into the head of the negro" by his advisers was a "standing invitation to every white man to break that head as soon as it insults him."

The atrocity stories were dismissed by Senator Cowan as being "too monstrous for belief," and as having "no foundation upon which to rest." The Radical measures had as their object a very different end, he asserted. The Southern states were to be put under military rule, and the advocates of force hoped and expected, he said, that new governments might be formed "upon the basis of political equality between the two different races," that the political power of the South might be "either paralysed or

---

[25] Thaddeus Stevens, February 7, 1867, *Congressional Globe,* 39 Cong., 2 Sess., 1076.
[26] Augustus Brandegee, *ibid.,* 1076–1077.

transferred to the radicals," and that the Southern states might be allowed no representation in Congress or the electoral college.

In order to justify this action before the country, the Radicals had affected "great concern" for the Negro, said the Senator. The freedman was depicted as utterly helpless in the hands of the whites, unable to defend himself from wholesale, mass murder. It was agreed that he could not even make a contract without "the guardianship of Government officials," yet it was avowed that, in a year or two, he would "burst his savage cocoon" and "soar away on painted pinion, a full-grown Radical bombyx. . . . Then will the day of Pentecost be fully come, and three or four million negroes are to be changed, not by the apostolic teaching of divinely-inspired men, but by virtue of amended constitutions and the pedagogic efforts of strong-minded school-marms." [27]

A careful examination of this controversy is not within the scope of this study. It is interesting to note, however, that the Congressional committee which investigated "affairs in the late insurrectionary states" could find only a few cases of outrage and atrocity for which dependable corroborative evidence was available. In many instances the cases reported to the committee were legitimate, no doubt, but often the character of the witnesses and of the evidence was such as to throw great doubt upon the validity of the case itself. For example, the committee based a portion of its report on the testimony of the Rev. A. S. Lakin, the representative of the Methodist Church in northern Alabama. Lakin was a man of very questionable character, but the testimony concerning him and his escapades covers over one hundred pages in the testimony of the Ku Klux Klan Committee, and three entire pages in the report of the majority.[28]

Another case rested upon the testimony of a twenty-three year

---

[27] *Congressional Globe*, 39 Cong., 2 Sess., February 16, 1867, Appendix, 154 *et seq.* B. B. Kendrick says that Cowan had been a consistent supporter of Lincoln, and simply adhered to the principles of Lincoln. His character was such that his words are "entitled to a great deal of respect and credence," says Kendrick. See *The Journal of the Joint Committee of Fifteen on Reconstruction, 39th Congress, 1865–1867*, Columbia University, 1914, *Columbia University Studies in History, Economics and Public Law*, LXII, 389–390.

[28] In one instance Lakin testified that he had seen a baby which "was a perfect representation and fac-simile of a disguised Ku Klux." The mother had been frightened by a visit of the Klan to her home some weeks before the birth of the child. See *K.K.K.*, VIII, Alabama I, 118–121.

old officer of a Negro regiment, a native of Iowa, who had entered the army at the age of nineteen. He was, in 1866, a sub-commissioner of the Freedmen's Bureau. He reported to his superior that he had "heard of" a murder, and that if the Commissioner wished to investigate he could refer him to a certain ferryman, who could "give the names of parties knowing the facts." [29]   Many cases were found to rest wholly or in part upon hearsay evidence. The details of the murder of a freedman, outrage upon a teacher, and burning of a school in Chambers County, Alabama, were related to a Congressional committee by a Negro who had heard about it "from everybody that lived in" that neighborhood.[30]   In 1871 the Rev. Lakin reported having seen, "in or about 1868," the ashes of "probably half a dozen school-houses" which, according to local gossip, had been burned by incendiaries.[31]   At Demopolis, Alabama, a Negro testified that he had heard that two schools had been burned in Choctaw County, possibly in 1869.[32]   The clerk of the court at Livingston testified that he had "heard of" the burning of one Negro school, in 1869, but that the white citizens had helped the Negroes rebuild. He faintly recalled another fire, but could give no details.[33]

Many similar cases might be given for Alabama. Similarly, in Georgia witnesses testified that they had "heard of" violence against the schools. William Jennings, Radical Republican tax assessor for the Fourth District, testified that he had heard of several cases. Such fires were "common" in 1867 and 1868, he said, but he knew of none after that period.[34]

The apparent inability of the Congressional committees to obtain conclusive evidence of alleged outrage, violence, and incendiarism does not mean, of course, that there were no such cases. Many factors tended to make the task of the committees a difficult one. Too, the letters of the Freedmen's Bureau afford ample evidence that schools were burned and teachers driven out. For

---

[29] Report of Captain J. H. Matthews to Lt. Stuart Eldridge, January 12, 1866, *Reconstruction Committee*, Part III, 146.
[30] Testimony of Oscar Judkins, October 18, 1871, *K.K.K.*, IX, Alabama II, 1042–1043.
[31] *K.K.K.*, VIII, Alabama I, 135.
[32] Testimony of Charles L. Drake, *K.K.K.*, X, Alabama III, 1548.
[33] *K.K.K.*, X, Alabama III, 1614.
[34] *K.K.K.*, VIII, Georgia II, 1133.

example, in November, 1868, the school at Athens, Georgia, was broken up and the teacher forced to leave the county.[35] In 1870 a school at Oxford, under the supervision of the Methodist Freedmen's Aid Society, was burned.[36]

A teacher at Chubb Institute, Floyd County, Georgia, reported an interesting and perhaps typical experience. In November, 1868, he went to Cedartown on business. Of his visit he wrote:

I was assaulted by one man by the name of Jo Blanch & one Daniel Blanch said I had come down there to incite & kick up a disturbance with the negroes. I said not so he said you get your Horse and leave here D—— quick, and never show yourself again. I said I would at my own convenience. He struck me in the mouth. Blanch call me out first I had said nothing to him up to then They do not favor an uneducated Republican. Blanch said Hello Poole what are you Union Republican you are a d—— mean low down man. You saying so do not make it so and in conclusion receiving other threats & intimidation. I do not know how long I will be allowed to remain here. My Politics is what makes them mad. I have been suffering from my assault ever since.[37]

This letter probably is a good example of the methods of intimidation used by Southerners who did not resort to secret orders, as well as an indication of the character and ability of some of the teachers. The Freedmen's Bureau agent at Albany, Georgia, described the situation in a letter to Superintendent Ware:

The whites of this country, as a mass, are prejudiced against and opposed to Northern teachers and look upon them as radicals and social equality propagandists. No matter how unfounded and unjust this presumption may be in a large majority of instances, it nevertheless exists and without using some influence to counteract and mitigate it and to show the whites that only simple primary school instruction is aimed at, these country schools will be opposed to all possible means to interfer [*sic*] with them and to break them up will be used, particularly in the more remote country districts.[38]

The Southern side of the controversy was well presented by General James H. Clanton in his testimony before the Ku Klux

[35] John J. Knox, sub-assistant commissioner, B.R.F.A.L., November 13, 1868, to E. A. Ware, B.R.F.A.L. MSS.

[36] R. S. Rust, Oxford, Georgia, to E. A. Ware, May 26, 1870, B.R.F.A.L. MSS.

[37] Louis N. Poole, teacher, Chubb Institute, Floyd County, Georgia, to E. A. Ware, November 5, 1868, B.R.F.A.L. MSS.

[38] October 5, 1868, B.R.F.A.L. MSS.

Committee. He declared that the teachers themselves were to blame for any prejudice which might exist. He had visited a public program at a freedmen's school at which a "radical delivered an address reciting the wrongs" which the Negroes had suffered at the hands of the whites. "The school was under radical regime," said the General, "the teachers were strangers to us, and it was a political nursery to prejudice the race against us. As the negroes number three to one white person among us it is a very serious question." [39]

The teachers considered the attitude of the Southern white people toward them to be an accurate reflection of Southern political and social feeling. The presence of a "Yankee teacher" in the South was "a thermometer of Southern feeling," wrote the editor of one of the leading association periodicals. "No more reliable sketches of Southern affairs" could be found than the letters of the teachers. [40]

The possibility that they were being persecuted as missionaries rather than as Yankees does not seem to have occurred to the teachers. The fact that the members of any group feel a keen resentment toward those who come into their midst as missionaries was well stated by a Republican tax assessor in Georgia, who was also a trustee of Atlanta University. His testimony before the Congressional Committee on Affairs in the Insurrectionary States is rather remarkable. He said that the Negroes were, in many cases, "insolent," and that they had demanded "certain rights without knowing exactly what their rights" were. The white people had been "exceedingly arrogant" and unwilling even to hear the requests of the Negroes. Sentiment was, in general, opposed to Negro education, and he had "heard of" the burning of schoolhouses. It was his opinion that teaching in a Negro school would exclude any individual from "what is called society" in Georgia.

"Even Republican families of reasonably good standing" would not recognize such teachers, for "by so doing they would exclude themselves from society." In response to the question, whether "people who go as missionaries to the heathen, even to the lowest

---

[39] June 19, 1871, *K.K.K.*, VIII, Alabama I, 236.
[40] Editorial, *American Missionary*, XII, 2 (February, 1868), 34.

type of heathenism, would not lose caste thereby," he said, "They would not lose caste at home, neither would these teachers from New England lose caste in New England, but the missionaries might lose caste in China." Further, it was believed that the teachers mixed "politics with their education," a practice to which the whites bitterly objected.[41]

The presence of the Yankee teacher often aroused the local press to opposition. The arrest of the editor of the Wilmington *Dispatch* because of criticism of the teachers has been noted. It is possible that the following editorial is the one which aroused the ire of the teachers:

This Southern land, it seems, will never escape the wrath of the Almighty, levelled at it because of the neglect to employ those means which he had given, a lack of appreciation of which caused the defeat that we sustained in our effort to achieve independence.

Curse after curse, like those which descended on the Egyptians, came spreading dismay throughout our land. Military rule first, Freedmen's-Bureau insolence, Yankee impertinence, all have been upon us, and all have been borne with a very commendable patience.

The worst of all the curses which we have been called upon to submit to, however, is the insupportable, intolerable nuisance of the schoolmarms in our midst, teaching the infant 'idea how to shoot.' We had hoped that this pestilential race would give us the go-by. We could stand any thing else that was sent; but when the benevolent societies of Boston sent out emissaries, we felt that we should sink under this, the last, the worst of all our punishments for a criminal failure to accomplish our own political salvation when the means were at hand.[42]

A similar note was struck by the editor of the Norfolk *Virginian,* who wrote:

They are gone or going.—The only joy of our existence in Norfolk has deserted us. The 'negro school-marms' are either gone, going, or to go, and we don't much care which, whereto, or how—whether it be to the more frigid regions of the Northern zone, or to a still more torrid climate; indeed, we may say that we care very little what land they are borne to, so not again to 'our'n,' even though it be that bourn whence no traveler returns. Our grief at their departure is, however, lightened somewhat by

[41] William Jennings, November 7, 1871, *K.K.K.*, VII, Georgia II, 1133. Jennings was a native of Ohio who had moved to Georgia in 1858.

[42] Wilmington (North Carolina) *Dispatch*, in *Freedmen's Record*, III, 2 (February, 1867), 20.

the recollection of the fact that we will get rid of an abominable nuisance.

Our only fear is that their departure will not be eternal, and like other birds of prey they may return to us in season, and again take shelter, with their brood of black birds, under the protecting wings of that gobbling and foulest of old fowls, the well known buzzard yclept Freedmen's Bureau.

In all seriousness, however, we congratulate our citizens upon a 'good riddance of bad baggage' in the reported departure of these impudent missionaries. Of all the insults to which the Southern people have been subjected, this was the heaviest to bear . . . to have sent among us a lot of ignorant, narrow-minded, bigoted fanatics, ostensibly for the purpose of propagating the gospel among the heathen, and teaching our little negroes and big negroes, and all kinds of negroes, to read the Bible and show them the road to salvation . . . but whose real object was to disorganize and demoralize still more our peasantry and laboring population. . . .

We hail with satisfaction the departure of these female disorganizers, and trust no favoring gale will ever return them to our shores, and that their *bureau* and other furniture may soon follow in their wake.[43]

Early in 1866 the Richmond *Times* published a satiric comment on the teachers:

White cravatted gentlemen from Andover, with a nasal twang, and pretty Yankee girls, with the smallest of hands and feet, have flocked to the South as missionary ground, and are communicating a healthy moral tone to the 'colored folks', besides instructing them in chemistry, botany, and natural philosophy, teaching them to speak French, sing Italian, and walk Spanish, so that in time we are bound to have intelligent, and probably, intellectual labor.[44]

In a later issue the editor of the *Times* again indulged his penchant for heavy sarcasm, and his effusion was reprinted, with approval, by the Augusta *Daily Press:*

TERRIBLE IN THE EXTREME

A Petersburg paper proclaims in the most heartless and cold-blooded manner a terrible calamity which has recently fallen upon the people of that heroic city. 'Seven schoolmarms left our city on yesterday for the North and may joy go with them', remarks the paper in question. . . . We feel assured that the people of Petersburg are bearing the loss of these attractive and interesting females with philosophic if not with Christian

[43] Norfolk *Virginian,* July 2, 1866, in Slaughter, *The Freedmen of the South,* 145–146.

[44] Richmond *Times,* January 16, 1866, in William H. Brown, *The Education and Economic Development of the Negro in Virginia.* Publications of the University of Virginia. Phelps-Stokes Fellowship Papers No. 6, p. 43.

resignation. . . . We hope the intercourse of these lovely missionaries and the colored heathen was mutually pleasant and advantageous. . . . Their opportunities for studying our domestic and social habits will no doubt enable them to write intelligently, spicily and pleasantly of high life in Petersburg.

Let us, for the sake of all strong-minded and lovely 'school-marms' who are now at the South, indulge the gallant hope that their sense of duty to the juvenile Cuffees of the late Southern Confederacy will not induce them to remain with us a moment longer than is required to fulfill their magnificent mission. . . .

We really stand in no need of Northern 'school marms' at the South, either for white or black pupils, but the 'first families' in Africa all desire to procure fresh, plump and tender missionaries. The invasion of the Confederate States by an army of 'school marms' after the collapse of the Confederacy was a mistake. We fear their anxiety to teach the Southern pickaninies made them forget the necessities—moral, educational and religious—of those unfortunate Northern negroes of whose horrible condition we read such shocking accounts in the Boston, New York and Philadelphia journals.[45]

Whatever may be said for the quality of the wit of the editor of the *Times,* there can be little doubt that the reprinting of his essay in Northern journals did not act as a sedative upon the nerves of those already antagonistic to the South.

Many teachers were visited by the Ku Klux Klan. Many were severely beaten, some tarred and covered with cotton, but less drastic steps usually proved successful. For example, one of the teachers employed by the American Missionary Association received a note bearing the following warning of a horrible fate in store:

1st quarter, 8th Bloody moon—Ere the next quarter be gone! Unholy teacher of the blacks, begone, ere it is too late! Punishment awaits you, and such horrors as no man ever underwent and lived. The cusped moon is full of wrath, and as its horns fill the deadly mixture will fall on your unhallowed head. Beware! When the Black Cat sleeps we that are dead and yet live are watching you. Fool! Adulterer and cursed Hypocrite! The far-piercing eye of the grand Cyclops is upon you! Fly the wrath to come.

Ku Klux Klan

D.B.R.P.[46]

[45] May 31, 1866.
[46] *American Missionary,* XII, 8 (August, 1868), 183.

A South Carolina teacher found on the door of his home a notice headed "IN HOC SIGNO." Beneath this were a cross, two daggers, a crescent moon, and the outline of a coffin, on which was printed "K K K." The note read:

Bretheren of the mystic order, assemble in solemn convocation. The bloody moon begins its course and there is work to be done; for the sacred serpent has hissed. FAIL NOT

Grand Skeleton
C. C. C. and T. S.[47]

Another K. K. K. warning read:

You are a dern aberlition puppy and scoundrel if We hear of your name in the papers again we will burn your hellish house over your head cut your entrals out.
The K K s are on your track and you will be in hell in four days if you don't mind yourself, mind that you don't go the same way that G.W.A. went some night
Yours in hell

K K K[48]

Frequently voices were raised in protest against such violent measures as the threatening and beating of teachers and the burning of schools. The Augusta *Chronicle and Sentinel* condemned the action of a group of young men who had forced a "Yankee negro school teacher" to leave his school. The action of the mob, said the *Chronicle and Sentinel,* was "deprecated" by every law-abiding citizen. Such acts were not only wrong in themselves, but caused "incalculable injury to the South" at a time when she was seeking restoration of her political status. It was true that many of the teachers were "doing mischief in embittering the blacks against the whites," but violence was not the remedy. Perhaps time would open the eyes of the teachers, or, better solution still, Southern communities might establish schools for the freedmen, and thus take away the occupation of the "fanatics" who were "usually selected to take charge of these schools under the

---

[47] *American Freedman,* III, 3 (June, 1868), 427.
[48] *Freedmen's Record,* IV, 5 (May, 1868), 80–81. "G. W. A." refers to G. W. Ashburn, prominent Radical politician in Georgia, who was murdered at Jonesboro, Georgia.
It should be noted that the K.K.K. notices given above were taken from journals of the associations.

Northern Commissions." The *Chronicle and Sentinel* admitted that the schools might "do great good," both in educating the Negro and in cultivating good feeling between the races. This would not be the case, however, if the schools were controlled by "narrow minded fanatics" who exerted a "mischievous influence" upon the Negro.[49]

The editor of another Georgia paper, the Macon *Telegraph,* confessed a certain admiration for the teachers who had "left home and all its comforts" to engage in such work among the Negroes. The Negroes were in the South, and free. To them the South must look for labor. Southerners, as the real friends of the Negro, should not object to his education. The Southern people were "eminently a missionary people," and must not condemn those who now engaged in real missionary work, even though the work was near at home.[50]

Nevertheless, the evidence clearly shows that, in most instances, the Northern teacher was socially ostracized, insulted, persecuted, and, in many cases, forced to abandon his school.[51]

This attitude did not extend to all Northerners who might have business in the South. Obviously, it would be absurd to assert that the Northerner was received with a glad hand and a warm heart throughout the South, but it is also incorrect to assume that the term "Yankee" (even when used with the stronger prefix) was, in itself, sufficient to bar an individual from "what is called society" in the South. Although an intensive study of this interesting phase of social relationships during the reconstruction period is impossible here, some pertinent items should be considered.

There is abundant evidence that Northern men who entered the South, or who remained there after the close of the war, for business purposes, were well received by the people. As in the case of the teachers, the Southern women were less inclined to extend

[49] Augusta (Georgia) *Chronicle and Sentinel,* October 14, 1866.

[50] Macon *Daily Telegraph,* in *American Missionary,* X, 3 (March, 1866), 62–63.

[51] As late as 1884 the Superintendent of Education for the American Missionary Association asserted that from the better class of Southerners the Northern teachers "got, and still get, simply social ostracism, the most severe letting alone that history records." He did not blame the Southern people, he said. The education of their former chattels merely added insult to injury. The result was violence from the lower classes and ostracism from all others. See address of Albert Salisbury to the National Educational Association, *Journal of Proceedings and Addresses, 1884,* p. 105.

social courtesies than the Southern men, but even among the women there was, to say the least, toleration.

General John Tarbell, U.S.A., in his testimony before the Committee on Reconstruction, denied the charge that Southern people were, as a whole, bitter against individual Northerners. After having travelled throughout Alabama, Mississippi, and northern Georgia he could say that he "would as soon travel alone, unarmed, through the south as through the north." "The south I left," he said, "is not the south I hear and read about in the north." From the picture drawn by the prevailing sentiment at the North he could "scarcely recognize" the people he had seen, and "except for their politics," liked so well. In his travels in the South he had always carefully made known his identity as "a Yankee and a black republican," yet he had not once received "anything like impoliteness or affront." The majority of the men to whom he had talked had told him that "it was not so much the matter as the manner of Northern men they objected to." The Southern business men wanted Northern men and Northern capital to come South, he said.[52]

General Meade expressed opinions in accord with those of General Tarbell. When Charles Sumner told Meade and Edward Bates that he was "fully convinced that a northern person could not safely go to the South," and that he had letters from various parts of the South which were of such a nature that they satisfied "everybody *but the prest.* of the bad state of feeling at the South" General Meade declared that his correspondents were "not trustworthy—they were there under strong prejudices," and that they had "so behaved as to excite the counter prejudices of the people— the schoolmarms wou[l]d insist upon *lit nigs* singing Old John Brown &c[.]"[53]

Major H. C. Lawrence, a native of Illinois, agent of the Freedmen's Bureau in North Carolina, told a Congressional Committee that he knew many Northern men who were engaged in business

[52] March 4, 1866. *Reconstruction Committee,* Part III, 156–157. General Tarbell had purchased a plantation in Scott County, Mississippi. The possible effect of this fact upon his testimony must be considered.

[53] *Diary of Edward Bates,* edited by Howard K. Beale. American Historical Association, *Annual Report, 1930,* Vol. IV, 554. Entry of March 15, 1866.

in North Carolina. He had not observed "any such prejudice against them as operates to their disadvantage." This, however, was not true of the teachers. He believed the women in North Carolina to be especially opposed to "white female teachers." [54] It was generally believed that a Northern man, "by exercising anything like a decent regard for private opinions," could work in the South with "self-respect, with safety, and with business prosperity." Northern business men were to be found everywhere. In the "out of the way" places they were "doing all the business," said one observer. [55]

Many Federal officers and men engaged in planting in the South after the war. A group of officers rented six thousand acres near Selma, Alabama, in 1865, and an officer of an Ohio regiment rented a plantation in Limestone County, Alabama. [56] Of sixteen plantations around Lake Concordia, Louisiana, ten were leased to Northern men in 1866. In fact, in 1866 the banks of the lower Mississippi were lined with plantations leased by Federal officers and other Northern men. [57] About forty-five Northern families settled in Morgan County, Georgia, soon after the war. The leader of the colony had been an officer under Sherman during the march to the sea, had liked the state, and determined to return after the close of hostilities. He and his associates were cordially received by their new neighbors, were treated "kindly and respectfully," and were not molested in any way. The leader, Captain True, was made a member of the executive committee of the State Agricultural Society. [58]

Northern business men were scattered all over the South. In western North Carolina a lieutenant colonel of the New Jersey Volunteers was engaged in gold mining in 1867. He had not been molested. [59] The President of the First National Bank of Galveston, Texas, in 1866 was Major-General Nichols, C.S.A., the cashier

---

[54] *Reconstruction Committee*, Part II, 293–294.

[55] See testimony of Stephen Powers, of the Cincinnati *Commercial*, in *Reconstruction Committee*, Part IV, 145; *Nation*, September 14, 1865, p. 322.

[56] *Nation*, September 28, 1865, p. 420, August 17, 1865, p. 208.

[57] Major Lorenzo Thomas, *Reconstruction Committee*, Part IV, 141; New York *Times*, May 8, 1866.

[58] Testimony of C. W. Howard, October 31, 1871, *K.K.K.*, VII, Georgia II, 830.

[59] James W. Lyon, Morganton, North Carolina, to J. W. Alvord, April 12, 1867, B.R.F.A.L. MSS.

was Major-General Clark, U.S.C.T., and ten members of the Board of Directors had served as officers in the Confederate army.[60] The postmaster and several business men of Athens, Alabama, were natives of the North, but were "socially well treated."[61] The editor of the Republican paper at Huntsville, Alabama, was a native of Ohio. When he visited his former home his friends "seemed delighted to see him back safe." They were surprised that he, a "cold and decided Republican," had returned from "the region of the Ku Klux and chimeras dire," and were "incredulous as to the description he gave them of the character of the people and the treatment he had received" in Alabama.[62]

Another Northerner, formerly an officer in the Federal army, in his testimony before the Ku Klux Committee asserted that Northern men who were gentlemen were "received with the civilities of a gentleman," but that Northern men were "subject to a closer scrutiny" than other men, and that there was "a disposition to investigate closely the character" of Northern immigrants. This tendency on the part of the Southerners was due to the fact that all over the South soldiers had remained, who, in many cases, would not have been socially acceptable in respectable circles in the North. He was aware, however, that it was impossible for men of opposing armies and sections to meet and associate in the same manner as if there had been no war.[63]

A former Federal officer, a native of Maine who had engaged in cotton planting in southwestern Georgia, declared, with evident enthusiasm, that he had not been insulted or injured in any way, that he had been "very kindly treated" in Georgia. He had brought his wife from Maine, and intended to remain in Georgia as long as he lived. "I have been exceedingly kindly treated since I have been in Georgia . . . much more so than I really expected to be when I first came here," he said. When he moved to the

[60] New York *Times,* May 8, 1866.
[61] Testimony of Daniel Coleman, County Solicitor, Athens, Alabama, *K.K.K.,* IX, Alabama II, 663.
[62] Testimony of William K. Lowe, native lawyer, *K.K.K.,* IX, Alabama II, 884.
[63] *K.K.K.,* VIII, Alabama I, 608. See, also, the testimony of Peter M. Dox, a member of the House of Representatives, *ibid.,* 435. Dox said he had told the House that the carpetbag officers of many Southern towns and counties would not be tolerated in the North. For example, the probate judge of Madison County was, Dox said, "a common jack-plane carpenter from Oregon," and the sheriff was practically illiterate.

farm which he had purchased, near Americus, he knew nothing about cotton. His neighbors came over on Sundays, rode over the plantation with him, and showed him "what to do." "They were really nice people," he said. "I cannot deny that because I was so nicely treated." He admitted that few citizens of Americus had called on him, but said that he and his wife had been "in society" to a much greater extent in Macon. In Atlanta, however, the Northerners had "a large society" of their own, and therefore were not "obliged to look to others." There was a very definite line of social cleavage in Atlanta, he thought. The Southerners did not accept the people from the North. He felt, as did many another Northern man, that the "ladies in the South" were "very much more bitter than the men." [64]

Evidence that at least one Northern farmer could go his way un-molested through the state of Georgia is given in a letter written in 1868 by a former officer of the Federal army:

Thomas county,
Georgia, *December* 28, 1868

Dear Sir: Your favor of today reached me, making inquiry concerning my treatment in this section by the people. I served as officer in the United States army during the late war. In the fall of 1865 I engaged in planting here, and have spent the entire time since within the State. In the spring of 1867 was appointed register under the reconstruction acts; registered three counties and managed the elections in two of them. In June, 1868, was appointed an agent of the Bureau of Refugees, Freedmen and Aban-doned Lands, with jurisdiction over three counties, and served in that capacity until the 1st instant. During this time I have driven through the State three times, have gone at all hours when and where I pleased, un-armed and unattended, have spoken openly at every place and to every-body, and used as strong republican language as I could command; have interested myself openly in three elections in behalf of the republican party, and we have carried the county by a large majority each time . . . and during all this time I have been treated as well as I could be at any place, and in no case have I been insulted in the least. The better class of people,

---

[64] Testimony of William C. Morrill, November 6, 1871, *K.K.K.*, VII, Georgia II, 1081–1099. Morrill and General Sheppard, of Maine, bought a plantation near Americus, which they sold to a third citizen of Maine. Morrill was agent of the B.R.F.A.L. and U.S. Commissioner at Americus and Collector of Internal Revenue at Macon, 1868–1871, in which office he was followed by William Gray, of Pennsylvania. In 1871 he was treasurer of the Western and Atlantic Railroad.

and particularly those who were good soldiers in the southern army, are very cordial in their treatment.

Hoping we may be 'let alone,' I subscribe myself your obedient servant,

O. T. Lyon [65]

A special correspondent sent south by the Boston cotton manufacturers association did not paint so favorable a picture. From Galveston, Texas, he wrote that Northern immigrants must "assimilate to these half-civilized Southerners," must sever all ties with the North, oppose Negro suffrage "to the death," and must subject themselves to "constant and untiring serveillance." If they would do these things, they would be "permitted" to remain in the South. He did not think, however, that many men could reconcile themselves to hearing their "friends, sentiments, and education made the subject of never-ceasing abuse and vituperation." The ministers, the women, and the young men hated the North "with a degree of intensity that cannot be exaggerated," he declared. As a rule the officers and men of the Confederate army were "more moderate, more reasonable, and milder" than the non-combatants, but even some of the soldiers were "most bitter and resentful." In short, military rule was necessary. The people of the South could only be held as "a conquered people," he thought.[66]

Another correspondent wrote that the Southern boys were being taught that the relations of the South to the North were those of "Venetia toward Austria, or of Poland to Russia." "As Hamilcar made Hannibal swear eternal enmity against old Rome, so every Southern matron is bringing up her children to hate and despise the Federal Union," he said. With rather interesting foresight, he prophesied that in the future the South would "present one solid, unanimous front." [67]

It is evident, then, that the Southern people were opposed to the Yankee teacher, often violently so, but that this opposition did not extend to all Northern men. Obviously not all Northern men

---

[65] House Miscellaneous Documents, 40 Cong. 3 Sess. no. 52 (Serial 1385), 157.

[66] The bitterness of this correspondent may be partially explained by the date—November, 1865—and partially by the fact that he had engaged in planting in Mississippi in 1864, where he had met violent opposition. *Nation,* December 7, 1865, p. 714.

[67] *Ibid.,* October 26, 1865, pp. 523–524.

were welcomed by all Southern people in all sections of the South, but the term "Yankee" was not a term of complete opprobrium, as is sometimes maintained.

There was little exception, however, to the hatred and contempt which the Southerner felt for the Yankee teacher. No doubt the very fact that the teachers closely associated with the Negroes contributed to this feeling. Such association, which broke down racial and traditional taboos, was a direct violation of the caste system. The advocacy of social and political equality further aggravated the estrangement between the Negro and his former master, and hence deepened the animosity which the whites felt toward the teachers.

It might be assumed that the Southern persecution of the Yankee teacher was merely evidence of universal opposition to the education of the Negro. Such was not the case. Immediately after the close of the war there arose a strong sentiment for the education of the Negro. This feeling was not universal, nor did it eventuate in the adoption of any definite program. Many Southern leaders expressed a strong belief that the Negro must now be educated. The details of the program which they might have proposed can only be surmised. By "education" they probably meant instruction limited to the rudiments, with the possible addition of manual and vocational training. Certainly the majority of those Southerners who wanted to see the Negro educated did not approve of the program of classical education introduced by the Northern teachers. They considered "higher education" for the Negro either impossible, foolish, or unwise and dangerous. Speculation on the possible result of the conviction that the Negro must be educated, and by Southerners, is idle, since the feeling was rendered sterile by the progress of social and political reconstruction under the Radical regime, and the consequent reaction of the South.

Certainly, there was no universal demand for free public schools for the Negro, and there was, in many sections, and on the part of many individuals, strong opposition to his education. It is also true, however, that many Southerners favored the education of the Negro, that they supported movements, both public and private, toward this end, and that, for a time at least, many native Southern whites were employed as teachers in freedmen's schools.

A prominent writer on the history of the reconstruction period, in discussing the attitude of the South toward the education of the Negro, declared that "on the part of the whites whose opinion was worth anything, there was no objection worth mentioning to negro schools in 1865 and 1866. . . . The evidence on this point that is worthy of consideration is conclusive. It is all one way." "For two years there was little or no opposition by the whites to the education of the negro, and to some extent they even favored and aided it." [68]

On the other hand, a well-known Negro scholar indignantly denies the truth of this statement. "Persistent propaganda represents the South after the war as being largely in favor of Negro education," he says. "This is a flat contradiction of plain historical evidence." [69]

Without quibbling over the language used by either of these writers, it is possible to submit evidence on both sides of the controversy. Any attempt to reach a definitive conclusion in the matter would be a task whose difficulty would be exceeded only by its length. As such it has no place here. The question impinges upon this study only in so far as it may have affected the Yankee teacher. Was the opposition to the teachers manifested by the Southern people merely the reflection of a general antipathy to the education of the Negro, or were there other reasons for this opposition? Is it possible that both Southerner and Northerner agreed on the desirability of educating the Negro, and that each wished to direct such education?

In the period prior to 1867 there seems to have been remarkably little violence among the Southern whites, although they manifested their disapproval of the Yankee teacher in no uncertain terms. In 1863 the schools at Memphis, Tennessee, were flourishing, but in the face of bitter opposition. The citizens were, it was said, "mad beyond expression," but the teachers continued their work, under the protection of Federal troops.[70] At Jacksonville,

---

[68] Fleming, *Civil War and Reconstruction*, 457, and note; 463.
[69] DuBois, *Black Reconstruction*, 645.
[70] *American Missionary*, VII, 5 (May, 1863), 111.

Florida, some opposition was felt because the school established in 1864 provided for the enrollment of both races. The white children objected, but the teacher showed them that opposition would be useless, since the Negroes would be educated whether the whites were or not. "This argument proved effective," she wrote.[71] Early in January, 1866, the Superintendent of Education for Florida reported "the bitterest opposition" to the education of the freedmen. Teachers were ostracized, and schools could operate only under the protection of Federal bayonets. By March, however, there was a strong demand for teachers and schools, not only from freedmen, but from former masters, especially the masters of large plantations. "Many" planters had offered to pay half the expenses of a school.[72]

In North Carolina many citizens were willing to see the Negro educated, but were determined that white and Negro children should not attend the same school. Nothing must be done which "looked towards the social equality of negroes and whites," wrote one observer. Some citizens felt that the Negroes should be educated as "intelligent and useful free laborers," but were unwilling to admit the possibility or desirability of higher education.[73]

Even in South Carolina, as early as 1865, there was some support of the education of the Negro. Some citizens believed that the Negro should be educated and given the ballot, since the whites could increase their political power by controlling the Negro vote.[74]

In 1866 northern Alabama was peaceful, there was no manifestation of opposition to Negro education, and no cases of violence had been reported to the authorities.[75] There were seven schools in northern Alabama taught by native white men, three schools taught by seven Negroes, and two schools taught by ex-

[71] William W. Davis, *Civil War and Reconstruction in Florida* (Columbia University, 1913), *Columbia University Studies in History, Economics, and Public Law*, LIII, 326, quoting letter from Mrs. Esther Hawks to New York *Tribune*.

[72] See H. H. Moore to F. G. Shaw, January 1, 1866, *National Freedman*, II, I (January 15, 1866), 3–5; H. H. Moore to T. W. Osborn, January 28, 1866, *Senate Executive Documents*, 39 Cong., 1 Sess., no. 27 (Serial 1238), 56–57; Davis, *Civil War and Reconstruction*, 389.

[73] *Nation*, October 5, 1865, p. 428.

[74] *Ibid.*, 426.

[75] Major J. Jones, B.R.F.A.L. Agent, *American Missionary*, X, 11 (November, 1866), 528–530.

soldiers of the Federal army. In fact, one observer reported that the citizens of Alabama were beginning to look favorably "on the education of the negro," and were now ready to give some support to Negro schools.[76]

Georgia, Tennessee, and Mississippi reported opposition. At LaGrange, Georgia, the Rev. J. H. Caldwell, formerly pastor of a Methodist Church in Georgia, and now a minister in the Northern branch of the Methodist Church, opened a school for six hundred pupils. In 1866 mobs fired into the building, breaking the windows, and both Caldwell and his wife received threatening letters. At Columbus, near LaGrange, some of the ladies of the town, "of the highest standing in society," were reported to have seriously planned to hang the Yankee teacher.[77] Schools were burned at Griffin, and violence was severe in Henry county.[78] In the Altamaha region the whites were united in their opposition to Negro education, but divided in their reasons for opposition— some thought any attempt to educate Negroes foolish, since they were believed to be mentally incompetent; some thought it dangerous to educate them, since no working class should ever be educated; while others feared the social and political power of the educated Negro. The citizens of Thomasville were also opposed to the establishment of Negro schools, but at Albany planters requested teachers for schools which they had established for their "hands." In fact, in most sections of the state the "better class of thinking men" favored the education of the Negro, and opposition was confined to the lower classes, according to the report of an official of the Bureau.[79] At Atlanta there was growing sentiment in favor of the education of the Negro. Many "secesh"—even some "secesh women"—visited the schools in 1866 and commended the work being done there. People were frequently heard to admit that they had changed their opinions, and had come to see that the schools were necessary and desirable. In many instances former masters bought books for their former

[76] New York *Daily Tribune*, February 3, 1866.
[77] MS. Report of the Superintendent of Education for Georgia, October 8, 1866, B.R.F.A.L. MSS.
[78] J. W. Alvord, *Report*, July 1, 1866; Augusta (Georgia) *Chronicle and Sentinel*, October 19, 1866.
[79] C. H. Howard, *Reconstruction Committee*, Part III, 43–44.

slaves, and encouraged them to attend school.[80] A Northern minister who visited Milledgeville in 1866 was "much encouraged" by the presence of prominent politicians, ministers, and teachers. He believed that prejudice against the schools was fast dying away.[81]

In his report for July, 1866, Superintendent Alvord reported a remarkable "change of sentiment" among the "better classes of the South." Many planters had become convinced that the Negro would be a more contented laborer if educated. The leading statesmen of the South were now urging that the Negro would be "safer" if "made moral and intelligent," and religious denominations all over the South had resolved to aid in the education of the Negro. In fact, the majority of the men of "higher intelligence" believed that the Negro should be educated, but "with the proviso that northern teachers" should "no longer be sent" and that the schools should be under Southern supervision.[82]

At about the same time General O. O. Howard told the members of the American Freedmen's Union Commission that although the South had been opposed to the education of the Negro, sentiment was now changing. He knew many planters who had been opposed to Negro education but who now urgently requested that teachers be sent to work in schools which they had set up on their plantations. He believed that soon planters would find it impossible to operate in any section of the South without first establishing schools for the freedmen.[83]

That the Southern people were not violently opposed to the education of the Negro was recognized by the benevolent associations. In November, 1866, the leading editorial in the *American Freedman* declared that although prejudice had not vanished from "the lower classes," the more thoughtful Southerners were now demanding the education of the Negro. It was recognized as "imperatively necessary to the welfare of the South," and this

[80] F. Ayer, *American Missionary*, X, 5 (May, 1866), 114.
[81] *Ibid.*, X, 4 (April, 1866), 86–88. One of the teachers, Professor Morton, of Oglethorpe College, established a school for freedmen in the spring of 1866. He had been a slaveholder, and a chaplain in the Confederate Army. See *American Missionary*, X, 5 (May, 1866), 111.
[82] *Report*, July 1, 1866, pp. 1–2.
[83] *American Freedman*, I, 9 (December, 1866), 133.

element of the Southern people was prepared to co-operate in the work, "provided it is offered in a kindly and Christian spirit."

The editorial suggested that since this was the existing state of sentiment in the South, the various associations must cultivate the feeling assiduously. The teachers must not depend upon bayonets, but "upon the kindly co-operation" of the Southern people. The teachers should refrain from unduly exciting the prejudices of the Southerners, who might be inclined to consider the coming of the Northern teachers "a sort of second invasion." Any assumption that the South was regarded as a missionary field would be "resented as an insult." Here was the difficulty. "The South no longer opposes the education of the freedmen. This it approves —it even attempts to provide. But it looks askance on Northern interference. Its hostility is excited not by the school-marm, but by the *Yankee* school-marm," said the editorial. If the teachers went into the South with the conviction that the Southern people were wholly hostile to Negro education, and that education must be supported by the bayonet; if they "contemptuously" disregarded "those race and sectional prejudices which are of a century's growth" or "openly and violently" assailed the beliefs of the Southern people, they would increase "the difficulties which a kindlier policy might remove," and "give some reasonable ground for an opposition which would otherwise be utterly without reason." The teacher might enter a Southern city, ignore the white citizens, confine himself wholly to the Negroes, select a site for a school—in short, conduct himself with "total disregard" of "local customs and life-long prejudices and opinions." If so, he need expect nothing but opposition. The teacher should first confer with "the mayor, alderman or clergyman, seek their advice, as much as possible conform to it." He should be "courteous, frank, and kind to all." If he conducted himself in this manner, and conformed to "local customs and practices" whenever such conformity would not "compromise principle," he would, no doubt, receive kindness, and even support, from the Southern people.[84]

In the following issue the same magazine declared that the

[84] *American Freedman*, I, 8 (November, 1866), 114.

teachers had no right to expect active support. Indifference must be considered toleration, and toleration would allow the work to prosper. Despite the withdrawal of many units of the Federal army, "outrages upon teachers" had been "by no means of common occurrence," and few schools had been forced to close.[85]

Had the teachers followed the excellent advice given them by the editor of the *American Freedman,* they might have been more successful in their efforts, and much of the bitter racial animosity of the reconstruction period might have been avoided.

In 1866 a correspondent of the New York *Herald* reported that there was "no objection to the education of the freedmen" in the South. The Southern people objected to, and found "a great deal of fault with," the missionaries who had come from the North, he said. They believed that the missionaries interfered with "other matters, in the relations between the servant and his employer." The Southern whites were willing to "undertake the education of the blacks themselves if they [were] only left alone."[86] The *Nation* observed an "increased interest . . . on the part of the better class of white people" but a continuation of outrages "among the ignorant and degraded," especially in Georgia, Mississippi, and Tennessee.[87] James D. B. De Bow declared that the "better informed people of the South" favored the education of the Negro to the limit of his capacity. They believed it to be "for their best interest" to educate the freedmen.[88] John Minor Botts asserted that the "more intelligent classes" would be glad to see the Negroes educated. "A great many" citizens of Virginia would give financial support to Negro schools, but, of course, there were "a great many" who would not.[89] One of the prominent teachers made a tour of inspection in Tennessee and Georgia in 1866. He found that the majority of the Southerners "spoke kindly of the

[85] Even the fiery Theodore Tilton understood this reason for Southern opposition. He urged that the associations employ Southern teachers in the freedmen's schools. In this way "the antipathy to Yankee schoolmasters and school marms would be disarmed," he wrote, and there would be no complaint about "a second Northern invasion." Southern opposition was "directed less against the institution than against those who control and conduct it," Tilton said. *Independent,* September 6, 1866.

[86] Thomas M. Cook, *Reconstruction Committee,* Part II, 278.

[87] *Nation,* September 20, 1866, p. 223.

[88] *Reconstruction Committee,* Part IV, 135.

[89] *Ibid.,* Part II, 122–123.

Negroes." They believed that the Negroes should be educated "both for their own good and that of the whites." They admitted that the teachers were not received socially, and many said *"they were afraid they taught them things they did not find in the books."* [90]

In Alabama there were, in 1866, many teachers and preachers who were anxious to teach the freedmen if some means of supporting the schools could be found. [91] Governor Parsons favored the work, and "some native white teachers" were willing to accept positions in freedmen's schools, according to the report of J. W. Alvord, Inspector of Schools. In the more remote districts, however, there was "much opposition," and women teachers from the North would require military protection, he wrote. [92] At Montgomery there was sympathy, even enthusiasm. The leading white men were formulating plans for the organization of a system of Negro schools. The son of one of the prominent citizens had opened a night school, with 150 pupils, and expected to open a day school in the near future. In this work he was supported by "the leading citizens." The ladies of the local churches proposed to teach in the Sunday Schools as soon as the Northern teachers could be persuaded to withdraw. [93] There was less opposition to freedmen's schools in Alabama than in other states, according to the report of the state Superintendent of Education. "Both schools and teachers" were "respected" in 1866. Some of the teachers were "natives of the State and from good families." [94]

Early in 1866 a Mississippi judge told the Committee on Reconstruction that there was "not only no opposition" to the education of the Negro in that state, but "a positive desire" that schools be established. There was, he said, a school in Aberdeen with more than one hundred pupils, and other schools in the vicinity, which were conducted by ministers. [95] The mayor and council of Aberdeen had formally endorsed the education of the Negro, and had

[90] Adam K. Spence, *American Missionary*, X, 8 (August, 1866), 184.
[91] Rev. J. Silsby, Montgomery, Alabama, October 22, 1866, *ibid.*, X, 112 (December, 1866), 281.
[92] *Senate Executive Documents*, 39 Cong., 1 Sess., no. 27 (Serial 1238), 110. Reports of Assistant Commissioners, B.R.F.A.L., Report of Inspector Alvord, January 1, 1866.
[93] Report of Agent at Montgomery, Alvord, *Report*, July 1, 1866, p. 6.
[94] C. W. Buckley, Report to Alvord, Alvord, *Report*, January 1, 1867, p. 16.
[95] Robert A. Hill, February 8, 1866, *Reconstruction Committee*, Part III, 68.

agreed to aid the benevolent associations in their efforts to establish schools for the freedmen.[96] By May, 1866, opposition had increased, however, and it was practically impossible for the teachers to carry on their work in Mississippi. Windows were smashed, schools destroyed, and teachers threatened. Rev. J. P. Bardwell, American Missionary Association teacher at Grenada, Mississippi, was severely beaten, other teachers threatened, and an officer of the Freedmen's Bureau murdered.[97]

Gradually the white people of Mississippi became convinced that the best defense against the Yankee teacher was active participation in Negro education. In October, 1866, Bardwell wrote that the people of Grenada had begun to "agitate the question" in "public assemblies." Their real motive was not interest in Negro education, he said. "The question with them is not so much *how they* shall *secure the education of the negroes*," but "how they can get rid of the *Yankee teachers*." [98] At Columbus the mayor and alderman gave special protection to the teachers, and strongly denounced those who had threatened and insulted them.[99] By the end of the year a favorable change was evident. Many citizens were giving lumber and money, and the "general tone of conversation" throughout the state showed that "a more friendly state of feeling existed." [100]

Opposition was very strong in many other sections of the South in 1866. The great Memphis riot of 1866, in which Negro churches and schools were burned, caused many teachers to abandon the work, and teachers were threatened in Alabama, Georgia, and Texas.[101]

South Carolina reported very little active opposition to the schools during 1866. Many citizens of Columbia were said to favor Negro education, but the majority were opposed, although

---

[96] *Senate Executive Documents*, 39 Cong., 1 Sess., no. 27 (Serial 1238), 46. Report of Colonel S. Thomas, Assistant Commissioner, B.R.F.A.L., January 31, 1866.

[97] *American Missionary*, X, 6 (June, 1866), 138, 200; Nashville (Tennessee) *Dispatch,* May 15, 1866.

[98] *American Missionary*, X, 10 (October, 1866), 218–219.

[99] Nashville (Tennessee) *Dispatch,* May 10, 1866.

[100] Report of A. C. Gillem, Assistant Commissioner, B.R.F.A.L., Alvord, *Report,* January 1, 1867, p. 18.

[101] *American Missionary*, X, 6 (June, 1866), 134–135; X, 10 (October, 1866), 223–224.

not violently. The Odd Fellows refused to rent their hall for use as a Negro school, but were willing to allow the teacher to use it "for a while." [102]   At Charleston George A. Trenholm, former Secretary of the Treasury of the Confederate States, was a member of a committee which visited the school of which F. L. Cardoza was principal. The committee asked Cardoza's advice in educational matters, as the Episcopal Convention of the state was planning to locate schools all over the state. This act was, Cardoza thought, impressive evidence of a strong interest in and sympathy toward Negro education.[103]   At about the same time Reuben Tomlinson, Superintendent of Education of the state, wrote Francis George Shaw, president of the National Freedmen's Relief Association, that he was "very much encouraged." A "genuine and surprising change" had taken place in "the minds of the people" of the state. A "large planter" had just called upon him, requesting permission to establish a school for freedmen in the vicinity of his plantation. His wife and niece were to be the teachers, and the planter was to erect the building. He was "only one of a number" who had recently made such offers, wrote Tomlinson. In his report to Superintendent Alvord, Tomlinson said that the bitterness which had been felt at first was abating, and that planters in various sections of the state had requested that Northern teachers be sent to set up schools on their plantations.[104]

In North Carolina many people were "indifferent" toward Negro education, some favored it, some opposed. In 1866 the Freedmen's Bureau knew of only one school which had been burned— at Elizabeth City. In some instances planters had established schools "as a means of promoting good order and contentment." Many local churches had established Sunday Schools for the Negroes.[105]   At Newton the white people favored the education of the Negroes, and set aside a building for their use. At Plymouth a Southern man, whose son had been a prisoner at Point Lookout, gave ten dollars to the Negro school.[106]   Major H. C.

---

[102] *National Freedman,* II, 1 (January 15, 1866), 9; II, 2 (February 15, 1866), 56–57.

[103] *American Missionary,* X, 4 (April, 1866), 79–80.

[104] *National Freedman,* II, 2 (February 15, 1866), 43; Alvord, *Report,* July 1, 1866, p. 5. For a similar statement by Tomlinson, see *Nation,* August 9, 1866, p. 103.

[105] Testimony of E. Whittlesey, *Reconstruction Committee,* Part II, 183, 192.

[106] New York *Tribune,* February 3, 1866.

Lawrence, B.R.F.A.L. agent in eastern North Carolina, asserted that all "intelligent and good citizens" in North Carolina favored the education of the Negro. They considered such a program "a social necessity," he said.[107]

In 1866 Virginia also reported growing sentiment in favor of the education of the Negro. "On the whole," wrote Superintendent R. M. Manly, "it is certain that there is an improving sentiment, particularly in centers of intelligence and influence." Newspapers and churches had expressed their approval of Negro education, "both as duty and sound policy."[108] There were dissenting voices, however, and the "milder modes of resistance" were frequently used, such as refusing to rent buildings for schools, or refusing to board teachers. In general, the Yankee teacher was "intensely hated," said Manly. Superintendent Alvord reported that favorable sentiment existed in the "better class," and that "a considerable number of earnest calls" had been made "for teachers and books." The religious conventions of the state had passed resolutions favoring the education of the Negro.[109] General John S. Mosby cordially received the leader of the group of teachers stationed at Warrenton, Virginia. It was his opinion that the Negroes should be educated. He saw "no reasonable objection to it," and offered to introduce the teacher to other citizens who might be sympathetic.[110] At Charlottesville, a professor of law in the University, several students in the University, and thirty or forty "sons and daughters of former slave-holders" were, in April, teaching an average of three hundred freedmen their "Three R's."[111]

The general increase in favorable sentiment toward Negro education continued throughout the spring and summer of 1867. Very little opposition was manifested until the fall of that year. E. L. Pierce, who was, in addition to his other duties, a member of

[107] *Reconstruction Committee,* Part II, 292–293.

[108] *National Freedman,* II, 2 (February 15, 1866), 57–58.

[109] *Report,* July 1, 1866, p. 3. Similar action had been taken by the Episcopal Church in South Carolina, as has been noted, and by the Southern Baptist Convention at Russellville, Kentucky, May 27, 1866. This action was cordially praised by the press. See Augusta (Georgia) *Chronicle and Sentinel,* June 9, 1866.

[110] Hiram Eddy, Warrenton, Virginia, *American Missionary,* X, 1 (January, 1866), 1–2.

[111] Nashville (Tennessee) *Dispatch,* May 1, 1866.

the Executive Committee of the New England Freedmen's Aid Society, in a report to the Annual Meeting of the Society, April 5, 1867, said:

> The disposition of the Southern people towards our schools has visibly improved. The baser sort continue their bitterness, though even these are becoming less violent, because more familiar with the spectacle. But the better-educated and more liberal-minded portion of the people . . . have, in a measure, abandoned opposition, and frequently expressed sympathy. Clergymen, editors, officials, and prominent citizens, have occasionally visited our schools, and . . . have testified their approval. . . .
>
> Even those who, from sectional antipathy, are hostile to our schools, admit the necessity of educating the colored people. They are alarmed lest Northern opinions on which republican society is founded, should come to have sway over the millions of this race, and see no other way to prevent what they reckon as a calamity, except by encouraging schools of their own for the colored people.

The work of the teachers had been of "great political importance." The Negroes would soon be enfranchised, said Pierce, and therefore must be educated. The Southern political leaders realized this fact, hence the wave of Southern interest in Negro education. The true friends of the Negro must take steps to thwart the "sinister calculations" of the Southerners, he declared.[112]

At this meeting, the Teachers' Committee reported violence at Warrenton and Richmond, Virginia, Smithfield and Snow Hill, North Carolina, and Savannah, Georgia, during the preceding year.[113] Since the New England Freedmen's Aid Society supported schools in most of the Southern states at this time, these reports of its committee are of especial importance.

In many of the states the prevailing opinion in the early months of 1867 was quite similar to that of the fall of 1866. In Alabama the Bureau inspector "found no opposition on the part of the better and influential class of white people to the education of the freedmen." [114] At Montgomery there was a day school of one hundred and fifty pupils and a night school of forty, both under the direction of a well educated Southern man. At Selma a school was supported by the local Presbyterian church; the

---

[112] *Freedmen's Record,* III, 5 (May, 1867), 76–83.
[113] *Ibid.,* 72.
[114] Alvord, *Report,* January 1, 1868, p. 32.

teachers were the pastor and his wife. Many planters, particularly in the Black Belt counties, favored the education of the Negro. In fact, plantation schools were "springing up in many localities." [115] In the Tennessee Valley no opposition was evident. It was not difficult to find well educated natives of the State who were willing to teach in colored schools. Among the applicants for such positions in 1867 were graduates of the University of Alabama and former county superintendents of education. [116]

Many planters in Arkansas "demanded" teachers for schools on their plantations. The Assistant Commissioner of the Freedmen's Bureau reported "with great satisfaction" the "increasing friendliness" toward both education and teachers. [117] The Superintendent of Education also reported widespread approval of schools for freedmen. Even in the extreme southwestern portion of the state planters were anxious to "extend every possible facility" to the schools "to furnish room, board the teachers, and guarantee protection." In only one Arkansas county was there any opposition. Even the clergymen extended "the courtesies of the profession" to the Assistant Superintendent of Schools, the Rev. E. K. Miller. [118]

Many Florida planters also wanted teachers in 1867, and "readily" supplied land for school sites. The freedmen furnished the labor, and the Freedmen's Bureau the windows, nails, and other materials. [119]

In August, 1867, the Bureau inspector reported that he had found in Mississippi a "very thorough earnestness on the part of the white people . . . to see the freedmen properly educated." The white people were organizing schools in all parts of the state. In practically all cases the white men had given land, and in Canton, Corinth, Jackson, and other cities the citizens had contributed liberally in cash. In fact, the inspector had not talked with a single leading influential white man who "did not express the opinion apparently with full earnestness, that the abolition of

[115] *Ibid.*, 33; *Report*, July 1, 1867, p. 31.

[116] *Ibid.*, 32.

[117] General C. H. Smith, in Alvord, *Report*, January 1, 1868, pp. 38–40.

[118] Alvord, *Report*, July 1, 1867, p. 44–45. Mississippi County. These details were given by Alvord because they showed "a kindliness of feeling on the part of the planters which had not been supposed to exist."

[119] General J. T. Sprague, Assistant Commissioner, B.R.F.A.L., Alvord, *Report*, January 1, 1868, p. 31.

slavery" was "a fixed fact, and that the freedmen ought to be educated." If the Negro was to be the laborer of the state, his education must be "thoroughly cared for." In the spring of 1867 Superintendent Pease was convinced that "all prejudice against the education of the freed people" would "soon disappear." He could have established fifty plantation schools if he had been able to secure the teachers, he said.[120] At Meridian there was a school taught by native white women, and at Canton a school under the direction of a Baptist minister of "fine reputation and broad influence." Another in the same town was taught by a Southern white man, and a third by a white woman. There was, however, some opposition at Oxford, Columbus, and Charleston. Several other towns were classed as "indifferent."[121]

The good feeling early manifested in eastern North Carolina continued during the first months of 1867. Sentiment at Edenton and Kinston was especially favorable.[122] At Smithfield, despite the slight unpleasantness of 1866, already referred to, there was great interest among the white people. Practically all the white citizens of the town attended a concert given by the pupils of the Negro school in April, 1867, and were so highly pleased that the local Methodist church offered the use of its auditorium for the next concert.[123] In short, Superintendent Fiske reported, sentiment in the state was "gradually strengthening in favor of schools for the freedmen" up to the close of the spring session, 1867.[124]

In South Carolina, Superintendent Tomlinson declared, in the summer of 1867, that while in 1865 he had not been able to find more than one white man of "social position" who would admit either the possibility or desirability of educating the colored children, he now doubted that a man could be found in the entire state who "whatever his private convictions may be, is not publicly in favor of educating them." "I question very much," said Tomlinson, "whether now a half dozen men of intelligence can be found" in the centers of greatest opposition in 1865 who would

---

120 *American Missionary*, XI, 9 (September, 1867), 201.
121 Alvord, *Report*, July 1, 1867, pp. 35–36.
122 Alvord, *Report*, January 1, 1868, p. 25.
123 *American Missionary*, XI, 9 (September, 1867), 195.
124 Alvord, *Report*, July 1, 1867, p. 18; *American Missionary*, XI, 3 (March, 1867), 51.

not "deem it a public calamity to have the schools discontinued." The people no longer spoke of the schools with bitterness, and "generally" treated the teachers "with politeness." There had been only one case of violence in 1867, and that very mild.[125]

In the spring of 1867 the officers of the Freedmen's Bureau agreed that opposition was disappearing in Georgia. The Superintendent of Education reported that a "truly wonderful change" in public sentiment had taken place. Conditions were better than "the most sanguine" could have hoped for. The Assistant Commissioner was pleased to report that opposition had practically ceased. There had been no interference since the early months of 1866 except the burning of one school "by unknown incendiaries."[126]

The people of Virginia were not, in the spring of 1867, violently opposed to the schools. They treated the teachers with "neglect" and carefully avoided all social contact with them, but by November there was active, though not serious, opposition. Groups of men marched around the homes of teachers, blowing horns and beating drums, tubs, and buckets. Teachers were burned in effigy, and ruffians swore to rid the "sacred soil of Virginia" of the contaminating influence of Yankee teachers and "nigger schools."[127]

By 1868 opposition was almost universal. In his report of January 1, 1868, Superintendent Alvord declared that the "revived rebel spirit of the South" had "thickened about" the schools. Many of the teachers had become discouraged and afraid to continue the work. "The truth is," said one of his assistants, "we are in the midst of a reign of terror, and unless something is done and done speedily for the relief of the persecuted Union people and friends of humanity, our educational work and interests must seriously suffer."[128] In July he reported continued bitterness toward the teachers. Almost all had received threats, both open and anonymous, and several had abandoned their schools under

[125] *American Missionary*, XI, 9 (September, 1867), 209; Alvord, *Report*, July 1, 1867, p. 19.

[126] Alvord, *Report*, July 1, 1867, pp. 26–27.

[127] John W. Pratt, Orange Court House, *Freedmen's Record*, III, 2 (February, 1867), 26; Rev. A. B. Corliss, *American Missionary*, XI, 11 (November, 1867), 27–28; *Congregationalist*, April 9, 1868.

[128] Alvord, *Report*, January 1, 1868, p. 46.

the pressure of opposition. He knew of none who had been injured, but he believed it advisable to withdraw all teachers from the small towns and rural districts, and to employ them in the larger towns and cities, where they could be protected "until after the November elections." [129]   Even in Alabama, heretofore reported as cordial toward Negro education, the Superintendent reported that the opposition was so strong that it would be "impossible for one at a distance to form any correct conception of the state of public sentiment." Everywhere there was determined opposition to the education of the freedmen. Schools had been burned, teachers threatened, even beaten and driven away. "Never was the spirit of opposition more bitter and defiant than at the present time," he said.[130]

Accounts of murders, outrages, and burnings now began to appear in the journals of the associations. For example, in September, 1868, the editor of the *American Missionary* warned his readers that a storm was gathering, and that the freedmen needed friends and advisers as never before. The September issue pointed with horror to the 968 murders in Texas, of which 379 were murders of freedmen by whites, and only ten of whites by Negroes. Outrages were said to be the order of the day in Mississippi, North Carolina, Texas, and Louisiana.[131]

Violent opposition increased as the presidential campaign of 1868 approached. In the words of Superintendent Alvord,

> Bitter opposition and frequent violence were "manifested quite up to the late presidential election. For a time it became doubtful whether schools in such localities could go on at all. Subsequently, however, to that election, asperity and bitterness . . . gradually subsided, open violence mainly ceased, and now, with very few exceptions, organized opposition no longer exists. Still, old prejudices remain, equality of rights is, more or less, resisted and the education of the freedmen throughout most of the southern states receives as yet too little practical encouragement." [132]

These conditions existed in most of the states. In Alabama the funds realized from the sale of Confederate property were ex-

---

[129] *Report*, July 1, 1868, p. 26 ff.
[130] Rev. R. D. Harper, Report to Alvord, Alvord, *Report*, July 1, 1868, p. 31.
[131] See *American Missionary*, XII, 9 (September, 1868).
[132] Alvord, *Report*, January 1, 1869, pp. 3–4.

hausted in 1868; many schools were closed because the *"increased violence of the people"* made it "unsafe for teachers to remain" at their posts. Many people believed that "no lower depth of degradation" could be reached than to teach Negroes.[133] Of eighteen districts in Arkansas, nine reported "opposition," three "favorable," one "passive," and five did not mention Negro education. Schools were burned and teachers flogged.[134] Even in West Virginia the Ku Klux Klan sent warnings to teachers, and the teachers were ostracized.[135] Of the 165 teachers remaining in Kentucky in August, 1868, only twenty-one were white, and they were located in towns, where they might be protected. The report of the Kentucky Superintendent of Education for 1868 contains a two page enumeration of outrages, threats, beatings, and burnings.[136] Opposition so great as to be almost prohibitive was reported from Louisiana, Texas, and even from Missouri and Kansas.[137]

In Tennessee the Klan was especially active in Montgomery, Stewart, and Dickson counties, and in the vicinity of such towns as Pulaski, Franklin, and Gallatin. Schools were burned, teachers threatened and beaten, and the usual pattern of violence followed.[138]

In Georgia opposition grew stronger as the election of 1868 approached. Schools were closed, or burned, teachers threatened and insulted. The teacher at Warrenton left in great haste, under threat of violence from the Klan. There was violence at Marietta, Jonesboro, Columbus, Newton, and in many rural areas.[139]

Superintendent R. M. Manly, an unusually well-balanced and sane school official, declared, in 1868, that there was intense hostility in Virginia toward Negro education. Efforts for Negro

---

[133] Superintendent Harper, Report to Alvord, Alvord, *Report*, January 1, 1869, p. 25.
[134] Superintendent Colby to Alvord, Alvord, *Report*, July 1, 1868, p. 45.
[135] Rev. John Kimball, *ibid.*, 10.
[136] Alvord, *Report*, January 1, 1869, pp. 43–49.
[137] Frank Chase, Louisiana, to J. W. Alvord, July 22, 1868, B.R.F.A.L. MSS. Alvord, *Report*, July 1, 1868, pp. 38–40, 41–42; January 1, 1869, pp. 32–34, 35–37, 50.
[138] Alvord, *Report*, January 1, 1869, p. 40.
[139] W. J. Bryan to E. A. Ware, November 9, 1868; R. C. Anthony to E. A. Ware, November 11, 1868; B.R.F.A.L. MSS.; *Freedmen's Record*, IV, 3 (March, 1868), 42; *American Missionary*, XII, 6 (June, 1868), 127–128.

education would be received "with comparative complacency if Southern white teachers—the widows, wives and daughters of Confederate soldiers—were exclusively employed," he observed.[140] Manly attributed the "unusual hostility" of the period to the "passions of the hour" and to "a very general dislike of the public school system of the North." By 1869, however, all violence had ceased in Virginia, and many native whites were seeking employment as teachers of Negro schools.[141]

In Florida, too, opposition had practically ceased by 1869. A great change of sentiment took place among the whites during the closing months of 1868, and both white and black expressed themselves as favoring education for the freedmen, according to the report of the Superintendent of Education.[142] By 1869 many of the leading men of the state were "avowed friends" of Negro education, and in several instances the wives of planters were teaching in Negro schools, even, in some instances, in co-operation with Northern teachers.[143]

Opposition had practically ceased throughout the South by 1870. General O. O. Howard, in an address to the National Education Association, at Trenton, New Jersey, in August, 1869, declared that he had not heard "for a long time of an instance of abuse of a teacher." Opposition had been severe but by this time it had "almost ceased."[144]

Notwithstanding Commissioner Howard's statement, however, there was to be some opposition in Mississippi. The quiet of 1869 was merely the lull before the storm. The passage of the School Law of 1870 led to violent opposition in 1871 and 1872, and even as late as 1876.[145]

There is ample evidence to support the conclusion that the Southern people were not united in complete opposition to the

140 Alvord, *Report,* July 1, 1868, p. 17.
141 Alvord, *Report,* July 1, 1869, pp. 20, 22.
142 Report of C. Thurston Chase, Superintendent of Education for Florida, February 10, 1868, B.R.F.A.L. MSS.
143 Superintendent George W. Gile, report to Alvord, Alvord, *Report,* July 1, 1869, p. 36.
144 National Educational Association, *Journal of the Proceedings and Addresses of the Annual Meeting,* Trenton, New Jersey, August 18–20, 1869, pp. 8–9.
145 See Dale S. Fleming, Development of Elementary and Secondary Schools in Mississippi during the Reconstruction, 1865–1875. Unpublished M.A. thesis, University of Mississippi, August, 1939. See also, Garner, *Reconstruction in Mississippi.*

education of the Negro. On the contrary, there was very little opposition until 1867, and it was not until 1868 that violence became prevalent throughout the South. After the election of 1868 this spirit of opposition declined, until by 1870, there was little outward manifestation of opposition.

If, then, the Southern people were not unanimously opposed to Negro schools in the period from 1865, can it be assumed that they actively supported such schools, and that they participated in the education of the Negro? Was their attitude merely one of indifference and mild opposition, or did they support Negro schools, and take part in educating their former slaves?

Here again there is evidence upon which to base a conclusion. Obviously no complete list of Southern participants in Negro education can be given, but it is clear that teaching in a Negro school was not considered disgraceful or shameful, for many Southern whites were engaged in this work.

Some instances of Southern co-operation and participation have already been noted. Many others might be given. For example, J. H. Clanton declared that "a great many Confederate soldiers" had been employed as teachers in Negro schools. Among those engaged in this work in Alabama were an orderly sergeant who had served under Clanton, the widow of a color-bearer who had also been in his command, a school-mate, and a cousin of his step-mother. The widow had sought Clanton's advice. He advised her to teach in a Negro school and secured a position for her. He said that he then asked the opinion of twelve prominent men, eleven of whom agreed that he had "done exactly right" in advising the woman to teach Negroes.[146] In Russell County, Alabama, the white people appointed a Methodist minister as teacher of the local freedmen's school. All went well "for more than two years, until politics alienated the races, and the Negroes demanded a Northern teacher or one of their own color."[147] The Montgomery *Advertiser* and the Selma *Times* advocated the employment of disabled veterans as teachers. In Dallas County the whites assisted in the construction of forty schools for the use of Negro chil-

[146] *K.K.K.*, VIII, Alabama I, 236.
[147] Fleming, *Civil War and Reconstruction*, 460. Dr. Fleming talked with Dr. O. D. Smith, of Auburn, one of the men who chose the teacher.

dren.[148] In Montgomery County a planter agreed to give the land and building material if his workmen would do the necessary work.[149]

The Superintendent of Schools for Georgia received many calls for Southern teachers and many applications from natives of the state. During 1865 and 1866 seven ex-Confederate soldiers were teaching in as many localities in the state, but when the opposition to Negro education became general they were forced to abandon the work. Another Southerner, a minister in the Methodist Episcopal Church, South, resigned his position when he learned that "Yankee teachers" were coming to help in the work. The Superintendent had, in 1866, many applications "from men and women, clergy and laity" for positions as teachers in freedmen's schools.[150] As economic conditions in the state grew worse, he received so many applications that he prepared a printed form on which to reply. "Lawyers, physicians, editors, ministers, and all classes" applied for positions as teachers of the freedmen. The Superintendent said they evidently believed that "anybody can teach niggers." [151]

Many schools were established by the native white people of Georgia. William Hauser, M.D., a native of the state, and former slaveholder, built a school on his plantation near Bartow.[152] A white woman taught a freedmen's school at Dawson for seven years, 1861 to 1868, with the support of the citizens of the town.[153] Citizens of Summerville, Albany, Ditmarsville, Clifton, Camilla, Griffin, Ft. Gaines, Hawkinsville, and many other villages and towns and plantations either built schoolhouses at their own expense, or gave land and lumber for the construction of the building, or, in many cases, took entire responsibility for the support of

---

[148] *Ibid.*, 626.
[149] *Nation,* October 5, 1865, p. 420.
[150] MS. report, Superintendent of Education for Georgia, Augusta, October 8, 1866, B.R.F.A.L. MSS.
[151] Report of Superintendent of Education for Georgia, Nashville (Tennessee) *Daily Press and Times,* August 14, 1867.
[152] William Hauser, Bartow, Georgia, to O. O. Howard, April 30, 1867, B.R.F.A.L. MSS.
[153] Andrew B. Clark, Agent, B.R.F.A.L., to E. A. Ware, November 6, 1868, B.R.F.A.L. MSS.

the schools.[154] Many people believed the Negro incapable of any great learning, but they were perfectly willing that he should "learn the rudiments," often supplying books for their servants, paying fees, drilling on the day's lessons, and assisting them in other ways.[155]

One of the most efficient teachers of Negroes in Buckingham County, Virginia, in the period immediately after the war was the son of Colonel Joseph Fuqua, a Confederate officer. In 1865 a native Southerner was teaching a Negro school at Charlotte Court House.[156] In the rural sections of North Carolina there were, in 1866, many schools for Negroes which were taught by Southern white men. They were not "started at the instance of the Freedmen's Bureau or the Freedmen's Aid Society," according to an agent of the Bureau, nor were they supported by either of these organizations. These schools were in "neighborhoods where there was nothing to repress any hostility towards them." Two schools near Fayetteville were taught by Southern men, one of whom was an ex-Confederate soldier. Of seven schools in Cumberland County all except the Fayetteville school were taught by Southern men, one or two by Southern Negroes. These men were working for "the sake of pay" and not from philanthropic motives, and their social standing had not suffered in the least because of their occupation, said the Bureau agent.[157] At Pendleton, South Carolina, a school was conducted by a daughter of Jasper Adams, "a renowned ante-bellum educator," and her husband. In Abbeville all the "eminent men of the town manifested the liveliest interest" in the education of the Negro.[158] The teacher of the school on Boykins plantation, near Camden, was a former drugstore clerk of Camden, who had served three years as a corporal in the Confederate Army.[159] Although many people considered

---

[154] See Mrs. M. F. Lamar, Pulaski County, April 7, 1870; C. A. de La Mera, Summerville, October 30, 1868; E. W. P. Smith, Albany, May 28, 1869; Hezekiah Brown, Savannah, June 2, 1869; James Z. Devaux, Clinton, June 3, 1869; W. L. Clark, Bainbridge, May 26, 1869, B.R.F.A.L. MSS. Many other examples might be given.

[155] Correspondence from Macon, Georgia, New York *Times*, June 18, 1866.

[156] Alrutheus A. Taylor, *The Negro in the Reconstruction of Virginia* (Washington, 1926), 150.

[157] Testimony of Major Henry C. Lawrence, *Reconstruction Committee*, Part II, 293.

[158] Horace Mann Bond, *The Education of the Negro in the American Social Order* (New York, 1934), 64.

[159] *Freedmen's Record*, III, 4 (April, 1867), 55.

a Negro in school a revolting sight, "a considerable number of native ladies" were teaching freedmen's schools in 1866. Most of them were employed by the aid societies, and there was little opposition from the people, according to press reports.[160] Even as late as 1869 ex-Confederate officers were teaching in the Negro schools of Arkansas.[161] In 1866 the mayor and council of Aberdeen, Mississippi, agreed to assist the benevolent associations in the establishment of freedmen's schools, and a local paper, *The Sunny South,* called upon all good citizens to give their aid.[162] As late as March, 1868, a Confederate officer residing in Mississippi requested advice from the authorities at Washington on the proper method of constructing schoolhouses for the freedmen.[163] At Canton the Baptist minister organized a school for the freedmen, and at Meridian land for a Negro church and school was donated by a prominent citizen.

In short, there were, in almost every Southern state, large numbers of white people "actively engaged in teaching" and supporting Negro schools.[164]

The strong opposition to Negro education which developed in the South after 1867–68 may be attributed to several causes. In the first place, the South objected not so much to the education of the Negro as to the education of the Negro by the Yankee teacher. Both Southerner and Northerner realized that the war had not ended with Appomattox. The Negro vote was the prize in the new phase of the contest. "When the combat was over and the 'Yankee school-m'ams' followed the train of the Northern armies, the business of educating the Negroes was a continuation of hostilities against the vanquished South, and was so regarded, to a considerable extent, on both sides," wrote a teacher at one of the prominent Negro schools.[165]

---

[160] New York *Times,* May 25, 1866.

[161] Statement of H. M. Wygant, National Teachers Association, *Proceedings,* Trenton, New Jersey, August 18–20, 1869, p. 14.

[162] Report of Col. Samuel Thomas, Assistant Commissioner, B.R.F.A.L., to O. O. Howard, January 31, 1866, Reports of Assistant Commissioners, B.R.F.A.L., *Senate Executive Documents,* 39 Cong., 1 Sess., no. 27 (Serial 1238), 46.

[163] E. W. Rice to O. O. Howard, March 22, 1868, B.R.F.A.L. MSS.

[164] Bond, *Education of the Negro,* 32–33, 34.

[165] Alice M. Bacon, "The Negro and the Atlanta Exposition," Trustees of the John F. Slater Fund, *Occasional Papers, No.* 7 (Baltimore, 1896), 56.

In 1867 the Montgomery *Advertiser* urged that the citizens of Alabama co-operate with the Freedmen's Bureau and the benevolent associations in educating the Negro. In an editorial the *Advertiser* said:

Our people have not been as prompt to teach the colored people themselves as they should be, trusting it to those who do not have very kind feelings for the South. A great many young men who are disabled for active work could find remunerative labor in teaching the colored children, and there is no discredit in it. It is a positive benefit to all concerned for the young men and women of the South to teach their former slaves. Some of the school books used by the teachers are embellished with all sorts of stories about the cruelties and persecutions of white people toward the blacks, and it will continue to be the case as long as strangers come in and teach them. . . . Let the colored people be educated and as far as we are able let the Southern people help them to build their school houses and teach them too.[166]

Eighteen months later the *Advertiser* declared that the Negro must be taught, and that if the task was not assumed by Southerners it would be taken up "by men and women imported from the Northern States, almost invariably of a class of people destitute either of money, character, or virtue, merely adventurers in search of the means of sustaining life, with little or no regard to the mode or manner in which it is obtained." [167]

The editor of the Petersburg, Virginia, *Index* expressed a similar sentiment. The Negroes could not now remain in a state of ignorance, said the *Index*. "They will be taught. Either we of the South must aid them in their moral advance, or the work will be undertaken by strangers and enemies, who will seek to alienate them from us, and use them as a power to perpetuate our political degradation." There had been, in the past, little animosity between the two races in the South, and it would be "the fault" of the white man if he should permit "outsiders" to come in and destroy the possibility of a continuation of the friendly feeling.[168] Bishop Elliott, of Georgia, expressed much the same feeling. The importation of persons from abroad to teach the Negro would

[166] Montgomery (Alabama) *Advertiser*, July 24, 1867, quoted in W. L. Fleming, *Documentary History of Reconstruction* (2 vols., Cleveland, 1906–1907), II, 181.
[167] January 27, 1869, quoted in Bond, *The Education of the Negro*, 33.
[168] Taylor, *The Negro in the Reconstruction of Virginia*, 151.

certainly "widen the breach" between the two races in the South, he declared. The work of educating the Negro must be done by Southerners.[169] Bishop Quintard, in an appeal for the support of freedmen's schools, warned his people that the education of the Negro was a spiritual and moral obligation. If there should be those who refused to admit the obligation, they should remember that the question was "not whether they shall be taught, but by whom they shall be taught." [170] A somewhat similar position was taken by the editor of the Augusta *Daily Press*. He believed that the people of the South were the "natural friends, guardians and protectors" of the Negro and, therefore, they should undertake his education. The Northern teachers were fit only to teach the Negro "hatred of the white people of the South," and various "insulting songs," he said.[171]

Many Southerners recognized the political importance of educating the Negro. "If we do not educate them someone else will, and whoever thus benefits them will win an influence over them which will control their votes," wrote certain citizens of Oxford, Mississippi. "If we perform this service," they said, "then we shall secure their identification with us in promoting all our interests." [172] The press of Mississippi pointed to the political implications of the education of the Negro. The Negro was determined to have an education, said the *People's Press*, of Hernando, and the chief problem before the South was whether to allow this education to be carried out by the Radical from the North, or to formulate plans for the immediate and active participation of native Southern whites in the work. The Negro educated by the "Cape Cod schoolmarms swarming into the South" would be more dangerous than the Radical Yankee himself. The Negro must be educated by the Southerner, said the Jackson *Clarion*. If properly educated he would double the voting strength of the South.[173] In fact, the Southerners were more than willing that the Negro

---

169 *De Bow's Review*, September, 1866, p. 313.
170 Nashville (Tennessee) *Republican Banner*, January 27, 1867.
171 Augusta (Georgia) *Daily Press*, May 3, 1866.
172 *De Bow's Review*, September 1866, pp. 309–310.
173 Fleming, Development of Elementary and Secondary Schools in Mississippi, 17–18. See, also, Garner, *Reconstruction in Mississippi*, 355 *et seq.*

should be granted the suffrage, since they believed they could control his vote, wrote a Northern correspondent.[174]

In Nashville, Tennessee, the *Republican Banner,* in commenting on a program presented by Fisk School, declared that even the most skeptical must now be convinced that the Negro was capable of "mental improvement." The Negro was in the South, said the *Banner,* and it was not to be hoped that he would leave; therefore, the South must "make the best of him" by educating him. He must be educated by those among whom he had lived, those who understood him, and those with whom "he must rise or fall." "The sooner we begin the better," said the *Banner.*[175] The education of the Negro was now one of the first duties of Southerners. The Northern teachers had done much good in Nashville, the *Banner* said, but some of them were essentially selfish in their opposition to any plan for city schools for Negroes, since they saw that if Nashville should establish schools for the freedmen "their occupation" would be "quite gone." Certain teachers were guilty of bad faith and "palpably dishonest misrepresentation" of the attitude of the local white people toward the Negro, the *Banner* charged. Through such misrepresentation they had drawn "ample support" from Northern benevolent associations. These "eminently philanthropic ladies and gentlemen" were not entirely unselfish when they sought to teach the Negro children "an unextinguishable hatred" for the white, said the *Banner.* Was it any wonder that the teachers were active in Radical political circles? [176]

Perhaps the feeling of the South is well expressed in the following quotation from the Augusta, Georgia, *Press:*

The education of the negro should now engage our earnest attention. They are now, by proclamation, free; and by law, citizens. It should be our duty to make them good citizens; and without education they cannot become good citizens. To have them educated by our enemies is an unwise policy. It teaches them to look upon us as their enemies instead of what we really are, their only true and sincere friends. We should, therefore, take this matter in hand, and establish schools for them wherever necessary,

[174] *Nation,* October 5, 1865, p. 426.
[175] June 1, 1867.
[176] April 9, 1867; July 28, 1867.

and furnish Southern teachers, who will not waste time in making them sing 'Down with the Rebels,' and urging them to believe that the people of the South dream of nothing else but to harrass and oppress them. It will harmonize the races, create better feelings between them, and, we believe, work for the general good. Besides this, it will enable the patriotic, self-sacrificing females of New England to remain at home, and make 'apple sass' and abuse the 'wicked South' at their little convivial back-biting tea-parties.

This will be more in accordance with their tastes and literary accomplishments, and much more agreeable to them; and, we are free to say, that it will be much more agreeable to our people. We are exceedingly obliged to them for the devoted interest which they have shown in the educational and spiritual and musical welfare of the negro; but we hope they will not put themselves to any trouble on this account, and, if they should come out this way again that it will be 'when they can't stay so long' as they did before.

But badinage aside, we seriously think that some steps should be taken by our people to educate the negro. In Mississippi some of the Professors of the University of that State and other gentlemen, have united in a circular on this subject, which they strongly advocate and urge upon the attention of the people. . . .

We do not know whether the County is, as yet, able to move in the premises; but we fear that neither the Inferior Court nor the City Council has the means to procure suitable buildings and pay the teachers, and provide for the other necessary expenses. But something should be done, and the sooner the better.[177]

Not only did the Southern whites fear the political domination of the enfranchised Negro, under the tutelage of the Yankee teacher, but they were bitterly opposed to the idea of "mixed schools" which was made a feature of the Radical program in most states. Superintendent Ruffner reported a "radical change" in sentiment in Virginia immediately after the passage of the first Civil Rights bill, which prohibited the segregation of the races in schools.[178] Even General Howard said that the opposition to freedmen's schools in the South arose largely from "the belief that the teachers [were] fostering social equality."[179] One of the teachers believed that the Southern people were opposed to the education of the Negro because they believed that such education meant "social

[177] Augusta (Georgia) *Daily Press,* June 21, 1866.
[178] Taylor, *Negro in Reconstruction of Virginia,* 154.
[179] Report, December, 1865, *House Executive Documents,* 38 Cong., 1 Sess., no. 11 (Serial 1255), 13.

as well as political equality." This belief would explain opposition and violence, for the Southerner would go to any extreme to prevent the accomplishment of such an aim.[180]

It is evident that the Yankee teacher went to the South with ideas and attitudes which were quite similar to those prevalent among the officers of the associations. In both cases one of the strongest motivating factors was a desire to complete a task which had been begun with the abolition crusade of Weld and Garrison. Among the teachers, as among the officers, there were many who were not professed abolitionists, but whose religious and emotional attitudes fitted them for participation in such a movement.

Without being aware of the inconsistency of their position, they professed to be individualists, to believe in the ability and the immediate responsibility of the individual, while, at the same time, they were humanitarians, upon whose souls the guilt and weakness of other men lay heavily. The Negro was an individual, a free man, a citizen, the equal of all other men, eminently capable of the assumption of the duties and responsibilities of the government of states. Yet—and here the individualist gives way to the humanitarian and reformer—he must be considered a ward, something less than a free man, an individual who must be protected, guarded, and carefully directed.

The ideals of the teachers were those of the most radical group in the North and in Congress. Obviously, in any group of individuals holding certain beliefs, those who voluntarily serve as missionaries are not those in whom the ideals of the group simply simmer, lukewarm. Those who go out with joy, as crusaders to the fray, are those in whom the fire burns fiercely. Thus it was that, in spite of certain notable exceptions, the Yankee teacher became an instrument in the hands of the Radical Republican reconstructionists. As such he conducted himself in such a manner as to incur the suspicion, contempt, and hatred of the Southern white.

This attitude did not extend to all Northern business men, many of whom engaged in business in the South with impunity and success. Indeed, Northern capital and enterprise were most wel-

[180] *Independent,* January 10, 1867.

come. Northern immigration was heartily encouraged, both officially and unofficially.

Nor was the violent reaction of the Southern people directed primarily at Negro education. The South was universally opposed to the education of the Negro by radical abolitionists from the North. Both groups understood the importance of the "Yankee schoolmarm" as a means of controlling the vote of the new citizens, and thus the education of the Negro became a point of conflict in the reconstruction of the South.

NOTES ON SELECTED OFFICERS OF THE EDUCATIONAL ASSOCIATIONS[1]

ABBOTT, LYMAN, 1835–1922

Secretary of the American Union Commission; member of the executive board of the American Missionary Association and of the American Freedmen's Union Commission.

While studying law in New York Abbott taught a Sunday School class in Plymouth Church. He was interested in the free-soil movement and contemplated going into Kansas with "Beecher Bibles" but did not follow the impulse. In 1860, through the instrumentality of Henry C. Bowen, he became pastor of the Congregational Church in Terre Haute, Indiana. He resigned this position in 1865 to become Secretary of the American Union Commission.

In 1870 Abbott became editor of the *Illustrated Christian Weekly,* a publication of the American Tract Society. In 1876 he became associated with Henry Ward Beecher in editing *Christian Union.* He succeeded Beecher both as editor-in-chief of this paper and as pastor of the Plymouth Church.

Lyman Abbott, *Reminiscences* (New York, 1915).

ALVORD, JOHN WATSON

Superintendent of Schools for Freedmen, Bureau of Refugees, Freedmen and Abandoned Lands; member of the executive board of the American Freedmen's Union Commission.

Alvord studied at Oneida Institute, Lane Theological Seminary, and Oberlin College. He was one of the "Lane Rebels"; others were George Whipple (*q.v.*), H. B. Stanton, who became the husband of Elizabeth Cady Stanton, Sereno W. Streeter, and James A. Thome. In 1835, while attending Lane Seminary, Alvord taught in a Negro school in Cincinnati. Some of his pupils became very important in freedmen's affairs in the South during the reconstruction period. Between 1835 and 1865 Alvord was pastor of Congregational churches in Litchfield County, Connecticut, and South Boston, Massachusetts.

---

[1] In the preparation of these sketches the following biographical dictionaries have been consulted:

Appleton's Cyclopaedia of American Biography (8 vols., New York, 1887–1889).
Dictionary of American Biography (20 vols., New York, 1928–1936).
National Cyclopaedia of American Biography (13 vols., New York, 1893–1906).

In 1865 Alvord became Inspector of Schools and Finances for Freedmen, and in the following year became Superintendent of Schools. He was instrumental in the founding of the Freedmen's Bank and served as both secretary and president of the organization. He was a member of the board of trustees of the National Soldiers and Sailors Orphans' Home, and was secretary of the Lincoln National Temperance Association. His doctrine of abstinence extended not only to intoxicating liquors but to tobacco.

J. W. Alvord was a distant relative of Corydon Alexis Alvord, New York printer. His son-in-law, John A. Cole, was Superintendent of the Lincoln Mission, Washington, D.C., and General Field Agent of the United States Christian Commission.

B.R.F.A.L. MSS. and private correspondence.

ANDREW, JOHN A., 1818–1867

President, Boston Educational Commission; president, New England Freedmen's Aid Society; Governor of Massachusetts.

Andrew was a graduate of Bowdoin. Both as a student and as a young lawyer in Boston he heartily opposed the extension of slavery. Andrew, Charles Sumner, Samuel G. Howe, and H. L. Pierce (brother of E. L. Pierce, *q.v.*), began the movement which resulted in the establishment of the Free-Soil party. He co-operated with Henry I. Bowditch (*q.v.*) and Samuel G. Howe in the case of the brig *Ottoman,* and in the formation of the Vigilance Committee of Boston. Among the other members of the Committee were Charles Sumner, Theodore Parker, Wendell Phillips, Charles Francis Adams, Richard Dana, Jr., Charles Hovey, George Minot, and Samuel Thayer. Andrew was deeply interested in John Brown, and secured legal counsel for him.

Much of Andrew's fame rests upon the success of his efforts in raising, organizing, and outfitting the Fifty-fourth and Fifty-fifth Regiments, U.S.C.T. During the war Andrew demanded that the government establish an agency to protect the interests of the freedmen. As a result of his insistence the American Freedmen's Inquiry Commission was created, with Robert Dale Owen, Samuel G. Howe, and James McKaye as members.

In 1865 Andrew became president of the American Land Company and Agency, a joint stock corporation seeking profitable investments for Northern capital in the South. [See Atkinson, Edward; Corson, R. R.; Hale, E. E.; Hallowell, R. P.; Higginson, T. W.]

Henry G. Pearson, *The Life of John Andrew* (2 vols., Boston, 1904).

ATKINSON, EDWARD, 1827–1905

Secretary, Boston Educational Commission; secretary, New England Freedmen's Aid Society; Boston Vigilance Committee; underground railroad operator.

Atkinson was an active member of the New England Cotton Manufacturers Association and treasurer and financial agent for six mills operating over 70,000 spindles. He was a prolific writer on economic and political questions, many of his pamphlets having very wide circulation. He advocated the immediate abolition of slavery, in order that the cotton lands of the South and Southwest might be opened to free labor. Atkinson was "by training and environment an Abolitionist and a Free-Soiler." In 1855 he became treasurer of a fund for the relief of Kansas. He contributed heavily to the support of John Brown. [See Hallowell, R. P.]

In 1862 Atkinson became associated with John A. Andrew (*q.v.*), Edward Everett Hale (*q.v.*), William Endicott, Jr., and others in the organization of the Boston Educational Commission, the predecessor of the New England Freedmen's Aid Society. At this time he was also a member of the New England Loyal Publication Society, of which John Murray Forbes was president. [See Pierce, E. L.]

In 1863 Atkinson, William Endicott, Jr., Edward S. Philbrick (*q.v.*), W. S. Bowditch, S. M. Standish and others organized the Free Labor Cotton Company for the operation of plantations in the South. In this venture Atkinson and his associates could rely on the knowledge and experience of Philbrick, who had realized a profit of over $80,000 from his previous operations in Sea Island cotton.

Atkinson actively influenced national legislation through his contacts with such Washington officials as Secretary of Treasury Hugh McCulloch and Senator Henry Wilson.

Harold F. Williamson, *Edward Atkinson, the Biography of a Liberal, 1827–1905* (Boston, 1934); [Edward Atkinson], *Cheap Cotton by Free Labor* (Boston, 1861).

BALDWIN, MATTHIAS W., 1795–1866

Port Royal Relief Association; Pennsylvania Freedmen's Relief Association.

In 1831 M. W. Baldwin built one of the first locomotives to be used in transportation in the United States. From this small beginning he developed the great Baldwin Locomotive Works, one of the largest enterprises of its kind in the world.

Baldwin's activities in support of abolition led to a boycott by Southern railroads before the war, but his losses from this action were more than compensated by the great demand for engines from the Federal government after the outbreak of war.

Baldwin was a very religious man, deeply interested in humanitarian movements. For thirty-five years he was a Sunday School teacher and superintendent. In 1835 he founded a school for Negro children and for years he helped support the Negro evangelist, Pompey Hunt. During the war his company appropriated ten per cent of its annual income to the United States Christian Commission.

Baldwin was a member of the American Philosophical Society and of the American Horticultural Society.

Encyclopedia Americana (30 vols., New York, 1937), XVII, articles entitled "Locomotive," and "Locomotive Industry."

BARKER, ABRAHAM

Pennsylvania Freedmen's Relief Association.

Abraham Barker was the son of Jacob Barker, prominent Philadelphia and New Orleans financier. The younger Barker founded the banking house, Barker Brothers, in 1842. Both Abraham Barker and his father were strong abolitionists. Abraham was active in raising Negro troops during the Civil War, and was one of the founders of the Union League of Philadelphia. His son, Wharton Barker, Philadelphia financier, helped organize the Third Regiment, U.S.C.T.

BISHOP, NATHAN, 1808–1900

Executive committee, American Freedmen's Union Commission.

Bishop entered the work among the freedmen after a lengthy experience in educational administration. He was superintendent of schools at Providence from 1838 to 1851, and filled the same office in Boston from 1851 until he moved to New York in 1857. Here he devoted his time to religious, educational, and philanthropic work. He was a member of the board of trustees of Brown University and of Vassar College, a member of the board of managers of the American Bible Society, a member of the New York Sabbath Commission, the American British Evangelical Alliance, the American Revision Committee, and the American Baptist Home Mission Society. He was chairman of the executive committee of the United States Christian Commission. In 1869 he became a member of the United States Board of Indian Commissioners. [See Fisk, Clinton B.]

BOND, HUGH L., 1828–1893

New England Freedmen's Aid Society; executive committee, American Freedmen's Union Commission.

Bond graduated from the University of the City of New York in 1848 and was admitted to the bar in 1851. In 1860 he became judge of the Criminal Court of Baltimore. In this position he charged the Grand Jury investigating the riot of April 19, 1861, that those who took part in the attack upon the Sixth Massachusetts Regiment as it passed through Baltimore were guilty of murder.

In 1870 President Grant appointed Bond judge of the Fourth Circuit Court. Here he heard the South Carolina Ku Klux cases and is said by one authority to have done much to break the reign of terror in that state.

He was deeply interested in the Negro, and helped organize the Baltimore Association for the Improvement of Colored People.

BOWDITCH, HENRY I., 1808–1892

Boston Educational Commission; New England Freedmen's Aid Society; Vigilance Committee; underground railroad operator.

Bowditch graduated from the Harvard Medical School in 1832. From his youth he was an ardent abolitionist. In 1834 he became a follower of William Lloyd Garrison (*q.v.*), and in 1842 he joined William E. Channing and F. S. Cabot in the formation of the Latimer Committee. Soon after the famous Burns case, Bowditch organized the Anti-Man-Hunting League for the purpose of rescuing fugitive slaves from their pursuers. Dr. Bowditch is best known for his work in establishing ambulance units in the Federal army. [See Andrew, John A.]

Pearson, *Andrew*, I, 57; M. A. De W. Howe, *Boston, the Place and the People* (New York, 1903), 267.

BOYNTON, CHARLES B., 1806–1883

Western Freedmen's Aid Society.

Although Boynton is best known for his abolitionist and religious work, he was also a politician and a railroad executive. He was the president of the first railroad in Berkshire County, Massachusetts, and was justice of Berkshire County and a member of the Massachusetts House of Representatives.

In 1840 he began his ministry in the Presbyterian church, holding pulpits in Massachusetts, New York, and Ohio before 1856. While in Ohio be became an ardent abolitionist. In 1854 Boynton was one of a party sent out to investigate the climate and general resources of Kansas. One result of this tour was the publication of *A Journey Through Kansas;* another was a strengthening of his opposition to slavery. [See Hale, E. E.; Walden, J. M.]

From 1865 to 1869 Boynton was pastor of churches in Washington, D.C., chaplain of the House of Representatives, and a teacher at the U.S. Naval Academy.

In addition to his book on Kansas Boynton was the author of several volumes on foreign policy and of a history of the navy during the Civil War.

BRYANT, WILLIAM CULLEN, 1794–1878

National Freedmen's Relief Association of New York.

Bryant was admitted to the bar in 1815. His famous "Thanatopsis" was published in 1817, and in 1829 he became editor of the New York *Evening Post*. By 1840 Bryant had begun his opposition to slavery. He supported

John Quincy Adams in the controversy over the right of petition and opposed the annexation of Texas. After 1848 the *Post* took a very active part in the anti-slavery crusade. By 1850 it had become violently abolitionist, and by 1856 it was "one of the most vigorous" of the Republican organs.

Bryant encouraged migration to Kansas, denounced the Dred Scott decision, and hailed John Brown as a hero. He denounced all plans of compromise and urged the energetic use of the sword against rebellion. He was in close contact with Salmon P. Chase (*q.v.*), whose appointment to a seat in the cabinet he urged upon President Lincoln.

CHASE, SALMON P., 1808–1873

President, American Freedmen's Union Commission.

The role of Salmon P. Chase as "attorney-general for runaway slaves" and as a member of the Liberty and Free-Soil Republican parties is well known. His activity in support of the benevolent associations is perhaps less well known. [For his action in assisting E. L. Pierce, see Chapter I. See, also, Bryant, W. C.; Jocelyn, S. S.; Pierce, E. L.]

American Freedmen's Union Commission, *First Annual Report,* 1866 (New York, 1866); *American Freedman,* I, 3 (June, 1866), 36–40.

CLAFLIN, WILLIAM, 1818–1905

President, New England Freedmen's Aid Society; member of executive committee, American Missionary Association; Governor of Massachusetts.

William Claflin was the son of Lee Claflin, a boot and shoe manufacturer. In 1838 he went to Missouri, where he became converted to abolitionism and, subsequently, became one of the charter members of the Free-Soil party. Claflin was the first Governor of Massachusetts to advocate woman suffrage. During his term legislation was adopted regulating divorce, improving the legal status of women, and regulating child labor. Claflin was a trustee of Boston University, Wellesley College, and Mount Holyoke College, and he and his father were the chief supporters of Claflin University, Orangeburg, South Carolina. [See Sleeper, Jacob.]

Claflin College, Sixty-ninth *Annual Catalogue of Claflin College 1937–1938* (Orangeburg, South Carolina, [1937]).

CLARK, EDWARD W., 1828–?

Treasurer, Port Royal Relief Association; treasurer, Pennsylvania Freedmen's Relief Association; American Freedmen's Union Commission.

Clark was a member of a prominent Philadelphia banking firm which included Jay Cooke among its members. He was president of the Lehigh Coal and Navigation Company and was receiver in bankruptcy of the Lehigh and Wilkes-Barre Coal Company.

Clark was "an advanced and early Republican," and his firm is said to have been of great influence in the maintenance of Federal credit during the war.

CLARKE, JAMES FREEMAN, 1810–1888

Vice-president, Boston Educational Commission; vice-president, New England Freedmen's Aid Society.

Clarke was a famous Unitarian minister. He founded the extremely liberal Church of the Disciples at Boston. He was a member of the Massachusetts State Board of Education, a lecturer at Harvard Divinity School, and editor of the *Western Messenger*.

Clarke was very active in temperance, anti-slavery, and woman suffrage.

COFFIN, LEVI, 1789–1877

Executive committee, American Freedmen's Union Commission; General Agent, Western Freedmen's Aid Society; underground railroad operator.

Levi Coffin was a native of North Carolina, a member of that group of Friends who left the slave-tainted soil of the South for the freedom of Indiana and Ohio. From 1826 Coffin became extremely active in the underground railroad, and in 1847 he opened a "free-goods-store" at Cincinnati. He was perhaps the outstanding operator of the underground railroad in the central states, and one of the most important in the entire nation.

Levi Coffin, *Reminiscences of Levi Coffin* (Cincinnati, 1876); Siebert, *Underground Railroad*.

COLLYER, ROBERT, 1823–1912

Advisory committee, American Freedmen's Union Commission.

Robert Collyer was a native of England. When he moved to Philadelphia in 1850 he became both a strong abolitionist and a sincere follower of Dr. William Furness, a leading Unitarian minister of that city. [See Furness, H. H.]

In 1859 Collyer became a Unitarian minister in Chicago. During the war he was a stanch supporter of the Union and was extremely active in the work of the U.S. Sanitary Commission.

COLWELL, STEPHEN, 1800–1871

Port Royal Relief Association; president, Pennsylvania Freedmen's Relief Association; American Freedmen's Commission; American Freedmen's Union Commission.

Colwell was an iron manufacturer with plants at Conshohocken, Pennsylvania, and Weymouth, New Jersey. He was a director of the Camden and

Atlantic Railroad, the Reading Railroad, and the Pennsylvania Central Railroad. He was a strong advocate of high tariff.

Colwell was an active member of the Colonization Society, attacking slavery as unprofitable and unwise. He was extremely active in both the United States Christian Commission and the United States Sanitary Commission.

Colwell was a trustee of the University of Pennsylvania and of the Princeton Theological Seminary.

COPE, FRANCIS R.

Port Royal Relief Association; Pennsylvania Freedmen's Relief Association; executive committee, American Freedmen's Union Commission.

Cope was a member of the firm of Cope Brothers, Philadelphia merchants. He was also a director of many banks and insurance companies.

Moses King, *Philadelphia and Notable Philadelphians* (New York, 1901), 42.

CORSON, ROBERT R., 1831–1904

Secretary, Pennsylvania Branch, American Freedmen's Union Commission.

Corson operated an extensive coal business at Pottsville and Philadelphia. During the war he was instrumental in the recruiting of fourteen thousand Negro troops without expense to the government. John Andrew (*q.v.*) appointed him Quartermaster-General of the state of Massachusetts. He was also aide-de-camp to Governors Smith and Gilmore of Rhode Island and New Hampshire.

Corson was a member of the Union League of Philadelphia, treasurer of the Association for the Prevention of Cruelty to Animals, a director of the Citizens Municipal Reform Association, member of the Philadelphia Society for Organizing Charity, inspector of state institutions for the deaf and dumb, and inspector of Moyamensing Prison. Robert Corson was a brother of George, Hiram, and Charles Corson, all of whom were extremely active in the underground railroad.

William Still, *The Underground Rail Road* (Philadelphia, 1901), 721 ff.

CROZER, JOHN P., 1793–1866

Pennsylvania Freedmen's Relief Association.

Crozer was a textile manufacturer. In 1845 he built a mansion, a church, and a normal school, at Upland, near Chester, Pennsylvania. He assisted in recruiting troops for the Federal army, and was a member of the United States Christian Commission.

Crozer endowed a professorship at Bucknell University, and by his will established a $50,000 memorial fund for missions among the Negroes. Crozer Theological Seminary was established by his family in his honor.

DEXTER, HENRY M., 1821–1890

Vice-president, Boston Educational Commission; New England Freedmen's Aid Society.

Dexter was a graduate of Yale University and of Andover Theological Seminary. In 1844 he became pastor of a Congregational Church at Manchester, New Hampshire, and five years later became pastor of Pine Street Church, Boston. From 1851 he was a member of the editorial staff of the *Congregationalist,* and a contributor to *Independent.* In 1865 he became editor of the *Congregationalist.* He was one of the founders of the *Congregational Quarterly* and was the author of several works on Congregationalism.

Dexter was a strong abolitionist. He organized the clergy of New England in protest against the Nebraska bill, and went to Washington to present their petitions to Congress.

FARWELL, JOHN V., 1825–1908

New England Freedmen's Aid Society; vice-president, American Freedmen's Commission.

In 1868 the dry goods firm headed by John V. Farwell was the leading store of its kind in Chicago, doing a business of ten million dollars annually. It maintained its commanding position until displaced by Marshall Field and Company.

Farwell was a very religious man, "dominated in his inner life by a puritanical moral code and a religious fervor." He was a member of the United States Christian Commission, gave the land for the first Y.M.C.A. in Chicago, and contributed liberally to Moody Bible Institute.

FISK, CLINTON B., 1828–1890

Executive board, American Missionary Association; vice-president, Freedmen's Aid Society of the Methodist Episcopal Church.

Early in childhood Fisk moved from New York to Michigan, where he later became a successful merchant and banker. In 1858 he moved to St. Louis, where he represented a large insurance company. His experience in Missouri confirmed a tendency toward abolitionism.

After promotion to the rank of brigadier-general Fisk was made assistant commissioner of the Freedmen's Bureau, with jurisdiction over Kentucky and Tennessee. While serving in this office Fisk assisted in the establishment of Fisk University, Nashville, Tennessee.

After his retirement from the Freedmen's Bureau, Fisk became commissioner of the South West Pacific Railroad, and subsequently, vice-president of the Missouri Pacific. From 1874 to 1890 he was a member of the U.S. Board of Indian Commissioners. [See Bishop, Nathan]

Fisk was very active in the Methodist Church. In 1886 he ran for the governorship of New Jersey on the prohibition ticket and was the candidate of this party in the presidential campaign of 1888.

FLETCHER, CALVIN, 1798–1866

Indiana Freedmen's Aid Commission.

Fletcher was well known as a lawyer, a banker, and a farmer. He was the first lawyer to begin practice at Indianapolis. He became a member of the state legislature in 1832. In 1843 he became president of the state bank branch at Indianapolis and later became head of the Indianapolis Banking Company.

FOWLER, JOSEPH S., 1820–1902

American Union Commission.

Joseph Smith Fowler was a native of Steubenville, Ohio. In 1845 he became Professor of Mathematics at Franklin College, Davidson County, Tennessee, and, in 1856, president of Howard Female Institute, Gallatin, Tennessee. His strong opposition to slavery forced him to leave the state, and in 1861 he moved to Springfield, Illinois. In 1862 he returned to Tennessee, and was appointed by Johnson to the office of Comptroller. In May, 1865, he was elected to the United States Senate. He refused to support the impeachment of President Johnson, and voted against the Fifteenth Amendment because it did not include a provision giving the suffrage to women.

FROTHINGHAM, OCTAVIUS B., 1822–1895

New England Freedmen's Aid Society; corresponding secretary, National Freedmen's Relief Association; committee on teachers and public, New York Branch, American Freedmen's Union Commission; executive committee, American Freedmen's Union Commission.

Frothingham was one of the strongest forces in New England Unitarianism. He graduated from Harvard in 1846, and was ordained in the following year. In 1855 he broke with the Salem church over the slavery question, and in 1859 he organized the Third Congregational Unitarian Society of New York, which later became the Independent Liberal Church. He was extremely unorthodox in his views, being even more liberal than the extremists among his followers. He was the author of biographies of Theodore Parker and of Gerrit Smith, of *Transcendentalism in New England,* and other works.

Frothingham was an active abolitionist, and was very prominent in the movement for woman suffrage and equal rights for women.

FURNESS, HORACE H., 1833–1912

Pennsylvania Freedmen's Relief Association.

Horace Howard Furness was the son of William H. Furness, a leading Unitarian minister of Philadelphia, who was an ardent champion of abolition as early as 1824. Horace Furness graduated from Harvard in 1854, and was admitted to the bar five years later. He, like his father, was a strong abolitionist, and served as both platform and field agent of the United States Sanitary Commission.

A student of Professor Francis James Child, he was one of the outstanding Shakespeare scholars and editors of his generation. He was a trustee of the University of Pennsylvania, a member of the Seybert Commission which investigated spiritualism, and the author of its *Report.* His wife was Helen Kate Rogers, author of *A Concordance to Shakespeare's Poems.*

GARRISON, WILLIAM LLOYD, 1805–1879

Vice-president, New England Freedmen's Aid Society; vice-president, American Freedmen's Commission; vice-president, American Freedmen's Aid Union; vice-president and member of executive committee, American Freedmen's Union Commission.

GRIFFITHS, GOLDSBOROUGH S., 1814–1904

President, Maryland Branch, American Union Commission.

Griffiths amassed a fortune in the paper and carpet business in Baltimore. An extremely devout Christian, he was a delegate to the Evangelical Alliance at Lubeck in 1856, president of the Maryland Sunday School Union, and president of the Baltimore Christian Association. A pioneer in penal reform, he organized the first prison Sunday School in the United States. He became "a relentless foe of the objectionable features of the prison system in the South." He was a prominent worker for the cause of temperance and supported both the Y.M.C.A. and the Baltimore home for newsboys.

HALE, EDWARD EVERETT, 1822–1909

Vice-president, Boston Educational Commission; vice-president, New England Freedmen's Aid Society.

Hale was pastor of the South Congregational Church, Boston, from 1856 to 1899. He was an active abolitionist and supported the New England

Emigrant Aid Company. He was the author of a book on the Kansas-Nebraska problem. [See Andrew, John A.; Atkinson, Edward; Boynton, C. B.]

Mr. Hale married Emily Baldwin Perkins, grand-daughter of Lyman Beecher.

HALLOWELL, RICHARD P., 1835–1904

American Freedmen's Union Commission.

As a young man, Hallowell was engaged in the wool business in Boston and Philadelphia, but resigned his first position because his firm purchased "slave products." During the abolition controversy he served as a member of the informal bodyguard which protected William Lloyd Garrison (*q.v.*) and Wendell Phillips. He was extremely active in abolitionism in Boston and Philadelphia, and was a member of the Pennsylvania Society for the Abolition of Slavery. After the execution of John Brown, he was a member of the group which escorted the body of the martyr to North Elba, New York, for burial. [See Andrew, J. A.; Atkinson, E.; Bryant, W. C.; Higginson, T. W.; McKim, J. M.]

During the war, Hallowell assisted in the recruiting of the Fifty-fourth and Fifty-fifth Massachusetts Volunteers, serving as treasurer of the recruiting fund. His brother, Norwood P. Hallowell, was Colonel of the Fifty-fifth Massachusetts Regiment.

After the close of the war, Hallowell spent much time and money in the interest of schools for Negroes. He was a trustee of Calhoun School, Lowndes County, Alabama. Hallowell was the author of *The Quakers in New England, The Quaker Invasion of Massachusetts,* and *Why the Negro Was Enfranchised*. Mrs. Hallowell was the former Anna Coffin Davis, granddaughter of James and Lucretia Mott.

In 1938 N. Penrose Hallowell and Mrs. J. Mott Hallowell, obviously members of the same family, were on the board of trustees of Calhoun School. *Bulletin,* 1937–38.

HATFIELD, EDWIN F., 1807–1883

American Freedmen's Union Commission.

From 1835 to 1856 Hatfield was pastor of the Seventh Presbyterian Church of New York. He was a Director of Union Theological Seminary, and in 1865 headed a campaign which added $500,000 to the endowment of the Seminary.

Hatfield was an ardent anti-slavery worker. He published *Freedom's Lyre,* "a collection of hymns for the slave and his friends."

HIGGINSON, THOMAS WENTWORTH, 1823–1911

Vice-president, New England Freedmen's Aid Society.

Higginson was one of the most interesting figures of his period. He was an abolitionist, an operator on the underground railroad, a member of the Boston Vigilance Committee, and a vigorous advocate of woman suffrage. In 1858 and 1859 he joined Gerrit Smith, Dr. Samuel G. Howe, Frank Sanborn, and George L. Stearns in supporting John Brown, and during the war he served as head of the First South Carolina Regiment. [See Andrew, J. A.; Atkinson, E.; Hallowell, R. P.; McKim, J. M.]

For a very interesting statement of Higginson's part in the John Brown raid, see Ralph V. Harlow, "Gerrit Smith and the John Brown Raid," *American Historical Review* XXXVIII (October, 1932), 32–60. See also, Harlow, *Gerrit Smith, Philanthropist and Reformer* (New York, 1939); Thomas Wentworth Higginson, *Army Life in a Black Regiment; Dictionary of American Biography,* IX, 16–18; Stanton, *History of Woman Suffrage.*

HUSSEY, CURTIS G., 1802–1893

American Freedmen's Commission.

In 1842 Hussey invested $110,000 in copper permits in the Lake Superior region. From this venture he realized a profit of $2,280,000. His organization, C. G. Hussey and Company, became the Pittsburgh Copper and Brass Rolling Mills, the first copper mill in the United States to turn out copper in great quantities. In 1859 Hussey entered the iron and steel field, organizing Hussey, Howe and Company.

Hussey was a member of the Society of Friends, and his views on slavery, temperance, war, and social morality were typical of the sect. He was deeply interested in the welfare of women in industry and business. He established the School of Design for Women, Pittsburgh, and was a member of the board of trust of the University of Pittsburgh, and president of the Allegheny Observatory.

JOCELYN, SIMEON S., 1799–1879

American Missionary Association.

As chairman of the Amistad Committee, Jocelyn assisted in the organization of the American Missionary Association, in which he held various offices for over thirty years.

Jocelyn began his ministerial career as pastor of a Negro church in New Haven under the control of the American Board of Home Missions. In 1829 he and Arthur Tappan proposed the organization of a Negro college at New Haven. In support of this project, Jocelyn and Tappan called a national convention of free Negroes, which, according to one authority, was the first "organized expression of Negro solidarity in the nation."

In 1863 Jocelyn visited Secretary Chase (*q.v.*) whom he found most enthusiastic in support of Negro education. "His aims," said Jocelyn, "correspond with the magnitude of the objects to be achieved."

Beard, *A Crusade of Brotherhood; American Missionary,* VII, 9 (September, 1863), 205; *Letters of Theodore Dwight Weld, Angelina Grimké Weld, and Sarah Grimké,*

1822–1844, edited by Gilbert H. Barnes and Dwight L. Dumond (2 vols., New York, 1934), I, 115.

KIDDER, HENRY P., 1823–1886

Treasurer, Boston Branch, American Union Commission.

In his youth Kidder was a dry goods clerk and an employee of the Boston and Worcester Railroad. In 1858 he became a partner in the firm of John E. Thayer and Brother. From 1865 until his death in 1886 he was a member of the firm of Kidder, Peabody and Company.

Kidder was a devout Unitarian and contributed heavily to various charities.

KIRK, EDWARD N., 1802–1874

President, American Missionary Association; New England Freedmen's Aid Society.

Kirk was one of the early abolitionists. In 1819, while a senior at Princeton University, he delivered an oration in support of the abolition movement and in condemnation of the Missouri Compromise.

As pastor of Mount Vernon Church, Boston, Kirk was an "aggressive" worker in evangelism and reform. He was intensely anti-slavery and was uncompromising and plain-spoken in his support of missions and temperance. During the war he was a fiery supporter of the Union.

Beard, *A Crusade of Brotherhood,* 131–132.

LANE, GEORGE W., 1818–1883

Chairman of the executive committee, American Union Commission.

For many years Lane was one of the leaders in mercantile business in New York. For thirty years he was a member of the Chamber of Commerce. He was connected with the Fulton National Bank, the Merchants National Bank, the Seamen's Bank, the Central Trust Company, the Continental Fire Insurance Company, and the Atlantic Mutual Insurance Company.

Lane was very active in philanthropic and religious work in New York.

LARNED, EDWIN C., 1820–1884

Secretary, Northwestern Branch, American Freedmen's Union Commission.

After graduating from Brown University, Larned became a professor of mathematics at Kemper College, Wisconsin. While there he studied law. In 1847 he moved to Chicago. He was an enthusiastic abolitionist and a warm friend of Abraham Lincoln. During the war he was a member of various defense committees and in 1861 was appointed Federal District Attorney by President Lincoln.

LOW, ABIEL A., 1811–1893

American Union Commission.

Low was the head of A. A. Low and Brothers, one of the leading American traders in Oriental goods. As president of the New York Chamber of Commerce from 1863 until 1866 Low led the New York businessmen in opposition to Great Britain's policy in regard to the Confederate navy. During this period he was also president of the Union Defense Committee of New York.

Low was the owner of two vessels destroyed by the Confederate navy, recovery for which was effected before the Joint Commission at Geneva.

Low was an active supporter of the first transatlantic cable and was associated with Collis P. Huntington and others in the construction of the Chesapeake and Ohio Railroad and in the building of Newport News, Virginia, and Huntington, West Virginia.

MILES, HENRY A., 1809–1895

Corresponding secretary, American Union Commission.

After his ordination as a minister in the Unitarian Church in 1832, Miles was pastor at Hallowell, Maine, and Lowell, Massachusetts. He was the author of *Lowell as It Was and Is,* a history which is said to have painted "an unduly roseate picture of industrial conditions" at Lowell.

McCLINTOCK, JOHN, 1814–1870

Vice-president, American Freedmen's Union Commission.

After serving one year as a minister in the Philadelphia Conference of the Methodist Episcopal Church, McClintock became a member of the faculty of Dickinson College, Carlisle, Pennsylvania. He was an extremely active abolitionist, and in 1847 was arrested on charges of having incited a riot while attempting to rescue a fugitive slave from his guards. Although feeling against him was very strong, he was acquitted.

In 1848 McClintock became editor of the *Methodist Quarterly Review,* and in 1865 he, with Bishop Matthew Simpson (*q.v.*), went to Europe as a delegate to the British Wesleyan Conference and to the Evangelical Alliance, Berlin.

During the war McClintock wrote many articles and letters in support of the Federal cause. Since he was considered "the most accomplished man" in American Methodism, his influence was of great value in "removing misapprehensions abroad."

McKIM, J. MILLER, 1810–1874

Port Royal Relief Association; Pennsylvania Freedmen's Relief Association; executive committee, American Freedmen's Union Commission; committee on teachers, New York Branch, American Freedmen's Union Commission; corresponding secretary, Western and Northwestern Branch, American Freedmen's Union Commission; corresponding secretary, American Freedmen's Commission.

McKim was widely known in the work of the associations, and among the abolitionists of the country. He became an abolitionist in early youth. At the age of twenty he represented the Negroes of Carlisle, Pennsylvania, at the Philadelphia Anti-Slavery Convention of 1837. John G. Whittier (*q.v.*), James Mott, and James Rhoads were also delegates to this convention. McKim was a member of that famous band of followers of Theodore Weld, "The Seventy," and was active in the work of the underground railroad and of the Philadelphia Vigilance Committee. He succeeded John G. Whittier as editor of the *Pennsylvania Freeman,* and was publishing agent for the Pennsylvania Anti-Slavery Society. In 1859 he and his wife were members of the party which escorted the body of John Brown to North Elba. [See Hallowell, R. P.] During the war McKim assisted in the organization of Camp William Penn, which sent eleven Negro regiments into the Federal forces.

In 1862 McKim organized the Port Royal Relief Committee, which became the Pennsylvania Freedmen's Relief Association. As corresponding secretary of the latter organization he traveled throughout the South establishing Negro schools.

Mrs. McKim was the former Sarah Allibone Speakman, "a Quaker beauty who used her feminine attractions to further the anti-slavery cause." Charles Follen McKim, the architect, was their son; their daughter, Lucy, became the wife of Wendell Phillips Garrison, son of William Lloyd Garrison (*q.v.*).

MANNING, JACOB M., 1824–1882

Vice-president, Boston Educational Commission; vice-president, New England Freedmen's Aid Society.

After his graduation from Amherst College in 1850 Manning became pastor of the Congregational church at Medford, Massachusetts. In 1857 he became assistant pastor of Old South Church, Boston. He assumed the pastorate in 1872.

Manning was chaplain of the Massachusetts Senate, chaplain of the Forty-third Massachusetts Regiment, a member of the Boston School Board, and a member of the board of trust of Harvard University.

MERRICK, SAMUEL V., 1801–1870

President, Pennsylvania Branch, American Freedmen's Union Commission.

Samuel Merrick was the head of Merrick and Sons, manufacturers of marine engines, heavy machinery, and boilers. This firm built the engines for a number of well-known naval vessels, including *New Ironsides,* one of the pioneer ironclads. Merrick and his associates also erected iron lighthouses on the coast of Florida and were interested in gas lighting in Philadelphia.

Merrick was the first president of the Pennsylvania Railroad Company. After 1849 he was a director of the Pennsylvania Railroad and of the Catawissa Railroad, and was president of the Sunbury and Erie. He was one of the founders of Franklin Institute.

After the war Merrick became interested in Southern education and made large contributions in support of schools in the South.

NAST, WILLIAM, 1807–1899

Freedmen's Aid Society of the Methodist Episcopal Church.

Nast was a native of Germany. In 1832 he became librarian and instructor in German at United States Military Academy at West Point. His next position was at Kenyon College, Gambier, Ohio, where he taught Greek and Hebrew.

About 1834 Nast joined the Methodist Church and in the following year became a missionary to the Germans of Cincinnati, where he organized the first German Methodist church in the city. For fifty-three years he was the editor of a religious periodical published in the German language.

NICHOLSON, TIMOTHY, 1828–1924

Secretary, Indiana Yearly Meeting of Friends.

Nicholson began his long work in educational and humanitarian movements as principal of Belvedere Academy, Belvedere, North Carolina. From 1855 to 1859 he taught at Haverford College, Pennsylvania, and in 1859 became head of the school.

Nicholson moved to Richmond, Indiana, about 1861, where he became very prominent in the Indiana Yearly Meeting. He led the Indiana Friends in their work for prison reform for over forty years. He was one of the most active agents in the work among the freedmen after the war.

Nicholson was a trustee of Earlham College, Richmond, and of the State Normal School.

OLMSTED, FREDERICK LAW, 1822–1903

General secretary, American Freedmen's Aid Union; general secretary, American Freedmen's Commission.

Olmsted was a man of varied interests. Among historians he is best known for his three volumes of observations on the ante-bellum South. He was a widely known and influential landscape gardener and architect.

During the war Olmsted was of great service as secretary of the United States Sanitary Commission. He was deeply interested in the work of the freedmen's relief societies and educational associations, and supported every effort in behalf of the freedmen. [See Pierce, E. L.]

PHILBRICK, EDWARD S.

Boston Educational Commission; vice-president, New England Freedmen's Aid Society.

In 1862 Philbrick went to Port Royal, South Carolina, under the auspices of the Boston Educational Commission. Upon his arrival at the Sea Islands, E. L. Pierce (*q.v.*) placed him in charge of three plantations.

In 1863 Philbrick proposed to John Murray Forbes, Boston railroad official and financier, that he and a group of associates invest twelve or fifteen thousand dollars in land in the Sea Islands of South Carolina, the land to be bought at the federal tax sales in April, 1863. A syndicate of thirteen Boston men, headed by Forbes, agreed that Philbrick should buy the land and manage the planting.

Philbrick also engaged in land and cotton speculation as a private venture. In 1862 he made only $5,000 from his private plantations instead of the $15,000 which he had expected, but in 1863, when he advised Edward Atkinson (*q.v.*) in regard to the Free Labor Cotton Company, he reported a net profit of $80,000.

E. L. Pierce, the special agent of the Treasury sent to the Sea Islands by Secretary Chase and President Lincoln, said of Philbrick that he, "combining a fine humanity with honest sagacity and close calculation," was the "leading purchaser of land at the tax sales." Whatever his humanitarian interests may have been, his "sagacity and close calculation" was such that by 1864 Philbrick was the owner of eleven plantations. On these plantations he set up stores from which he sold goods valued at thousands of dollars monthly. The great demand for dry goods, hardware, and similar manufactured products led Philbrick to advise his New England friends, including Edward Atkinson, that the emancipation of the Negro would open a vast market to the Northern merchant.

Philbrick was bitterly criticized for his speculation in land and cotton, but he asserted that he was not ashamed of his profit, which he considered to be merely the reward for having performed a service which was "very much needed by the community."

Pearson, *Letters,* VIII, 101–102, 219–220, 229, 237, 248; *Independent,* April 21, May 5, 1864; John Murray Forbes, *Letters and Recollections of John Murray Forbes,* edited by Sarah Forbes Hughes (2 vols., Boston, 1899), II, 71. For an interesting discussion of the "tax sales" controversy see Guion G. Johnson, *A Social History of the Sea Islands* (Chapel Hill, 1930).

PIERCE, EDWARD L., 1820–1897

Vice-president, New England Freedmen's Aid Society; governing board, American Freedmen's Union Commission.

Pierce was a graduate of Brown University and of the Harvard University law school. He worked in the office of Salmon P. Chase (*q.v.*) in Cincinnati and was his secretary in Washington. In the first week of the war Pierce enlisted as a private (a "three months man") in the Third Massachusetts Regiment. He was soon detailed to supervise the work of a detachment of Butler's "contrabands" at Fortress Monroe.

In 1862 Secretary Chase sent Pierce to the Sea Islands of South Carolina as special agent of the Treasury. From his report to Secretary Chase, and his conversations with the Secretary and with other interested individuals, there developed the idea that schools might be supported by the proceeds from the sale of confiscated cotton. Pierce's report to Chase, the report of the Rev. Mansfield French, and appeals from various officials of the Federal army and navy led to the creation of the Boston Educational Commission. [See Chapter I; see, also, Andrew, J. A.; Atkinson, E.; Philbrick, E. S.]

Charles Sumner was also interested in the "Port Royal Experiment." He wrote Pierce that he was "proud" of his report, and that it would be printed as a Congressional document. "There is great ignorance in the chamber in regard to the pending cotton bill, and I fear there will be delay," wrote Sumner.[1]

Pierce accompanied the teachers and labor superintendents who sailed for the Sea Islands in March, 1862, on board the steamer *Atlantic*. As the vessel bearing the "Gideonites" approached the shore Pierce exhorted them to undertake their task with courage, for, said he, "never did a vessel bear a colony on a nobler mission, not even the Mayflower, when she conveyed the Pilgrims to Plymouth." [2]

Of this group John Murray Forbes, who was also a passenger on the *Atlantic*, wrote:

"Our passengers consist chiefly of the 'villiantropic' society . . . bearded and mustached and odd-looking men, with odder-looking women. . . . You would have doubted whether it was the adjournment of a John Brown meeting or the fag end of a broken-down phalanstery! . . . Frantic women, unprotected females, appealed to the captain and to Mr. E. L. Pierce to let them go and teach young nigs; others in despair about their traps, some tearful at parting. . . ." [3]

[1] Edward L. Pierce, *Memoir and Letters of Charles Sumner* (4 vols., Boston, 1877–1893), IV, 82. Pierce was the official biographer of Sumner. The bill under consideration was prepared by F. L. Olmsted (*q.v.*), whom Sumner called "an admirable man."
[2] Pierce, "Freedmen at Port Royal," *Atlantic Monthly*, XII (September, 1863), 298.
[3] Forbes, *Letters*, I, 294–296.

After the war Pierce held several public offices. He was Collector of Internal Revenue at Boston, District Attorney, and a member of the Massachusetts legislature. He was widely recognized as an authority on railroad law.[1]

[1] See, also, Pierce to Chase, May 18, 1864, Salmon P. Chase MSS., Library of Congress; Pierce to Alvord, May 14, 1867, B.R.F.A.L. MSS.; Port Royal Correspondence, the National Archives.

POLLOCK, JAMES, 1810–1890

American Union Commission.

Pollock was admitted to the bar in 1833, became deputy attorney general for Northumberland County, Pennsylvania, in 1835, and, in 1844, was elected to the House of Representatives, a position which he held until 1849. While in the House he served as chairman of the special committee appointed to consider the construction of a trans-continental railroad.

In 1850 Pollock became judge of the Eighth Pennsylvania district and five years later was elected governor of the state by a combination of Whig and Know-Nothing groups. He served as Governor of Pennsylvania until 1858. During his term he sold the state-owned canals and railroads which connected Reading and Philadelphia to the Pennsylvania Railroad and others.

Pollock represented Pennsylvania at the peace conference of 1860–1861. In May, 1861, he was appointed director of the Philadelphia mint.

REID, JOHN M., 1870–1896

Board of Managers of the Freedmen's Aid Society of the Methodist Episcopal Church.

After graduating from the University of the City of New York in 1839 and from the Union Theological Seminary in 1841 Reid taught at Mechanics Institute, New York. In 1846 he entered the ministry, serving churches in New York and Connecticut. From 1858 to 1864 he was president of Genesee College, the predecessor of Syracuse University. It was largely through his efforts that the library of Leopold von Ranke came into the possession of the University.

Reid served as editor of the *Western Christian Advocate* and of the *Northwestern Christian Advocate*. He was also secretary of the Missionary Society of the Methodist Episcopal Church. [See Rust, R. S.; Walden, J. M.]

ROBERT, CHRISTOPHER RHINELANDER, 1802–1878

American Union Commission.

Robert began his career as a clerk and in 1835 he established the firm of Robert and Williams, importers of sugar, cotton, and tea. This venture was so successful that in 1862, when the partnership was dissolved, Robert was a very wealthy man.

From 1858 to 1863 Robert was president of the Delaware and Lackawanna Railroad.

After 1828 Robert was closely associated with the work of the Home Missionary Society. In 1838 he was chosen a member of the executive committee of the Society and from 1855 to 1870 he was treasurer. In addition to this work he personally gave large sums to Hamilton College, Beloit College, and Auburn Theological Seminary. In 1863 he founded Robert College, at Constantinople. After the war he bought from the government its hospital buildings at Lookout Mountain, Tennessee, and established there in 1866 a college for the "poor whites" of the South, but "local opposition to its Yankee origin led him soon to abandon the experiment."

RUSSELL, LEBARON

Committee on teachers, Boston Educational Commission; New England Freedmen's Aid Society; American Freedmen's Commission.

In 1862 Governor Andrew (*q.v.*) sent Russell as his personal representative to Port Royal, instructing him to investigate and report on conditions among the freedmen there. One of the results of Russell's report was the demand by Governor Andrew that the government establish an agency for the protection of the freedmen. This demand led, as has been noted, to the creation of the American Freedmen's Inquiry Commission.

Russell was active in assisting Andrew in recruiting Negro troops. He was a member of the Committee for Colored Troops, which was composed of Russell, George L. Stearns (John Brown's friend and adviser), John Murray Forbes, Amos H. Lawrence, Richard P. Hallowell (*q.v.*), and William I. Bowditch. [See Pierce, E. L.]

Pearson, *Andrew*, II, 67, 82.

RUST, RICHARD S., 1815–1906

Secretary, Freedmen's Aid Society of the Methodist Episcopal Church; secretary, Western Freedmen's Aid Commission; executive committee, American Freedmen's Union Commission.

In his youth Rust attended Phillips Academy, at Andover, Massachusetts. When he and several other students were expelled from the school because of their refusal to resign from an anti-slavery society, Rust went to Canaan, New Hampshire, where he entered an academy which admitted Negroes to the student body. When local opposition forced this institution to close he went to Wilbraham Academy, Wilbraham, Massachusetts, and then to Wesleyan University, Middletown, Connecticut. He graduated from the latter institution in 1841. Throughout his school career he supported himself by delivering anti-slavery lectures.

In 1846 Rust became principal of the New Hampshire Conference Seminary, and, in the same year, became state school commissioner. In 1859 he moved to Cincinnati, and became president of Wilberforce University. He was head of the University until it was sold to the African Methodist Church in 1863. He assisted in the organization of the Contraband Relief Association, which became the Western Freedmen's Aid Commission. He was corresponding secretary of the Commission.

Rust was strongly dissatisfied with the non-denominational character of these organizations. He believed that there was great danger that the work of the Methodist Church would suffer if it continued to co-operate with the non-denominational associations. He especially feared the power and influence of the Catholic Church. In a letter to J. W. Alvord he asserted that all the other evangelical churches had organized their own societies for the relief and education of the freedmen before the organization of the Methodist Freedmen's Aid Society, in August, 1866.[1] Such organizations were necessary, Rust believed, because of "peril from Romanists" who were "working to proselyte the freedmen." Should the evangelical churches fail to provide schools for the freedmen they would attend the schools of the Romanists, "whose instructions [would] disqualify them from becoming loyal citizens or intelligent Christians."[2] Rust believed that the teachers sent into the South should evangelize as well as educate. This belief forced him into the controversy over the function of the schools. [See Reid, J. M.; Walden, J. M.]

[1] Rust to Alvord, January 15, 1868, B.R.F.A.L. MSS.
[2] R. S. Rust, *The Freedmen's Aid Society of the Methodist Episcopal Church,* 16.

SCAMMON, J. YOUNG, 1812–1890

Advisory committee, American Freedmen's Union Commission.

Scammon was one of the leading business men in Chicago. He was also well known as a lawyer. It is said that he, more than anyone else, was responsible for the establishment of the system of free public schools in Chicago.

In 1844 Scammon began publishing the Chicago *Journal,* in 1865 he helped found the Chicago *Republican,* and in 1872 he began publishing *Inter-Ocean.* He was the founder and president of the Marine Bank of Chicago, president of the Mechanics National Bank of Chicago, and of the Chicago Fire and Marine Insurance Company. He was instrumental in bringing the Michigan Central Railroad to his city and was prominent in the development of the Galena and Chicago Union Railroad.

Scammon was a delegate to the Republican convention in 1864 and in 1872. He was a member of the state senate in 1861.

SELLERS, WILLIAM, 1824–1905

Pennsylvania Freedmen's Relief Association.

After serving as apprentice in various machine shops Sellers began the manufacturing of machine tools and mill gearing. In 1855 he organized William Sellers and Company, of which he was president until 1905.

Sellers was one of the leading inventors of machine tools. He received ninety patents on basic machines, such as steam injectors, rifling machines, riveters, hydraulic machinery, steam hammers, and the spiral-geared planer. The system of uniform screws, bolts, and nuts now used in the United States is known as the "Sellers or U.S. Standard" system.

In 1868 Sellers organized the Edge Moor Iron Company. This company furnished the iron work for the Philadelphia Centennial and for the Brooklyn Bridge. In 1873 he organized the Midvale Steel Company, which soon "became a leader in the production of heavy ordnance."

Sellers was a member of Franklin Institute, and a trustee of the University of Pennsylvania.

SHAW, FRANCIS G., 1809–1892

New England Freedmen's Aid Society; president, National Freedmen's Relief Association; vice-president and member executive committee, American Freedmen's Union Commission; American Freedmen's Aid Union; American Freedmen's Commission.

Shaw was the grandson of Francis Shaw and the son of Robert Gould Shaw, both of whom, by judicious investment in Maine lands, made large fortunes, which Francis George Shaw inherited. Shaw was a follower of Henry George and was deeply interested in Brook Farm and other socialistic communities. Both he and his son-in-law, George William Curtis, were apostles of Fourierism. Shaw translated the works of Fourier, Zschokke, and George Sand. He was the father of Josephine Shaw Lowell (Mrs. Charles Russell Lowell, Jr.,) who was very active in freedmen's aid; of Robert Gould Shaw, who was killed at Fort Wagner; and of Mrs. George W. Curtis, Mrs. Frances C. Barlow, and Mrs. Robert B. Minturn.

W. A. Hinds, *American Communities and Co-operative Colonies* (Chicago, 1908), 248; Forbes, *Letters,* II, 113.

SIMPSON, MATTHEW, 1811–1884

American Freedmen's Aid Commission; American Freedmen's Union Commission; New England Freedmen's Aid Society; Pennsylvania Freedmen's Relief Association.

After a varied career as a student of law and of medicine Simpson was admitted to the Methodist ministry in 1836. In the following year he became a member of the faculty of Allegheny College and in 1839 assumed the presidency of Indiana Asbury University, at Greencastle, Indiana.

As editor of the *Western Christian Advocate,* a position which he held from 1848 until his election to the bishopric in 1852, Simpson exercised great influence. His forceful opposition to slavery attracted wide attention, and he received the support of Salmon P. Chase (*q.v.*). During the war he became a confidant of Stanton and Lincoln. He favored strong action against the Confederacy, and was sometimes called "the War Bishop." [See McClintock, John.]

SLEEPER, JACOB, 1802–1889

Vice president, Boston Educational Commission; New England Freedmen's Aid Society.

Between 1825 and 1850 Sleeper amassed a fortune in the wholesale clothing business and in real estate, and retired. In 1855 he assisted in the organization of the New England Educational Society. He was for fifty-five years superintendent of a Sunday School in Boston. Among his other activities were temperance and missions. He was president of the Massachusetts Bible Society, vice-president of the American Bible Society, and president of the Massachusetts Temperance Association.

Sleeper was a director of the Bank of Commerce, of the North American Insurance Company, and of several Western railroads. He served as a member of the Governor's Council under Governors Banks and Andrew (*q.v.*). [See Claflin, W.]

SPELMAN, HARVEY B.

Cleveland Freedmen's Aid Commission; executive committee, American Freedmen's Union Commission.

Harvey B. Spelman was the father-in-law of John D. Rockefeller. He was a prominent merchant in Cleveland, a representative in the Ohio legislature, and a leader in anti-slavery, temperance, and humanitarian work in Cleveland and New York.

STORER, BELLAMY, 1796–1875

Governing board, American Freedmen's Union Commission.

As a youth Storer was a member of a group of young men calling themselves the "Flying Artillery," who went about promoting revivals.

After his admission to the bar in Boston in 1817 Storer moved to Cincinnati, where he became an outstanding Whig. In 1834 he was a member of Congress. Ten years later he became a judge of the Superior Court of Cincinnati. He was professor of law in the Cincinnati Law School.

THOMPSON, JOSEPH P., 1819–1879

President, American Union Commission; executive committee, American Freedmen's Union Commission; National Freedmen's Aid Commission; American Missionary Association.

Thompson was one of the leaders of the Congregational home missionary movement. For years before the outbreak of war he worked unceasingly and tirelessly to arouse public opinion in behalf of the slaves.

For a time Thompson was associated with Richard S. Storrs, Leonard Bacon, and Joshua Leavitt on the editorial staff of the *Independent*. He resigned in 1862, after a disagreement with Henry C. Bowen on matters of policy.

Thompson's second wife was Elizabeth Coit Gilman, a sister of Daniel Coit Gilman.

TOBEY, EDWARD S., 1813–1891

American Missionary Association.

Tobey was a man of wide and varied interests. His position as director or president of many concerns made him one of the outstanding business men of Boston. He was an officer of the Fall River Line, a director of many Boston banks, treasurer of a large textile mill and of an insurance company, and president of the Boston Board of Trade. He was also interested in education and in church history. He was president of the Boston Y.M.C.A., and a trustee of Bradford Academy and of Dartmouth College.

During the war Governor Andrew (*q.v.*) placed Tobey on the special committee for the defense of Boston, and Secretary Chase (*q.v.*) made him a member of the special advisory committee on Federal finances. In 1863 Secretary Stanton asked him to serve on a board to consider methods for destroying the *Merrimac*.

In 1866 Tobey served a term as state senator, and three years later he was appointed to the United States Board of Indian Affairs. [See Bishop, N.; Fisk, C. B.] From 1875 to 1886 he was postmaster of Boston.

WALES, THOMAS C., 1805–1880

American Union Commission.

At the age of fourteen Wales began working in a shoe store, and four years later he established his own business. In 1825, when twenty years of age, he sold the first India rubber shoe purchased in the United States. Between 1830 and 1833 he, as an agent for the Goodyear Company, was active in the introduction of rubber goods. In 1858 he patented "Wales Patent Arctic Gaiter," from the sale of which he made a large fortune.

WALDEN, JOHN MORGAN, 1831–1914

Secretary, Cleveland Freedmen's Aid Commission; secretary, Northwestern Freedmen's Aid Commission; secretary, American Freedmen's Commission; executive committee, American Freedmen's Union Commission; New England Freedmen's Aid Society; secretary, Freedmen's Aid Society of the Methodist Episcopal Church.

Walden was a native of Lebanon, Ohio. As a youth he followed the skepticism of Tom Paine, but in 1849 he experienced a violent conversion. In 1854 he moved to Fairfield, Illinois, where he published the *Independent Press,* in which he strongly opposed liquor and "squatter sovereignty." He received little support in this venture, however, and soon returned to Ohio. In 1856 he went to Kansas, where he began publishing the Quindaro *Chindowan,* a free-soil paper. He became very active in the Kansas controversy, acting as delegate to five free-soil conventions, including the Leavenworth constitutional convention of 1858. He "stumped the state" in opposition to the Lecompton constitution. [See Boynton, C. B.; Hale, E. E.]

In 1858 Walden returned to Cincinnati, where he was admitted to the Cincinnati Conference of the Methodist Church as an active minister. He was pastor of the York Street Church, Cincinnati. During the war he was very active in the work of the Defense Committee, and was personally responsible for recruiting two regiments.

Walden co-operated with R. S. Rust (*q.v.*) in the organization of the Methodist Freedmen's Aid Society. He had been active in the Contraband Relief Society of Cincinnati and in the Western Freedmen's Aid Society, and is said to have led the withdrawal of the Methodists from the Western Society in August, 1866. In this effort he was joined by R. S. Rust, Bishop Clark, Luke Hitchcock, J. M. Reid (*q.v.*), Adam Poe, and other prominent Methodist clergymen and laymen.

In 1867 Walden became presiding elder of the Eastern Cincinnati Conference. In the following year he became agent of the Western Methodist Book Concern, and in 1884 was chosen Bishop.

WALKER, JAMES B., 1805–1887

New England Freedmen's Aid Society.

A native of Philadelphia, Walker was a newspaper publisher and lawyer in Ohio until his conversion by Theodore Weld. After a year in study at Western Reserve College, Hudson, Ohio, he became an agent for the American Bible Society. In 1837 he became pastor of a Presbyterian church at Akron, Ohio. In 1839 he moved to Cincinnati, where he published his famous work, *The Philosophy of the Plan of Salvation.* By 1855 this work was used as a textbook in seminaries in all sections of the United States, and had been translated into French, German, Italian, Welsh and Hindustani.

Walker was a powerful force in abolitionism. In 1840 he established at Cincinnati *The Watchman of the Valley,* in which he attacked slavery and advocated abolitionism, temperance, and similar doctrines. In 1842 he became pastor of a Congregational church at Mansfield, Ohio, "composed chiefly of abolitionists and temperance reformers." In 1846 he began publishing another periodical, *The Herald of the Prairies.*

From 1859 to 1865 Walker was a member of the faculty of Chicago Theological Seminary. During this period he attempted to set up a college community "on the Oberlin model," in Benzie County, Michigan. This adventure in Christian socialism, which Walker called "Benzonia," was abandoned in 1870.

After the failure of Benzonia Walker taught intellectual and moral philosophy at Wheaton College and was pastor of the local Congregational church.

WHIPPLE, GEORGE, d. 1876

Secretary, American Missionary Association; executive committee, American Freedmen's Union Commission.

George Whipple was one of the most active and influential workers in the abolition and education movements. He received sound training in abolitionist principles as a student at Oneida Institute, Lane Seminary, and Oberlin College. During his vacations he was an earnest anti-slavery agitator.

In 1836, immediately after his graduation from Oberlin College, he was made principal of the preparatory department of the college, and two years later was appointed professor of mathematics. This position he held until 1847, when he became secretary of the American Missionary Association. In this position he was extremely active in the work among the freedmen. He was an intimate friend of J. W. Alvord (*q.v.*) and many other leaders in the movement. He was the virtual director of the work of the American Missionary Association among the freedmen until his death in 1876.

Weld-Grimké Letters, 51n, 57–58; James H. Fairchild, *Oberlin, the Colony and the College* (Oberlin, 1883), 289.

WHITTIER, JOHN GREENLEAF, 1807–1892

Vice-president, New England Freedmen's Aid Society; American Freedmen's Aid Union; American Freedmen's Commission.

His first published poem appeared June 8, 1826, in the Newburyport *Free Press,* edited by William Lloyd Garrison. Whittier became an abolitionist in 1832, after reading Garrison's *Thoughts on Colonization,* and from that date was increasingly active in the movement. From March, 1838, to

February, 1849, he edited *The Pennsylvania Freeman*. [See McKim, J. M.] He was an intimate friend of Theodore and Angelina Grimké Weld.

Like Bryant (*q.v.*), Whittier took an active interest in national politics. He bitterly attacked Polk because of the Mexican War, and castigated Webster because of his famous "Seventh of March Speech." Whittier was among those who induced Sumner to run for the Senate in 1851 on a Free-Soil-Democratic ticket.

Whittier was "one of the first to suggest the formation of the Republican party and always considered himself one of its founders."

Pierce, "Freedmen at Port Royal," *Atlantic Monthly*, XII (September, 1863), 291–315; *Weld-Grimké Letters; American Freedman*, I, 2 (May, 1866), 23; Julia M. Stuart, Whittier, as an Abolitionist, 1833–1863 (unpublished M.A. thesis, Vanderbilt University, 1939).

WISE, DANIEL, 1813–1898

American Freedmen's Union Commission.

Wise was born in Portsmouth, England. At the age of twenty he went to Grafton County, New Hampshire, where he was employed as a teacher. In 1834 he became pastor of a church at Lisbon, New Hampshire, and began to attract attention because of the vigor of his attack on slavery.

Between 1838 and 1844 Wise was editor of the *Sunday School Messenger* and of *The Ladies Pearl*. From 1845 to 1857 he held pastorates at Nantucket, Providence, Fall River and New Bedford. As editor of *Zion's Herald* and editor of the Sunday School literature of the Methodist Church he strongly supported the movement for the exclusion of all slaveholders from the Methodist Church.

After serving sixteen years as secretary of the Sunday School Union and editor of its publications he took the same position with the American Tract Society.

YEATMAN, JAMES E., 1818–1901

New England Freedmen's Aid Society; American Freedmen's Commission.

James Yeatman was the son of Thomas Yeatman, iron manufacturer, of Wartrace, Tennessee. After an apprenticeship in his father's business the younger Yeatman moved to St. Louis, where he became one of the leaders in the business and commercial life of the city. He was one of the founders of the Merchants Bank of St. Louis, and one of the incorporators of the Missouri Pacific Railroad Company.

Yeatman is best known for his work as head of the Western Sanitary Commission. Under his direction great progress was made in the care of the sick and wounded. He introduced the first railroad hospital cars ever used by military forces. In his work with the Sanitary Commission he assisted Dorothea Dix in the hospital and nursing service.

OFFICERS OF THE LEADING EDUCATIONAL ASSOCIATIONS[1]

AMERICAN FREEDMEN'S UNION COMMISSION

Abbott, Lyman
Alvord, J. W.
Beecher, Henry Ward
Bishop, Nathan
Blanchard, Jonathan
Bond, Chas. W.
Bond, Hugh L.
Brimmer, Martin
Brooks, Phillips
Burroughs, J. C.
Butler, William Allen
Cabot, Samuel
Chapin, J. H.
Chase, Salmon P.
Chase, Supply
Clark, E. W.
Clark, J. B.
Coffin, Levi
Colfax, Schuyler
Collins, James B.
Collyer, Robert
Colwell, Stephen
Cope, Francis R.
Corson, Robert R.

Crawford, M. D. C.
Dike, Henry A.
Endicott, Wm., Jr.
Field, H. M.
Frothingham, O. B.
Garrison, Wendell Phillips
Garrison, William Lloyd
Gookins, S. B.
Hallowell, R. P.
Hammond, Chas. B.
Hatfield, Edwin F.
Haynes, D. C.
Hogarth, William
Holmes, H. B.
Hooper, Edw.
Israel, Fielder
Jay, John
Kennedy, Crammond
Kennedy, Thos.
Knight, H. B.
Larned, E. C.
McClintock, John
McKim, J. Miller

Merrick, Samuel V.
Parkman, John
Parmly, E.
Parrish, Jos.
Patterson, R. W.
Perkins, Joseph
Pierce, E. L.
Plumb, David
Rhoads, James E.
Rust, R. S.
Scammon, J. Young
Shaw, Francis Geo.
Shipherd, J. R.
Simpson, Matthew
Skinner, Thomas H.
Spelman, H. B.
Storer, Bellamy
Storrs, H. M.
Thompson, Jos. P.
Walden, J. M.
Ward, Geo. Cabot
Whipple, Geo.
White, Sam. S.
Wise, Daniel

AMERICAN UNION COMMISSION

Abbott, Lyman
Allen, R. H.
Bond, L. Montgomery
Booth, Wm. A.
Bowen, James H.
Bridges, J. C.
Brimmer, Martin
Brown, John N.
Buddington, Wm. I.
Butler, Chas.
Cameron, James
Chase, C. Thurston

Claghorn, John W.
Coffin, Arthur G.
Colgate, C. C.
Cope, Francis R.
Dickson, C.
Dows, David
DuBois, Henry N.
Duryea, J. T.
Eddy, T. M.
Fancher, E. L.
Fell, J. G.
Foster, Dwight

Fowler, J. S.
Frazier, J. M.
Gardner, James H.
Gilman, Daniel Coit
Griffiths, G. S.
Hall, E. G.
Hammond, C. G.
Harrison, Jos., Jr.
Hill, Ham.
Israel, F.
Kent, Horace L.
Kidder, Henry P.

[1] These lists, compiled from the published reports of the associations and from various manuscripts, may not include all the officers of the associations listed.

172 *Appendix II*

AMERICAN UNION COMMISSION—Continued

Kitchell, H. D.
Lambert, Wm. G.
Lane, Geo. W.
Lathrop, D. W.
Low, A. A.
Meade, Geo. G.
Merrick, Sam. C.
Miles, H. A.
Mingins, Geo. J.
McMichael, Morton
Morgan, Henry T.

Odiorne, T. G.
Parker, Jos.
Patten, W. H.
Pierce, H. M.
Pollock, James
Reynolds, James L.
Robert, Christopher R.
Root, E.
Ryder, W. H.
Scovill, H. G.
Stewart, Benedict D.

Stout, A. V.
Strong, J. W.
Thatcher, L. A.
Thompson, Joseph P.
Turner, David
Tyng, S. H., Jr.
Wales, Thomas C.
Welsh, John
White, M. C.
Work, Sam.
Wray, Sam. W.

AMERICAN MISSIONARY ASSOCIATION

Abbott, Lyman
Ball, Alonza S.
Barstow, A. C.
Beadle, J. P.
Beecher, Edw.
Beecher, Henry Ward
Belden, Henry
Bennett, J. O.
Blanchard, Jonathan
Boynton, Chas. B.
Brown, Wm. B.
Butler, Jacob
Chapin, Wm. C.
Claflin, Wm.
Cleveland, Chas. D.
Cravath, E. M.
Crooks, Adam
Davis, S. N.
Eustis, W. T.
Fanning, T. C.
Farish, F. D.
Farnworth, Ezra
Field, John

Fisk, Clinton B.
Graham, D. M.
Hallock, Horace
Harris, Sam.
Holmes, J. M.
Holmes, Sam.
Holton, E. D.
Jocelyn, S. S.
Ketchum, Edgar
Kirk, E. N.
Lester, Andrew
Martin, Sella
McKeen, Silas
Noble, F. A.
Palmer, Julius A.
Palmer, Ray
Parker, Leonard S.
Patton, W. W.
Pike, G. D.
Porter, A. H.
Prindle, Cyrus
Ritter, Thomas

Sabin, Oscar C.
Shepard, Geo.
Shipherd, J. R.
Smith, E. P.
Smith, J. J.
Snow, Franklin
Straight, Seymour
Strieby, M. E.
Sturtivant, J. M.
Swain, Leonard D.
Tappan, Arthur
Tappan, Lewis
Thompson, J. B.
Thurston, David
Thurston, Stephen
Tobey, E. S.
Washburne, Emory
Washburne, I.
Whiting, Wm. E.
Whipple, Geo.
Williston, J. P.
Woodworth, C. L.

FREEDMEN'S AID SOCIETY OF THE METHODIST EPISCOPAL CHURCH

Allyn, Robert
Bonner, B. R.
Boyd, W. F.
Chalfant, J. F.
Clark, D. W.
Crews, H.
DeCamp, Harvey
Dobbins, J. G.
DuBois, John
Duval, B. F.
Dymond, R.
Eddy, T. M.

Fay, B. St. J.
Ferguson, C.
Fisk, Clinton B.
Foster, Geo. F.
Fowler, C. H.
George, A. C.
Gee, A. A.
Goodrich, Grant
Goodwin, A. S. W.
Gray, B. F.
Hagans, M. B.
Harrison, J. C.

Hartuppe, G. H.
Hatfield, H. M.
Hight, J. J.
Hitchcock, Luke
Hoyt, F. S.
Ketchum, C. W.
Larkin, J. F.
Leonard, A. B.
Liebhart, H.
Magee, J. P.
M'Donald, David
Merrill, S. M.

FREEDMEN'S AID SOCIETY OF THE M. E. CHURCH—Continued

Miller, J. V. R.
Nast, Wm.
Ninde, Wm. X.
Pfaff, John
Phillips, J. M.
Poe, Adam
Reid, J. M.

Ridgeway, H. B.
Rogers, H. B.
Ross, J. H.
Runyon, Wm.
Rust, R. S.
Scranton, A. B.
Shaw, T. F.

Shinkle, Amos
Shutt, J. D.
Taylor, M. W.
Van Cleve, L. F.
Walden, J. M.
Wiley, I. W.

FRIENDS' ASSOCIATION OF PHILADELPHIA FOR THE RELIEF OF COLORED FREEDMEN

Albertson, Henry
Bettle, Edw.
Cadbury, Joel, Jr.
Cadbury, John W.
Cadbury, Rich.
Canby, W. M.
Coates, Benj.
Cope, Marmaduke C.
Evans, Chas.
Evans, J. Wistar

Evans, Wm., Jr.
Garrett, Geo. W.
Garrett, John B.
Garrett, Phillip C.
Haines, Henry
Hillis, John H.
Hillis, Sam.
Janney, Rich. M.
Kimber, Anthony M.

Longstreth, Wm. C.
Morris, Elliston P.
Rhoads, Chas.
Scattergood, Thomas
Scull, David, Jr.
Shipley, Sam.
Stokes, Francis
Tatum, John C.
Vaux, George
Whitall, James

NATIONAL FREEDMEN'S RELIEF ASSOCIATION OF NEW YORK

Bryant, William Cullen
Butler, William Allen
Collins, Charles
Collins, Joseph B.
Davison, Edw. F.
Dike, Henry A.
Estes, E. C.
Fox, Henry J.

Frothingham, O. B.
Gould, Charles
Hallowell, N. P.
Hawkins, William G.
Jay, John
Ketchum, Edgar
Kingsley, E. M.
Leigh, Charles C.

McKim, J. Miller
Noyes, Geo. F.
Parmly, Eleazar
Shaw, Francis Geo.
Tathum, Chas. B.
Tyng, S. H.
Ward, Geo. C.
Woolsey, J. J.

NEW ENGLAND FREEDMEN'S AID SOCIETY

Andrew, John A.
Atkinson, Edward,
Barnard, Charles F.
Bond, Hugh L.
Bowditch, Henry I.
Brimmer, Martin,
Butler, William Allen
Brown, John Carter
Burnside, A. E.
Cabot, Samuel
Cabot, Mrs. Samuel
Caswell, A.
Chapin, J. H.
Cheney, Mrs. Ednah D.
Child, Francis J.
Claflin, William
Clarke, James Freeman

Codman, Chas. R.
Collins, James B.
Coney, Samuel
Crocker, Miss L.
Cummings, Charles A.
Curry, Cadwallader
Dexter, H. M.
Elliott, T. D.
Ellis, Miss Lucy
Emerson, Geo. B.
Endicott, Mrs. A. T.
Endicott, William, Jr.
Farwell, John V.
Felton, Miss M. S.
Frothingham, Fred.
Frothingham, O. B.
Gannett, E. S.

Gannett, Wm. C.
Gardner, A. B.
Garrison, William Lloyd
Goodwin, I.
Gurney, Mrs. E. W.
Hague, William
Hale, E. E.
Harris, Edward
Hawkins, W. G.
Hepworth, G. H.
Higginson, James J.
Higginson, Thomas Wentworth
Hill, Hamilton A.
Hooker, R. W.
Hooper, Edward W.
Hooper, R. W.

NEW ENGLAND FREEDMEN'S AID SOCIETY—Continued

Jackson, James J.
Kidder, Henry P.
Kimball, M. G.
Kirk, E. N.
Lane, J. A.
Leverett, T. H.
Loomis, Henry
Loring, Mrs. Chas. B.
Lothrop, Loring
Lowe, Chas.
Lowell, Miss Anna
Lowell, Mrs. Geo. Russell
Manning, Jacob M.

May, Miss Abby W.
May, Fred. W. G.
Miner, A. A.
Padelford, Seth
Parker, J. W.
Parkman, John
Philbrick, E. S.
Pierce, E. L.
Poland, Luke
Rogers, Wm. B.
Rowland, L. P.
Russell, LeBaron
Russell, Thomas

Seaver, Norman
Sleeper, Jacob
Shaw, Francis G.
Simpson, Matthew
Stevenson, Miss Hannah E.
Stevenson, Miss M. C.
Thayer, J. B.
Walden, J. M.
Walker, J. B.
Waterston, R. C.
Whittier, John Greenleaf
Willard, C. W.
Yeatman, James

PENNSYLVANIA FREEDMEN'S RELIEF ASSOCIATION

Baldwin, M. W.
Barker, Abraham
Biddle, William
Blight, Atherton
Bond, L. Montgomery
Brooks, Phillips
Buckley, Edw. S.
Coates, Benj.
Clark, E. W.
Colwell, Stephen
Cope, Francis R.
Cope, Marmaduke
Corson, Robert R.
Crozer, John P.
Evans, Wm., Jr.

Frauciscus, A. H.
Furness, Horace H.
Garrett, Phillip G.
Hallowell, Morris L.
Hunn, John
Hunt, B. P.
Jones, J. Huntington
Jones, Jacob P.
Morris, Wistar
McKim, J. Miller
Newton, Rich.
Parrish, Jos.
Platt, Clayton
Randolph, P. P.
Rathbun, R. M.

Rhoads, Chas.
Rhoads, J. E.
Sellers, Wm.
Simpson, Matthew
Smith, J. Wheaton
Wetherill, Edw.
Wheeler, Chas.
White, James W.
White, Sam. S.
Whitney, Geo.
Winsor, Henry
Wood, Horatio C.
Wright, Jas. A.
Yarnall, Ellis

WESTERN FREEDMEN'S AID COMMISSION

Allen, D. H.
Boynton, C. B.
Clark, J. B.
Coffin, Levi
Cravath, E. M.
Goodwin, E. P.
Harwood, Edw.
Hills, O. H.

Hoyt, Wayland
Kennedy, Thos.
Larkin, J. F.
Maxwell, G. M.
Nixon, Wm. Penn
Pullan, R. B.
Ritchie, A.
Rust, R. S.

Stewart, J. B.
Storer, Bellamy
Storrs, H. M.
Sumner, Wm.
Walden, J. M.
Walker, J. P.
White, R. M.
Wright, J. F.

NORTHERN TEACHERS IN SERVICE IN THE SOUTH, 1862–1870, WHOSE HOMES HAVE BEEN LOCATED [1]

NAME	HOME	STATION
Abbot, Mrs. C. P.	Montreal, C. E.	Fortress Monroe, Virginia
Abbott, Ellen	Bangor, Maine	Jacksonville, Florida
Abbott, Mrs. Melinda	Bangor, Maine	Jacksonville, Florida
Aborn, Henry T.	Boston, Massachusetts	Williamsport, Maryland
Ackley, A. B.	Granville, Ohio	Montgomery, Alabama
Adams, C. H.	Clyde, Ohio	Montgomery, Alabama
Adams, Mrs. C. H.	Clyde, Ohio	Montgomery, Alabama
Adams, Lucy O.	Marion, New York	Trent Camp, North Carolina
Adams, Miss M. V.	Spencerport, New York	Montgomery, Alabama
Adams, Mary E.	Canaan, Connecticut	Beaufort, North Carolina
Adams, Sarah A.	Marion, New York	Trent River Camp, North Carolina
Adlington, Ellen E.	Weymouth, Massachusetts	Wilmington, North Carolina, and St. Mary's, Georgia
Alcott, Miss P. A.	Auburndale, Massachusetts	Fortress Monroe, Virginia
Alden, William H.	Westville, Connecticut	St. Helena, South Carolina
Aldrich, Mrs. L. G.	Newark, New York	Petersburg, Virginia
Alexander, Louisa	Oberlin, Ohio	Marietta, Georgia
Alford, Caroline	Ellington, Connecticut	Columbus, Georgia
Allen, Anna W.	Keene, New Hampshire	Washington, D.C.
Allen, D. T.	Kalamazoo, Michigan	Galveston, Texas
Allen, Jane Van	Gloversville, New York	Charleston, South Carolina
Allen, Mrs. Julia G.	Kalamazoo, Michigan	Galveston, Texas
Allen, Ruth A.	Black Earth, Wisconsin	Mobile, Alabama
Allen, Willard S.	Wilbraham, Massachusetts	Bermuda Hundred, Virginia
Allen, William F.	West Newton, Massachusetts	Charleston and St. Helena, South Carolina
Allen, William H.	Dorchester, Massachusetts	St. Helena, South Carolina
Allender, Miss A. E.	New London, Connecticut	Augusta, Georgia
Alson, Henry T.	Boston, Massachusetts	Williamsport, Maryland
Alvord, Major H. E.	Greenville, Massachusetts	Beaufort, South Carolina
Alvord, Miss S. S.	Austinburg, Ohio	Athens, Alabama
Ames, Mary	Springfield, Massachusetts	Beaufort, South Carolina
Anders, Lymas	Brattleboro, Vermont	Mitchelville, South Carolina
Anderson, Matilda	Brooklyn, New York	Gray's Inn, Maryland
Andrews, Miss E. H.	Swampscott, Massachusetts	Norfolk, Virginia
Andrews, Emma D.	Milltown, N.B.	Fortress Monroe, Virginia
Andrews, H. H.	Middletown, Connecticut	James Island, South Carolina

[1] This is not a complete list of Northern teachers. It includes only the teachers whose homes have been located. It was compiled from official lists, published reports, and manuscripts.

NAME	HOME	STATION
Andrews, Julia C.	Milltown, N.B.	Fortress Monroe, Virginia
Andrews, O. L.	New York, New York	Cleveland, Tennessee
Andrews, Miss S. E.	Hartford, Connecticut	Augusta, Georgia
Angier, Annie L.	Westboro, Massachusetts	Richmond, Virginia
Armstrong, Jennie M.	New York, New York	Charleston, South Carolina
Armstrong, Miss M. J.	New York, New York	Savannah, Georgia
Armstrong, S. C.	Hawaii	Hampton, Virginia
Arnold, George F.	Hamilton, New York	Beaufort District, South Carolina
Arnold, James D.	New Hampshire	Huntsville, Alabama
Ashley, Mrs. M. E.	Northboro, Massachusetts	Wilmington, North Carolina
Ashley, Mary A.	Northboro, Massachusetts	Wilmington, North Carolina
Ashley, Rev. S. S.	Northboro, Massachusetts	Wilmington, North Carolina
Auld, Lydia P.	E. Boston, Massachusetts	Fortress Monroe, Virginia
Ault, Anna M.	Newberry, Pennsylvania	Nashville, Tennessee
Ausman, Mrs. Sarah	Belle Prairie, Minnesota	Atlanta, Georgia
Ayer, Miss E. C.	Tonawanda, New York	Athens, Georgia
Ayer, Mrs. E. F. (T.?)	Belle Prairie, Minnesota	Atlanta, Georgia
Ayer, Rev. F.	Belle Prairie, Minnesota	Atlanta, Georgia
Ayres, Miss C. F.	Worcester, Massachusetts	Macon, Georgia
Ayres, Martha D.	Worcester, Massachusetts	Macon and Albany, Georgia
Ayres, Miss N. M.	Worcester, Massachusetts	Macon, Georgia
Babbitt, Mary R.	Southbury, Connecticut	Norfolk, Virginia
Babcock, Sarah A.	Plymouth, Massachusetts	Darlington, South Carolina
Bacheler, Daniel T.	Potsdam, New York	Lawrenceville, Virginia, and Roanoke Island, North Carolina
Bacheler, Ella B.	Potsdam, New York	Lawrenceville, Virginia, and Roanoke Island, North Carolina
Bacon, Miss D. A.	Gilead, Ohio	Greenville, North Carolina
Bacon, Miss H. E.	Hartford, Connecticut	Beaufort District, South Carolina
Baker, Alma	Quasquiton, Iowa	Cairo, Illinois
Baker, Miss M. A.	Goodale's Corner, Maine	Richmond, Virginia
Baker, Mary F.	Hopkinton, Massachusetts	Hilton Head, South Carolina
Ball, Angelina	Concord, Massachusetts	Norfolk and Richmond, Virginia
Ball, Elizabeth A.	Concord, Massachusetts	Norfolk and Richmond, Virginia
Banfield, J. S.	Dover, New Hampshire	Alexandria, Virginia, and Columbus, Georgia
Bardwell, Rev. J. P.	Oberlin, Ohio	Vicksburg, Mississippi
Barker, Edward	Massachusetts	Richmond, Virginia
Barnard, Francis E.	Boston, Massachusetts	Port Royal, South Carolina
Barnes, Miss E. M.	Bakersfield, Connecticut	Macon, Georgia
Barnes, Harriet R.	Norwich, Connecticut	Jacksonville, Florida
Barnes, Sara C.	Concord, Massachusetts	Columbus, Georgia
Barnes, Sarah M.	Woodbury, Connecticut	Houston, Texas
Barnett, Miss L. D.	Parshallsburg, Michigan	Memphis, Tennessee
Barnum, Jennie E.	Oberlin, Ohio	Atlanta, Georgia

NAME	HOME	STATION
Barnum, Joseph H.	Oberlin, Ohio	Memphis, Tennessee
Barnum, Mrs. Joseph H.	Oberlin, Ohio	Memphis, Tennessee
Barrett, Miss G. N.	Rose Valley, New York	Trent Camp, North Carolina
Bartemus, Miss A. M.	Boston, Massachusetts	Augusta, Georgia
Bartemus, Anna M	Groton Junction, Massachusetts	Jacksonville, Florida
Barton, R. S.	New London, Connecticut	Lynchburg, Virginia
Bas, Ella F.	North Adams, Massachusetts	Baltimore, Maryland
Bassett, J. A.	New Haven, Connecticut	Augusta, Georgia
Bates, Elia	Scituate, Massachusetts	Raleigh, North Carolina
Bath, Enoch	Ogdensburg, New York	Alexandria, Virginia
Battey, Mary S.	Barrington and Providence, Rhode Island	Andersonville, Georgia
Beals, Miss E. E.	Watertown, New York	Columbia, South Carolina
Beals, Mrs. H. N.	Angelica, New York	Beaufort, North Carolina
Beals, Sarah	Angelica, New York	Beaufort, North Carolina
Beckwith, Mrs. D.	Ashland, Ohio	Mound City, Illinois
Beebe, Phoebe	Adrian, Michigan	Talladega, Alabama
Beede, Lindley	Amesbury, Massachusetts	Baltimore, Maryland
Beigle, Jennie	Warriors Mark, Pennsylvania	Murfreesboro, Tennessee
Belden, Mrs. Diana A.	Eaton, New York	Trent River Camp, North Carolina
Bemis, L. C.	Athol Depot, Massachusetts	Smithfield, North Carolina
Bemis, Mrs. Mary O.	Athol Depot, Massachusetts	Smithfield, North Carolina
Benedict, Julia A.	Woodbury, Connecticut	Hilton Head, South Carolina
Bennett, Miss E. P.	Gloucester, Massachusetts	Roanoke Island, North Carolina
Bennett, Rev. H. E.	Wakeman, Ohio	Nashville, Tennessee
Benson, Mary A.	Potsdam, New York	Jacksonville, Florida
Bent, Catherine R.	Newburyport, Massachusetts	Jacksonville and Gainesville, Florida
Benton, Miss M. W.	Northampton, Massachusetts	Selma, Alabama
Bigelow, A. M.	Middletown, Connecticut	James Island, South Carolina
Bigelow, Mrs. R. M.	Washington, D.C.	Washington, D.C.
Billings, Mrs. H. S.	Andover, Massachusetts	Greenville, North Carolina, and Madison, Georgia
Bingham, Amorette W.	Vergennes, Vermont	Beaufort District, South Carolina
Blackman, Miss E. C.	Montrose, Pennsylvania	J. E. Tucker plantation, near Okolona, Mississippi
Blaisdell, Nicholas	Boston, Massachusetts	Edisto Island, Charleston, South Carolina
Blake, James P.	New Haven, Connecticut	Beaufort, South Carolina
Blanchard, Miss I. C.	Portland, Maine	Alexandria, Virginia
Bliss, Emily T.	Springfield, Massachusetts	Beaufort, South Carolina
Blood, Miss C. M.	Worcester, Massachusetts	Raleigh, North Carolina
Blood, John E.	Pepperell, Massachusetts	Wilmington, North Carolina
Bond, S. A.	Michigan	Murfreesboro, Tennessee
Booth, George C.	Chicago, Illinois	Houston, Texas
Booth, Miss L. A.	Montgomery, New York	Beaufort, South Carolina
Botts, Fannie J.	Syracuse, New York	St. Augustine, Florida, and Milford, Delaware

NAME	HOME	STATION
Botume, Elizabeth H.	Wyoming, Massachusetts	Beaufort, South Carolina
Boutelle, Miss M. L.	Leominster, Massachusetts	Washington, D.C.
Bowe, Daniel	Yale, Andover	Port Royal, South Carolina
Bowen, Agnes M.	Mallet Creek, Ohio	Macon, Georgia
Bowethorpe, Samuel T.	Boston, Massachusetts	Ladies Island, Beaufort, South Carolina
Bowker, Abbie A.	East Boston, Massachusetts	Wilmington, North Carolina, and Savannah, Georgia
Boyden, M. Louise	Leominster, Massachusetts	Georgetown, Delaware; Memphis, Tennessee; Charleston, South Carolina
Brackett, Mrs. Louise W.	Farmington and Phillips, Maine	Staunton, Virginia
Brackett, Rev. N. C.	Phillips and Farmington, Maine	Staunton, Virginia, and Harpers Ferry, West Virginia
Bradley, Amy M.	New Hanover, Connecticut	Wilmington, North Carolina
Bradley, Celia M.	Wayne, Ohio	Lexington, Kentucky
Franch, E. C.	Coldwater, Michigan	Mobile, Alabama
Brand, Rev. James	Saco, Maine	Washington, D.C.
Breck, Elizabeth P.	Northampton, Massachusetts	Charleston and Sumter, South Carolina
Brewer, Rev. F. P.	New Haven, Connecticut	Raleigh, North Carolina
Brewer, M. Adele	Stockbridge, Massachusetts	Raleigh, North Carolina
Brooks, Nancy D.	Berlin Heights, Ohio	Lexington, Kentucky and Gallatin, Tennessee
Brower, Miss T. R.	Milford, Ohio	Columbus, Kentucky
Brown, Charles H.	Boston, Massachusetts	Port Royal, South Carolina
Brown, Miss E. J.	Nashua, New Hampshire	Alexandria, Virginia
Brown, Emily J.	Belfast, Maine	Newbern, North Carolina
Brown, Emma B.	Georgetown, (D.C.?)	Washington, D.C.
Brown, Eunice M.	Worcester, Massachusetts	Washington, D.C.
Brown, Rev. H. E.	Columbus, Nebraska	Talladega, Alabama
Brown, Mrs. H. E.	Columbus, Nebraska	Talladega, Alabama
Brown, Minnie L.	Watertown, New York	Charleston, South Carolina
Brown, Sarah C.	Watertown, New York	Fernandina, Florida
Brown, Sarah G.	Barre, Massachusetts	Townfield, Virginia
Browne, Joseph W.	Springfield, Massachusetts	Baltimore, Maryland
Brownson, Mary	Richmond, Vermont	Fortress Monroe, Virginia
Buchanan, Mrs. A.	Barnet, Vermont	Murfreesboro, Tennessee
Buchanan (or Buchan), Bell	Ashland, Ohio	Memphis, Tennessee
Buchanan, C. W.	Barnet, Vermont	Murfreesboro, Tennessee
Buchanan, Cordelia	Pennsylvania	Nashville, Tennessee
Buchanan, J. E.	Barnet, Vermont	Murfreesboro, Tennessee
Buchanan, John	Pennsylvania	Nashville, Tennessee
Bullard, Annie M.	Westboro, Massachusetts	Richmond, Virginia, and Charleston, South Carolina (d. 1868)
Bullard, Miss H. C.	Boston, Massachusetts	Charleston, South Carolina
Bumstead, Horace	Boston, Massachusetts	Atlanta, Georgia
Burchard, O. R.	New Haven, Connecticut	Raleigh, North Carolina

NAME	HOME	STATION
Burke, Margaret	Pittsfield, Massachusetts	Hilton Head, South Carolina, and Thomasville, Georgia
Burnett, Mary A.	Southampton, Long Island, New York	Norfolk, Virginia
Burns, Mrs. E. V.	Cincinnati, Ohio	Nashville, Tennessee
Burt, Sarah M.	Northampton, Massachusetts	Augusta, Georgia
Bushee, Mrs. J. A.	East Boston, Massachusetts	Wilmington, North Carolina
Buttrick, Harriet	Concord, Massachusetts	Charleston, South Carolina, and Richmond, Virginia
Buxton, Mrs. M. B.	Topsham, Vermont	Norfolk, Virginia
Caldwell, W. L.	Cleveland, Ohio (?)	Lagrange, Georgia
Campbell, Annie	Belleville, C.W.	Trent River, North Carolina
Campbell, Annie M.	Norwalk, Connecticut	Baltimore, Maryland
Campbell, E. F.	New Ipswich, New Hampshire	Portsmouth, Virginia, and Savannah, Georgia
Campbell, Emma	Ironton, Ohio	Atlanta, Georgia
Campbell, Letitia G.	Nashua, New Hampshire	Richmond, Virginia
Campbell, Maria L.	Portsmouth, New Hampshire	Jacksonville, Florida
Campbell, Sarah	Norwalk, Connecticut	Baltimore, Maryland
Canedy, Anne C. G.	Fall River, Massachusetts	Newbern, North Carolina (d. August 15, 1866)
Canedy, B. L. (Betsy L.)	Massachusetts	Newbern, North Carolina
Canedy, Bessie L.	Fall River, Massachusetts	Richmond, Virginia
Canfield, Mrs. S. A. Martha	Ohio	Maysville, Kentucky
Carber, D. Lena	Lowville, New York	Washington, D.C.
Cardozo, Rev. F. L.	New Haven, Connecticut	Charleston, South Carolina
Cardozo, Mrs. M. H.	New Haven, Connecticut	Charleston, South Carolina
Carkin, Philena	N. Chelmsford, Massachusetts	Charlottesville, Virginia
Carpenter, Mrs. F. E.	Nelson, New York	Hilton Head, South Carolina
Carpenter, Rev. George C.	Nelson, New York	Hilton Head, South Carolina
Carr, Lena	Norfolk, Virginia	Roanoke Island, North Carolina
Carrol, Eunice E.	Villa Ridge, Illinois	
Carter, Harriet	Old Cambridge, Massachusetts	Washington, D.C.
Case, Abbie	Fitchburg, Massachusetts	Savannah, Georgia
Case, Mrs. L. F.	Milbury, Massachusetts	Albany, Georgia
Cathon, Miss M. S.	Townshend, Vermont	Ladies' Island, South Carolina
Celburn, Miss M. K.	Worcester, Massachusetts	Savannah, Georgia
Chace, Lydia B.	Providence, Rhode Island	Louisa Court House, Virginia
Chamberlain, E. A.	Barnstable, Massachusetts	Georgetown, D.C.
Chamberlain, J. M.	Oberlin, Ohio	Gerard, Alabama
Chamberlain, Melissa	Dover, New Hampshire	Charleston, South Carolina
Chamberlain, Phebe	Barnstable, Massachusetts	Georgetown, D.C.
Chamberlin, Miss L. A.	Montrose, Pennsylvania	Okolona, Mississippi (J. E. Tucker plantation)
Chapman, Miss A. L.	Palmyra, New York	Beaufort, North Carolina

NAME	HOME	STATION
Chase, Lucy	Worcester, Massachusetts	Charleston, South Carolina; Richmond and Norfolk, Virginia
Chase, Luella J.	Exeter, New Hampshire	Charleston, South Carolina
Chase, Martha H.	Providence, Rhode Island	Norfolk and Richmond, Virginia
Chase, Sarah E.	Worcester, Massachusetts	Norfolk, Virginia
Chidester, William E.	Oberlin, Ohio	Natchez, Mississippi
Christrer, Mary E.	N.E. Brunswick, Maine	Americus, Georgia
Chute, Benjamin P.	Massachusetts or New Brighton, Pennsylvania	Nashville, Tennessee; Stevenson, Alabama; and Lynchburg, Virginia
Clapp, Ada	Hillsdale, Michigan	Nashville, Tennessee
Clark, Abbie B.	Malden, Massachusetts	Wilmington, North Carolina, and Bainbridge, Georgia
Clark, Mrs. Martha	New Lyme, Ohio	Mound City, Illinois
Clark, Mary E.	Parma, New York	Richmond and Norfolk, Virginia
Clark, Sarah	Dorchester, Massachusetts	Richmond and Norfolk, Virginia
Clark, Rev. Silas	New Lyme, Ohio	Mound City, Illinois
Clark, Susan H.	Meadville, Pennsylvania	Fortress Monroe and Mill Creek, Virginia
Clark, William L.	Malden, Massachusetts	Wilmington, North Carolina, and Bainbridge, Georgia
Clark, William S.	Boston, Massachusetts	Port Royal, South Carolina (d. 1863)
Clarke, Anna F.	Wellesly, Massachusetts	Columbus, Georgia
Clarke, Jane E.	Boston, Massachusetts	Sandy Spring and Annapolis, Maryland; Columbus, Georgia
Clary, Miss M. H.	Conway, Massachusetts	Hilton Head, South Carolina
Clemmons, G. H.	Northboro, Massachusetts	Wilmington, North Carolina
Clift, Miss A. J.	Strykersville, New York	Oxford, North Carolina
Clift, W. L.	North Mansfield, Massachusetts	Wilmington, North Carolina
Coggesball, Anna E.	St. Charles, Illinois	Mobile, Alabama
Cogswell, Catherine A.	Foxboro, Massachusetts	Sommerville, South Carolina
Coit, Rosetta A.	Hastings Centre, New York	Fernandina, Florida
Cole, Mrs. Hannah W.	Elizabeth City, New Jersey	Roanoke Island, North Carolina
Coleman, Rev. N.	Berlin, Connecticut	Poplar Grove, Virginia
Coleman, Mrs. Sarah G.	Berlin, Connecticut	Poplar Grove, Virginia
Colburn, Mary K.	Worcester, Massachusetts	Savannah, Georgia
Collins, George	Oberlin, Ohio	Danville, Kentucky
Collins, Mrs. George	Oberlin, Ohio	Danville, Kentucky
Colton, Mrs. M. F.	Croton, Iowa	Montgomery, Alabama
Comings, Charles F.	Oberlin, Ohio	Brookhaven, Mississippi
Condol, N. T.	Elmira, New York	Aberdeen, Mississippi
Condon, Elizabeth	Boston, Massachusetts	Newbern, North Carolina
Conkling, William	Rensselaerville, New York	Savannah, Georgia

NAME	HOME	STATION
Conkling, Mrs. Wm. T. (M.J.)	Rensselaerville, New York	Augusta, Georgia
Cook, Miss S. S.	Milford, Massachusetts	Macon, Georgia
Cooke, Martha A.	Nashua, New Hampshire	Richmond, Virginia
Cooke, Mary J.	Nashua, New Hampshire	Richmond, Virginia
Cooley, Jane	Ludlow, Massachusetts	Hilton Head and Charleston, South Carolina
Cooley, Mary A.	Chicago, Illinois	Mobile, Alabama
Corliss, A. B.	Princeton and Bound Brook, New Jersey	Edenton, North Carolina, and Franklin Depot, Virginia
Corliss, Mrs. A. B.	Princeton and Bound Brook, New Jersey	Edenton, North Carolina, and Franklin Depot, Virginia
Cornoer, Mrs. Mary T.	E. Cleveland, Ohio	Montgomery, Alabama
Cortes, Sarah	Baltimore, Maryland	Ellaville, Georgia
Cortes—(daughter of Sarah C.)	Baltimore, Maryland	Ellaville, Georgia
Corwen, Mrs. D. C.	Brooklyn, New York	Norfolk, Virginia
Corwin, Duke	Brooklyn, New York	Alexandria, Virginia
Cotrell, Anna T.	Chicago, Illinois	Linneaus, Missouri
Couch, Miss F. A.	Pottsville, Pennsylvania	Murfreesboro, Tennessee
Crane, Miss J. E.	Yonkers, New York	Columbia, South Carolina
Crane, Kate G.	Brownsville, New York, or Farmington, Maine	Washington, D.C.
Cravath, Laura A.	Troy, Minnesota	Nashville, Tennessee
Crockett, Miss	Portland, Maine	Shenandoah Valley, Virginia
Cromwell, J. Wesley	Philadelphia, Pennsylvania	Norfolk, Virginia
Crosby, Mrs. C.	Pepperell, Massachusetts	Nashville, Tennessee
Crosby, Charles	Pepperell, Massachusetts	Nashville, Tennessee
Cross, Emma E.	Richmond, New York	Lexington, Kentucky
Curtis, Mrs. Annie C.	New York, New York	Trent River Camp, North Carolina
Curtis, Cordelia	Woodbury, Connecticut	Petersburg, Virginia
Curtis, Mary C.	Hillsdale, Massachusetts	Cairo, Illinois
Curtis, Miss S. L.	S. Egremont, Massachusetts	Augusta, Georgia, and Norfolk, Virginia
Daffin, Miss S. L.	Philadelphia, Pennsylvania	Arlington, Virginia
Daggett, Hattie C.	Downers Grove, Illinois	Houston, Texas
Damon, Mrs. Caroline	Worcester, Massachusetts	Augusta and Atlanta, Georgia
Dann, Miss C. A.	Chatham Four Corners, New York	Habeshaw Plantation, Paris Island, South Carolina
Davis, Emily E.	New York, New York	Portsmouth, Virginia
Day, Deborah	Mt. Vernon, Ohio	Atlanta, Georgia
Day, Delia M.	Sheffield, Ohio	Montgomery, Alabama
Day, Miss L. J.	Sheffield, Ohio	Montgomery, Alabama
Day, Mary C.	Sheffield, Ohio	Macon and Andersonville, Georgia
Day, Tabitha	Ohio	Murfreesboro, Tennessee
Dayton, Emma	Janesville, Wisconsin	Houston, Texas
Dean, Clara A.	Fabius, New York	Farmville, Virginia

NAME	HOME	STATION
Dean, Hattie A.	Amherst, Massachusetts	Fortress Monroe, Virginia
Deering, E.	Portland, Maine	Harper's Ferry, Virginia
Denison, Rev. J. H.	Williamston, Massachusetts	Fortress Monroe, Virginia
Dewey, Miss C.	Auburn, New York	Washington, D.C.
Dewey, Miss F. H.	Hanova, New Hampshire	Tallahassee, Florida
Dickinson, Mrs. L. S.	Beloit, Wisconsin	Galveston and Hempstead, Texas
Dickson, Mr.	Philadelphia, Pennsylvania	North Carolina
Dickson, Mrs.	Philadelphia, Pennsylvania	North Carolina
Dickson, C. F. (?)	Nashua, New Hampshire	
Dickson, Miss C. S.	Groton, Massachusetts	Albany, Georgia
Dickson, Julia F. P.	Boston, Massachusetts	Cambridge, Maryland
Dimick, O. W.	Lyme, New Hampshire	Savannah, Georgia
Dimick, Mrs. O. W.	Lyme, New Hampshire	Savannah, Georgia
Disbrow, Mrs. E. H.	New York, New York	Washington, D.C.
Dixon, Elizabeth O. V.	Boston, Massachusetts	Bay Side, Maryland
Dore, Rev. J. S.	South Dover, Maine	Uniontown, D.C.
Dore, Mrs. J. S.	South Dover, Maine	Uniontown, D.C.
Douglas, A. B. C.	Meridian, New Hampshire	Smyrna, Tennessee
Douglas, Mrs. A. B. C.	Meridian, New Hampshire	Smyrna, Tennessee
Douglass, Miss E. W.	Decorah, Iowa	Savannah, Georgia, and Seays, Tennessee
Dow, Charlotte S.	Elyria, Ohio	Montgomery, Alabama
Dow, Lucy E.	Hampton, New Hampshire	Raleigh, North Carolina
Dowd, Hattie W.	New Haven, Connecticut	Augusta, Georgia
Dowling, Lucinda M.	Van Wert, Ohio	Natchez and Vicksburg, Mississippi
Doxey, Miss M. J.	Brooklyn, New York	Newport News, Virginia
Drake, Miss C. A.	Waterbury, Connecticut	Savannah, Georgia
DuBois, Adelle	Ann Arbor, Michigan	Athens, Alabama
Dudley, Annie S.	Lewiston, Maine	Martinsburg, Virginia
Duncan, Miss J. W.	Nashua, New Hampshire	Norfolk, Virginia
Dunham, Miss S. T.	E. Dennis, Massachusetts	Thomasville, Georgia
Dunlapp, John	Oxford, Ohio	Shelbyville, Tennessee
Dunn, Mrs. A. A.	Greenwich, Massachusetts	Staunton, Virginia
During, E.	Portland, Maine	
Dyer, Miss M. E.	Spencerport, New York	Athens, Georgia
Eaman, Miss M. A.	Salnie, Michigan	Memphis, Tennessee
Eddy, Mrs. Mary E.	Fall River, Massachusetts	Fortress Monroe, Virginia
Elliot, Rebecca E.	Cincinnati, Ohio	Nashville, Tennessee
Ellis, Frances E.	Boston, Massachusetts	Newbern, North Carolina
Elwell, Miss R. H.	Hartford, Connecticut	District of Columbia
Emerson, Miss A. E.	Weymouth, Massachusetts	St. Mary's, Georgia
Emlette, Miss M. C.	Portland, Maine	
Engleman, Emma	New York, New York	Augusta, Georgia
Enmonds, Alden	Crawfordsville, Maryland	Cahaba, Alabama
Etheridge, Miss A. S.	Montrose, Pennsylvania	Augusta, Georgia
Ethridge, Eliza J.	Dover, Illinois	Mobile, Alabama
Evans, Elizabeth M.	Columbus, Wisconsin	Houston, Texas
Evans, Henrietta J.	Concord, New Hampshire	Beaufort District, South Carolina

NAME	HOME	STATION
Eveleth, Miss E. B.	Williamsburg, L.I., or Brooklyn, New York	Beaufort, North Carolina and Magnolia, Florida
Eveleth, Mrs. M. E.	Portland, Maine	Charleston, Virginia
Everson, Miss C. E.	Palmyra, New York	Petersburg, Virginia
Everett, Albert	Groton, Massachusetts	Edisto Island, South Carolina
Falles, Mary E.	East Boston, Massachusetts	Norfolk, Virginia
Farrand, G. A.	Cleveland, Ohio	Alabama
Farrand, Mary	Ypsilanti, Michigan	Palmyra, Missouri
Fay, Miss E. S.	Burlington, Vermont	Norfolk, Virginia
Fenton, Ella	Mt. Kisco, New York	Hilton Head, South Carolina
Fernold, Anne Shaw	Portsmouth, New Hampshire	Washington and Elizabeth City, North Carolina
Fish, Mr. Henry	Long Island, Delaware	Alexandria, Virginia
Fisher, Mrs. H. C.	Brooklyn, New York	Norfolk and Alexandria, Virginia
Fisher, Louise	Boston, or Salem, Massachusetts	Norfolk and Richmond, Virginia
Fitch, Miss E. F.	East Sheffield, Massachusetts	Athens, Georgia
Fitch, Miss J. S.	Elyria, Ohio	Montgomery, Alabama
Fitch, Mary M.	Medway or Holleston, Massachusetts	Atlanta, Georgia
Fitts, Hannah	West Boyleston, Massachusetts	Hilton Head, South Carolina
Flagler, Sara	Washington, D.C.	Washington, D.C.
Fletcher, Harrison T.	Harvard, Massachusetts	Charleston, South Carolina
Fletcher, Mary C.	Grafton, Massachusetts	Norfolk, Virginia
Fogg, Mrs. Emma M.	Concord, New Hampshire	Beaufort District, South Carolina
Foote, Emma L.	Wisconsin	Huntsville, Alabama
Foote, Mrs. H. C.	Watertown, Connecticut	Macon and Augusta, Georgia
Foote, Miss H. G.	Detroit, Michigan	Newton, Georgia
Ford, Rev.	Minnesota	Kentucky
Ford, Abby C.	Morristown, New Jersey	Washington, D.C.
Ford, Julia B.	Morristown, New Jersey	Washington, D.C.
Ford, Laura L.	Parishville, New York	Jacksonville, Florida
Forrest, Frank R.	Brandywine Manor, Pennsylvania	Lynchburg and Liberty, Virginia
Forten, Charlotte S.	Philadelphia, Pennsylvania	St. Helena, South Carolina
Fortune, Gertrude	Cromwell, Connecticut	Savannah, Georgia, and Port Royal, South Carolina
Fortune, Mrs. Julia S.	Cromwell, Connecticut	Savannah, Georgia
Foster, Jennie R.	Delavan, Wisconsin	Houston, Texas
Foster, Mrs. M. C.	Troy, New York	Norfolk, Virginia
Foster, Mrs. S. A.	Troy, New York	Norfolk, Virginia
Foster, Sarah E.	Somerville, Massachusetts	Richmond, Norfolk, and Gordonsville, Virginia; and Annapolis, Maryland
Fowler, L.	Mt. Kisco, New York	Hilton Head, South Carolina
Fowler, Mary A.	Foxboro, Massachusetts	Columbus, Georgia, and Edisto Island, South Carolina

Name	Home	Station
Fowler, Myra M.	Fishkill, New York	Augusta, Georgia
Fowler, Sarah	Mt. Kisco, New York	Hilton Head, South Carolina
Fox, Mrs. G. C.	New York State	Georgetown, South Carolina
Francis, Abby B.	Cambridge, Massachusetts	Richmond, Virginia and Washington, D.C.
Francis, Rev. C. W.	New Haven, Connecticut	Atlanta, Georgia
Freeman, Rev. E. H.	New Jersey	Franklin, Tennessee
Freeman, Mrs. E. H. (Sophia)	New Jersey	Franklin, Tennessee
Freeman, Mrs. S. P.	Maine	Roanoke Island, North Carolina
Fubley, Mrs. Catherine A.	Pennsylvania	Nashville, Tennessee
Gannett, William C.	Boston, Massachusetts	Port Royal, South Carolina
Gardener, Maggie	W. Bloomsfield, New York	Savannah, Georgia
Gardener, Polly	Mallet Creek, Ohio	Macon, Georgia
Gardner, Anna	Nantucket, Rhode Island	Charlottesville, Virginia and New Bern, North Carolina
Garland, Miss E.	Ann Arbor, Michigan	Chattanooga, Tennessee
Garland, Elizabeth H.	Brattleboro, Vermont	Charleston, South Carolina
Garrison, Thirza	Wasioja, Minnesota	Houston, Texas
Gates, Ellen A.	Petersham, Massachusetts	Darlington and Camden, South Carolina
Gay, Fannie H.	Rochester, New York	Ladies Island, South Carolina
German, George L.	Baltimore, Maryland	
Gibbins, Isabella	W. Roxbury, Massachusetts	Charlottesville, Virginia
Gibbs, Miss S. L. (L. L.?)	Wells, Maine	Lexington, New York
Gibson, Isaac T.	Salem, Iowa	Macon City, Missouri
Gilbert, William P. M.	Brattleboro, Vermont	Talladega, Alabama
Gilchrist, Miss E. G.	Manlius, New York	Beaufort, South Carolina, and Washington, D.C.
Gillespie, Miss S. E.	Hampton, New Hampshire	Staunton, Virginia
Gilmore, Lizzie A.	Westboro, Massachusetts	Staunton, Virginia
Gleason, Fannie	Glenns Falls, New York	Norfolk, Virginia
Goodell, Miss M. L.	New Haven, Connecticut	Fortress Monroe, Virginia, and Albany, Georgia
Goodell, Miss S. F.	Amherst, Massachusetts	Washington, D.C., and Augusta, Georgia
Goodenow, Miss	Portland, Maine	Washington, D.C.
Goodman, Miss H. W.	Worcester, Massachusetts	Savannah, Georgia
Goodman, Hanna L.	Worcester, Massachusetts	Macon, Georgia
Goodrich, Mary F.	Elmira, New York	Plymouth, North Carolina
Gordon, Carrie	Norwich, Connecticut	Atlanta, Georgia
Gordon, Mrs. E. A. R.	Blackstone, Massachusetts	Norfolk, North Carolina (?)
Gordon, Helen	New Bedford, Massachusetts	Washington, D.C.
Gould, Miss C. E.	New Hartford, Connecticut	Macon, Georgia
Gould, Effie J.	Groton Junction, Massachusetts	Hilton Head, South Carolina
Gould, F. J.	Boston, Massachusetts	Thomasville, Georgia
Gould, Mrs. F. J.	Boston, Massachusetts	Thomasville, Georgia
Graham, Emma	New Albany, Indiana	Atlanta, Georgia
Graves, Fannie	Hatfield, Massachusetts	Raleigh, North Carolina

NAME	HOME	STATION
Green, J. Porter	Hawaii	Hampton, Virginia
Green, Martha E.	Ottawa, Illinois	Shelbyville, Missouri
Green, Mary	Hawaii	Hampton, Virginia
Green, Mary A.	Boston, Massachusetts	Charleston, South Carolina
Greenbrier, Miss L.	Cleveland, Ohio	Marietta, Georgia
Greenbrier, Sarah	Cleveland, Ohio	Arlington, Virginia
Greene, Miss J. E.	Newfield, New York	Beaufort, South Carolina
Gregg, Miss F. E.	Baldwinsville, New York	Beaufort, South Carolina
Gregory, James M.	Washington, D.C.	Mt. Tabor, Maryland
Griffiths, Miss M. F.	New York, New York	Charleston, South Carolina
Grosvenor, Miss H. M.	Canterbury, Connecticut	Wilmington, North Carolina, and Macon, Georgia
Groves, Mrs. C. H.	Washington, D.C.	Washington, D.C.
Groves, Miss P. G. (C.?)	Washington, D.C.	St. Mary's County, Maryland
Guild, Abbie	Walpole, Massachusetts	Fortress Monroe, Virginia
Gunn, Mary C.	Campville, Connecticut	Roanoke Island, North Carolina
Hagar, Miss A.	Springfield, Ohio	Shelbyville, Tennessee
Hagerman, J. L.	New York City	Atlanta, Georgia
Haines, Carrie	Oberlin, Ohio	Memphis, Tennessee
Haines, Emily S.	Mariton, New Jersey	Liberty, Virginia
Haines, W. M.	West Connelsville, Ohio	
Hale, S. C.	E. Cleveland, Ohio	Lexington, Kentucky
Haley, Caroline C.	Portsmouth, New Hampshire	Raleigh, North Carolina
Haley, Rev. Frank	Wolfboro, New Hampshire	Macon, Georgia
Haley, Mrs. J. R.	Wolfboro, New Hampshire	Macon, Georgia
Haley, Miss S. A.	Biddeford, Maine	Columbia, South Carolina
Hall, Alice	Lansingburgh, New York	Baltimore, Maryland
Hall, Mrs. L. A. (Miss?)	Worcester, Massachusetts	Norfolk and Alexandria, Virginia
Hamilton, Miss E. L.	Conshohocken, Pennsylvania	Farmville, Virginia
Hamilton, Miss H. E.	Hartford, Connecticut	Washington, South Carolina
Hamilton, Miss L. E.	Oberlin, Ohio	Newton, Georgia
Hamlin, Mrs. J. H.	Melmore, Ohio	Evansville, Indiana
Hammond, Mrs. C. M.	Chatham, New York	Dawfuskie Island, South Carolina
Hammond, H. C.	Watertown, New York	Columbia, South Carolina
Hanford, Mrs. Harriet	Ithaca, New York	Augusta, Georgia
Hanley, Mrs. J. P. R.	Philadelphia, Pennsylvania, or Tom's River, New Jersey	Washington and Plymouth, North Carolina
Hanley, Maggie	Philadelphia, Pennsylvania	Washington, North Carolina
Harper, Zilpha R.	Limerick, Maine	Lexington, Virginia
Harris, Adeline	North Bridgewater, Massachusetts	Raleigh, North Carolina
Harris, Miss B.	Oberlin, Ohio	North Carolina
Harris, Miss Blanche V.	Oberlin, Ohio	Natchez, Mississippi, and Goldsboro, North Carolina
Harris, Cicero	Cleveland, Ohio	Fayetteville, North Carolina
Harris, Harriet L.	Portland, Maine	Beaufort District, South Carolina
Harris, Robert	Cleveland, Ohio	Fayetteville, North Carolina

Name	Home	Station
Harris, Rev. W. D.	Cleveland, Ohio	Richmond, Virginia
Hart, Mrs. Martha C.	Clinton, Massachusetts	Washington, D.C., and Vicksburg, Mississippi
Hartwell, Mrs. F. M.	East Avon, New Jersey	Washington, D.C.
Hartwell, Henry T.	South Walpole, Massachusetts	Baltimore, Maryland
Harvey, Kate B.	New York Mills, New York	Washington, D.C.
Harward, Anna C.	Moulton, Illinois	Grenada, Mississippi
Haskell, George M.	St. Paul, Minnesota	Pine Bluff, Arkansas
Haskell, Miss H. M.	Clinton, Massachusetts	Savannah, Georgia, and Wilmington, North Carolina
Hastings, Mary	Lawrence, Massachusetts	Memphis, Tennessee
Hatch, Hattie E.	Woodstock, Vermont	
Haven, Ellen B.	Portsmouth, New Hampshire	Columbus, Georgia, and Norfolk, Virginia
Haven, Isabella T.	Portsmouth, New Hampshire	Charleston, South Carolina
Haviland, Mrs. Laura S.	Adrian, Michigan	Memphis, Tennessee
Hawkins, Ester H.	Boston, Massachusetts	Jacksonville, Florida
Hawks, Mrs. J. M. (Esther H.)	Manchester, New Hampshire	Jacksonville, Florida
Hawks, Dr. J. Milton	Manchester, New Hampshire	
Hawley, Emeline A.	Terre Haute, Indiana	Atlanta, Georgia
Hawley, Emma R.	Bristol, Connecticut	Edenton, North Carolina, and Alexandria, Virginia
Hay, Martha L.	Williamsburg, New York	Trappe, Maryland
Hazee, Lizzie	Shoemakertown, Pennsylvania	Lebanon, Kentucky
Heacock, Annie	Jenkinton, Pennsylvania	Port Royal, South Carolina
Heacock, Eliza	Jenkinton, Pennsylvania	Washington, D.C.
Heacock, Miss Gayner	Shoemakertown, Pennsylvania	Port Royal Island, South Carolina
Heacock, Jessie	Jenkinton, Pennsylvania	Port Royal, South Carolina
Healy, Mr.	Greenwich, Ohio	Gerard, Alabama
Heinly, J. R.	Vincennes, Indiana	Orville, Alabama
Henderson, Miss M.	Hartford, Connecticut	Columbia, South Carolina
Hendry, Elmira	Angola, Indiana	Lexington, Kentucky
Henley, Miss L. A.	Waynesville, Ohio	Memphis, Tennessee
Henning, Amanda	Ann Arbor, Michigan	Memphis, Tennessee
Henry, Charlotte J.	Cohoes, New York	Jacksonville, Florida
Herbert, Miss E. A.	Leon, New York	Trent Camp, North Carolina
Hewitt, L.	Providence, Rhode Island	Maryland
Hewitt, Mrs. L.	Providence, Rhode Island	
Heyser, Emanuel	Philadelphia, Pennsylvania	
Hibbard, O. D.	Wyandotte, Michigan	
Hicks, Mrs. C. M.	Albany, New York	
Higgins, Melvina	Ithaca, New York	Atlanta, Georgia, and Petersburg, Virginia
Hill, Agnes	Bridport, Vermont	Washington, D.C., and Memphis, Tennessee
Hill, Miss E.	Hingham, Massachusetts	Hilton Head, South Carolina
Hill, Ellen S.	Saco, Maine	Milledgeville, Georgia

NAME	HOME	STATION
Hill, Minnie A.	Nashua, New Hampshire	Petersburg and Pocahontas, Virginia
Hilliard, Miss M. E.	Northfield Farms, Massachusetts	Savannah, Georgia
Hine, Jennie	Tallmadge, Ohio	Atlanta, Georgia
Hine, Mary A.	Waterbury, Connecticut	Plymouth, North Carolina
Hitchcock, Miss J. L.	Southington, Connecticut	Norfolk, Virginia
Hitchcock, Mary B.	Waverly, Illinois	Pine Bluff, Arkansas
Hitchcock, Mrs. S. S.	Putnam, Connecticut	Beaufort District, South Carolina
Hoit, Maria A.	South Petersburg, New York	Norfolk, Virginia
Holden, Miss L. J. S.	Cuttingsville, Vermont	Beaufort District, South Carolina, and Louisville, Kentucky
Hooper, Edward W.	Boston, Massachusetts	Port Royal, South Carolina
Hopson, Mrs. Cynthia M. (Mrs. H. V.?)	Hudson and Cleveland, Ohio	Talladega, Alabama
Hosley, Mary A.	Chesterfield, New Hampshire	Summerville, South Carolina
Hosmer, Jane	Concord, Massachusetts	Gordonsville, Virginia
Hosmer, Miss S. A.	Ashby, Massachusetts	Augusta, Georgia, and North Carolina
Houghton, Mrs. Catherine B.	New York City	Beaufort District, South Carolina
Hovey, Horace W.	Montpelier (Vermont?)	Richmond, Virginia
Howard, Adeline J. (T.?)	Boston, Massachusetts	Quaker Neck, Maryland
Howard, Climena G.	South Easton, Massachusetts	Raleigh, North Carolina
Howard, Jennie E.	Fairhaven, Massachusetts	Elizabeth City, North Carolina
Howard, Martha A.	Fall River, Massachusetts	Chestertown, Maryland
Howard, Oliver	South Easton, Massachusetts	Raleigh, North Carolina
Howe, Abbie E.	Oxford, Massachusetts	Fortress Monroe, Virginia, and Albany, Georgia
Howels, Horace G.	Gardner, Massachusetts	
Howells, Miss T. Weld	Pittsburgh, Pennsylvania	Petersburg, Virginia
Hoy, Miss M. L.	Brooklyn, New York	Prince Frederick and Burkittsville, Maryland
Hubbard, Miss E. A.	Utica, New York	Washington, D.C.
Hubbard, Miss E. M.	Northampton, Massachusetts	Augusta, Georgia
Hubbard, Emily	Corning, New York	Petersburg, Virginia
Hubbard, William A.	Chicago, Illinois	Pine Bluff, Arkansas
Hughes, Miss Hannah	Medina, Ohio	Louisville, Kentucky
Hulbert, Sarah P.	Seville, Ohio	Natchez, Mississippi
Hulstart, C. Elizabeth	Romeo, Michigan	Memphis, Tennessee
Humaston, Mary L.	Windsor, New York	
Humphreys, Miss M. G.	Fort Wayne, Indiana	Atlanta, Georgia
Hunn, Miss E. A.	Camden, Delaware, and Philadelphia, Pennsylvania	St. Helena, South Carolina
Hunn, Hannah	Camden, Delaware	St. Helena, South Carolina
Hunt, Fanny M.	Sonderland, Massachusetts	Savannah, Georgia
Hunt, Miss S. A.	Sonderland, Massachusetts	Savannah, Georgia

NAME	HOME	STATION
Hunt, Sarah D.	North Amherst, Massachusetts	Norfolk, Virginia
Huntoon, Miss E. A.	Wallingford, Vermont	Milledgeville, Georgia
Ireson, Helen M.	Lynn, Massachusetts	Newbern, North Carolina
Isham, Emeret B.	Watertown, New York	Fernandina, Florida
Jackson, Mrs. E. G.	Concord, New Hampshire	Port Deposit, Maryland
Jackson, S. S.	South Middleboro, Massachusetts	Winchester, Virginia
Jackson, W. A.	South Middleboro, Massachusetts	Winchester, Virginia
Jacobs, Miss M. P.	Kennett Square, Pennsylvania	Atlanta, Georgia
James, Elizabeth	Medford, Massachusetts	Roanoke Island, North Carolina
James, William L.	Philadelphia, Pennsylvania	Sandy Springs, Maryland
Janes, Miss C. M.	Lima, New York	Nashville, Tennessee
Jarvis, Martha A.	Oberlin, Ohio	Meridian, Mississippi
Jencks, Miss E. F.	Killingly, Connecticut	Wilmington, North Carolina
Jenkins, Annie L.	Dorchester, Massachusetts	Columbus, Georgia
Jennes, Miss S. A.	Wolfboro, New Hampshire	Savannah, Georgia
Jennings, Katie	Philadelphia, Pennsylvania	Richmond, Virginia
Jennings, Mrs. M. M.	Philadelphia, Pennsylvania	Richmond, Virginia
Jennings, William	Ohio	Georgia
Jillson, Justus K.	Warwick, Massachusetts (?)	Camden, South Carolina
Job, William	Wernersville, Pennsylvania	
Johnson, Abbie W.	North Brookfield, Massachusetts	Fernandina, Florida
Johnson, Ezra	Philadelphia, Pennsylvania	Buchanan, Virginia
Johnson, Mrs. J. B.	Washington, D.C.	Washington, D.C.
Johnson, Miss K. K.	Binghampton, New York	Petersburg, Virginia
Jones, ———	Warsaw, New York	Hopeton, Georgia
Jones, Cornelia	Schenectady, New York	Richmond, Virginia
Jones, Ellen M.	North Woburn, Massachusetts	Washington, North Carolina, and Charleston, South Carolina
Jones, Hellen M.	Tabor, Iowa	Louisville, Kentucky
Joy, Rev. Wellington	Carbondale, Illinois	Bristol, Indiana
Judkins, Thomas	Eugene City, Oregon	Morehead City, North Carolina
Judson, J. R.	Litchfield, Ohio	Jonesboro, Tennessee
Keith, Charlotte M.	Middleboro, Massachusetts	Hilton Head, South Carolina
Kelley, L. J.	Yarmouth, N.S.	Athens, Georgia
Kellogg, Martha L.	Avon, Connecticut	Wilmington, North Carolina, and Hilton Head, South Carolina
Kempton, Anna L.	New Bedford, Massachusetts	Culpepper, Virginia
Kempton, Ellen S.	New Bedford, Massachusetts	Charleston, South Carolina
Kennedy, Mary	Philadelphia, Pennsylvania	Norfolk, Virginia
Kennedy, Mary A.	New York, New York	Norfolk, Virginia
Ketchum, Mrs. E. J.	Philadelphia, Pennsylvania	Oxen Run, Prince George County, Maryland
eyes, Sarah E.	Westford, Massachusetts	d. 1866

NAME	HOME	STATION
Kidder, Miss A. H.	Peacham, Vermont	Wilmington, North Carolina
Kiddoo, Miss F. A.	Hillsboro, Illinois	Memphis, Tennessee
Kimball, Mary R.	Salem, Massachusetts	Roanoke Island, North Carolina, and Columbus, Georgia
King, Miss E. E.	Danville, New York	Petersburg, Virginia
Kinne, A. E.	Syracuse, New York	Fernandina, Florida
Kinne, Mrs. A. E.	Syracuse, New York	Fernandina, Florida
Kinney, Rose	Oberlin, Ohio	Atlanta, Georgia
Kinsley, Mary B.	Bennington, Vermont	Fortress Monroe, Virginia
Kittridge, Elizabeth	Pennsylvania	South Carolina
Knapp, Amelia	Greenwich, Connecticut	Raleigh, North Carolina
Knapp, Emily	New Castle, New York	Norfolk, Virginia
Knapp, Eunice	New Castle, New York	Norfolk, Virginia
Knapp, Miss S. A.	Tarrytown, New York	Jacksonville, Florida
Knight, A. Jane	Lancaster, Pennsylvania	Edisto Island, South Carolina
Knight, L. A.	N. Bennington, Vermont	Baltimore, Maryland
Lakeman, Sarah E.	Salem, Massachusetts	Charleston, South Carolina
Lamson, Miss A. W.	Sebec, Maine	Washington, D.C.
Lane, H. L.	Franklin, Pennsylvania	Washington, D.C.
Lane, Mary	Chelsea, Massachusetts	Townfield, Virginia
Lane, Mary	Four Corners, Ohio	Chattanooga, Tennessee
Lane, Sara F.	Franklin, Pennsylvania	Washington, D.C.
Langford, Fanny S.	Wyoming and Boston, Massachusetts	Beaufort, South Carolina
LaRue, Rachel	Philadelphia, Pennsylvania	J. E. Tucker Plantation, near Okolona, Mississippi
Lawrence, Laura A.	Potsdam, New York	Petersburg, Virginia
Lawton, E. Mariana	Cambridge or Leicester, Massachusetts	Alexandria, Virginia, and Salisbury, Maryland
Lawton, F. L.	Skaneateles, New York	Jones's Church, D.C.
Lawton, Fred A.	Washington, D.C.	Fairfield, Maryland
Lawton, L. Virginia	Cambridge or Dorchester, Massachusetts	Frederick City, Maryland, and Alexandria, Virginia
Learned, Helen A.	Watertown, Massachusetts	Baltimore, Maryland (d. 1866)
Leary, Mrs. Mary L.	Cleveland, Ohio	Marietta, Georgia
Leavitt, Ellen A.	Hampton, New Hampshire	Staunton, Virginia, and Covington, Kentucky
Lee, B. K.	Boston, Massachusetts	Hilton Head, South Carolina
Lee, Miss C. B.	Hillsdale, Michigan	Nashville, Tennessee
Lee, Ellen M.	Templeton, Massachusetts	Charleston, South Carolina, and Columbus, Georgia
Lee, Maria	Wayland, Massachusetts	Fortress Monroe, Virginia
Leeke, Mary A.	Hamden, Connecticut	Norfolk, Virginia
Leigh, Dr. E.	New York, New York	Washington, D.C.
Leland, Eunice H.	North Abington, Massachusetts	Raleigh, North Carolina (d. 1867)
Leland, Harrison	Neponsett, Massachusetts	Columbus, Georgia, and Raleigh, North Carolina
Lennon, Mary I.	New York, New York	Charleston, South Carolina
Leonard, Elizabeth A.	Stafford, Connecticut	Raleigh, North Carolina

NAME	HOME	STATION
Leonard, Miss H. M.	New Bedford, Massachusetts	Americus, Georgia
Lewis, Harriet A.	Oberlin, Ohio	Aberdeen, Mississippi
Lewis, Hattie	Tallmadge, Ohio	Atlanta, Georgia
Libby, Phebe	Wells, Maine	Harrisonburgh, Virginia
Lillie, Sarah P.	Hopedale, Massachusetts	Hilton Head, South Carolina
Littlefield, Frances	Hallowell, Maine	Savannah, Georgia
Littlefield, J. Sherman	East Stoughton, Massachusetts	Charleston, South Carolina
Litts, Palmer	Oberlin, Ohio	Fortress Monroe, Virginia
Lloyd, Mark R.	Pottstown, Pennsylvania	Fincastle, Virginia
Loomis, Miss C. H.	Cheming, New York, or Hartford, Connecticut	Columbia, South Carolina
Lord, Julia A.	North Yarmouth, Maine	Washington, D.C.
Lucas, William P.	Brattleboro, Vermont	Gordonsville, Virginia (?)
Luckey, Helen E.	Sing Sing, New York	Beaufort, North Carolina
Lyman, James O.	Hartford, Wisconsin	Pine Bluff, Arkansas
Lynch, Miss J. M.	Brooklyn, New York	Elkton, Maryland
Lyon, M. E.	Putnam, Connecticut (?)	Port Royal, South Carolina
Lyon, Miss R. J.	Oberlin, Ohio	Macon, Georgia
McCarthy, James	Syracuse, New York	Alabama
McCleland, Miss H. A.	Oberlin, Ohio	Meridian, Mississippi
McConnell, Jennie	Tecumseh, Michigan	Macon, Georgia
McCulloch, A. W.	Spring Garden, Pennsylvania	Huntsville, Alabama
McCulloch, Mrs. A. W.	Spring Garden, Pennsylvania	Huntsville, Alabama
McDowell, Miss	Philadelphia, Pennsylvania	Columbia, South Carolina
McGill, Hattie (Mrs. H. M.)	Fredericktown, Ohio	
McKay, C. E. (Charlotte?)	Boston, Massachusetts	Poplar Grove and Petersburg, Virginia
MacKay, G. B.	Linton, Ohio	Summerville, Tennessee
McKinney, Miss J. A.	Mecklenburgh, New York	Columbia, South Carolina
McMahon, Charles W.	Plymouth, Massachusetts	Appomatox Court House, Virginia
McMath, J. D.	Allegheny City, Pennsylvania	Hilton Head, South Carolina
Mahoney, Sarah	Somers, Wisconsin	Mobile, Alabama
Mallory, Rev. W. W.	Springfield, Massachusetts	Nashville and Chattanooga, Tennessee
Mann, Maria R.	Concord, Massachusetts	Harpers Ferry, Virginia
Marrell, H. W. H.	Bath, Maine	
Marrell, Mrs. H. W. H.	Bath, Maine	
Marshall, Mrs. Ada S.	Newport, Rhode Island	Baltimore, Maryland
Marshall, Julia M.	Williamsburg, Long Island	Savannah, Georgia
Mather, Mrs. R. C.	South Boston, Massachusetts	Beaufort, South Carolina
Mattson, Henrietta	North Bloomfield, Ohio	Memphis, Tennessee
Maxwell, Miss A. W.	Charlmont, Massachusetts	Trent River Camp, North Carolina
Maynard, Susan	Ann Arbor, Michigan	Memphis, Tennessee
Means, Kate A.	Andover, Massachusetts	Newbern, North Carolina
Mecorney, Charles J.	Worcester, Massachusetts	Norfolk, Virginia
Merriam, Anne J.	Worcester, Massachusetts	Newbern, North Carolina, and Columbus, Georgia

NAME	HOME	STATION
Merrick, Caroline H.	Cortland, New York	Savannah and Augusta, Georgia
Merrick, Chloe	Syracuse, New York	Fernandina, Florida, and Newbern, North Carolina
Merrill, Arabella	Brunswick, Maine	
Merritt, Rev. E. W.	North Madison, Connecticut	Charleston, South Carolina
Miller, Ada L.	Chicago, Illinois	Macon, Georgia
Miller, Rev. E. K.	Milwaukee, Wisconsin	Pine Bluff, Arkansas
Miller, Eliza M.	Chicago, Illinois	Macon, Georgia
Mitchell, Annie M.	Nantucket, Massachusetts	Nashville, Tennessee
Mitchell, Eliza	Oberlin, Ohio	Tennessee, and Atlanta, Georgia
Mitchell, Harriett	Richfield, New York	Alexandria, Virginia
Mitchell, William F.	Nantucket, Massachusetts	Nashville, Tennessee
Mobly, Rev. Hardy	Brooklyn, New York	Savannah, Georgia
Moore, C. W.	Lamberton, New Jersey	Georgetown, D. C.
Morgan, Miss F. A.	New Haven, Connecticut	Plymouth, North Carolina, and St. Augustine, Florida
Morgan, Miss F. E.	Bernardstown, Massachusetts	Athens, Georgia
Morse, Arthur T.	Bradford, New Hampshire	Charleston, South Carolina
Morse, George H.	Walpole, Massachusetts	Warrenton, Virginia
Morse, Louisa A.	Bradford, New Hampshire	Charleston, South Carolina
Murray, Ellen	Milton, Massachusetts	St. Helena, South Carolina
Murray, Harriet W.	Pennsylvania	South Carolina
Murray, Hattie A.	Melmore, Ohio	Evansville, Indiana
Neal, Miss F. M.	Cincinnati, Ohio	Memphis, Tennessee
Neibling, ——	Poughkeepsie, New York	Demopolis, Alabama
Newcomb, Fanny	Dedham, Massachusetts	Elizabeth City, North Carolina
Newcomb, Rev. George	Dedham, Massachusetts	Elizabeth City, North Carolina
Newcomb, Hattie L.	Prescott, Wisconsin	Demopolis, Alabama
Newman, Sarah P.	Brunswick, Maine	Newbern, North Carolina
Newsome, Hugh	Oberlin, Ohio	Greensburgh, Kentucky
Newton, A. E.	Boston and West Cambridge, Massachusetts	Washington, D.C.
Newton, Charles A.	West Cambridge, Massachusetts	Washington, D.C.
Newton, Chloe B.	Kinsman, Ohio	Memphis, Tennessee
Newton, Isaac M.	Kinsman, Ohio	Summerville, Tennessee
Nichols, J. A.	New Haven, Connecticut	Goldsboro, North Carolina
Nicholas, Mrs. J. A.	New Haven, Connecticut	Goldsboro, North Carolina
Nichols, Mrs. K. H.	Sing Sing, New York	Portsmouth, Virginia
Nichols, Mary M.	Fairhaven, Massachusetts	Elizabeth City, North Carolina, and Richmond, Virginia
Nickerson, Mrs. P. B.	Farnsworth, New Hampshire	Harper's Ferry, Virginia
Nickerson, Rev. S. S.	Farnsworth, New Hampshire	Harper's Ferry, Virginia
Niles, Kate	Post Mills, Vermont	Charleston, South Carolina
Odell, Susan	Biddeford, Maine	Roanoke Island, North Carolina

NAME	HOME	STATION
Ogden, John	Columbus, Ohio, and St. Paul's, Minnesota	Nashville, Tennessee
Ogden, Mrs. John	St. Paul's, Minnesota	Nashville, Tennessee
Oliver, Mrs. E. L.	Georgetown, Maine	Charlestown, Virginia
Oliver, Mrs. M. E.	Lynn, Massachusetts	Fernandina, Florida
O'Riordan, John	New York State	Clinton, South Carolina
Orr, L. H. (Lilia)	Cleveland, Ohio	Montgomery, Alabama
Orton, Miss C. S.	Brooklyn, New York	Alexandria, Virginia
Osborne, Mary S.	East Bridgewater, Massachusetts	Church Creek, Maryland
Osgood, Miss L. E.	Fryeburgh, Maine	Fernandina, Florida
Owen, H. F.	Philadelphia, Pennsylvania	Island Creek, Maryland
Page, Octavia C.	Lawrence and Watertown, Massachusetts	Norfolk, Virginia, and Charleston, South Carolina
Palmer, Miss J. T.	Cooperstown, New York	Uniontown, D. C.
Palmer, James H.	South Hampton, New Hampshire	Port Royal, South Carolina
Palmer, Miss L. C.	Windham, Ohio	Chattanooga, Tennessee
Parish, Miss A. W.	New Haven, Connecticut	Dathaw Island, South Carolina
Park, Anna C.	Bennington, Vermont	Washington, D.C.
Park, William E.	Andover, Massachusetts	Port Royal, South Carolina
Parker, Miss M. A.	Kalamazoo, Michigan	Clarksville, Tennessee
Parker, Miss M. A.	Northboro, Massachusetts	Wilmington, North Carolina
Parker, Maria M.	Salem, Massachusetts	Alexandria, Virginia
Parker, Mrs. R.	Grand Rapids, Michigan	Atlanta, Georgia
Parker, Russell	Grand Rapids, Michigan	Atlanta, Georgia
Parmelee, Miss L. A.	Toledo, Ohio	Cuthbert, Georgia
Parsons, Elizabeth	Utica, New York	Wadmalaw Island and Columbia, South Carolina; Richmond, Virginia
Parsons, Miss S. P.	Utica, New York	Washington, D.C.
Passmore, Louise	Woonsocket, Rhode Island	Trent River Camp, North Carolina
Patrick, Ellen M.	Hopedale, Massachusetts	Charleston, South Carolina
Patton, Miss R. G. C.	Brooklyn, New York	Newport News, Virginia
Paul, Mary L.	Saratoga Springs, New York	Jacksonville, Florida
Payne, Etta	Boston, Massachusetts	Snow Hill, North Carolina, and Sumter, South Carolina
Payne, Helen A.	Hamilton, New York	Atlanta, Georgia
Pearson, Sarah M.	Boston, Massachusetts	Newbern, North Carolina
Pease, G.	Boston, Massachusetts	Darien, Georgia
Pease, N. R.	Lowell, Massachusetts	Louisiana
Peck, Ellen	Roxbury, Massachusetts	Port Royal, South Carolina
Peck, George B.	Roxbury, Massachusetts	Port Royal, South Carolina
Peck, Solomon	Roxbury, Massachusetts	St. Helena, South Carolina
Peckham, Miss Abbie C.	Woonsocket, Rhode Island, and Worcester, Massachusetts	Pocahontas and Petersburg, Virginia

NAME	HOME	STATION
Peduzzi (Reduzzi?), Miss Emily T.	Portsmouth, New Hampshire	Washington, North Carolina
Peebles, David	Northville, Michigan	Matagorda, Texas
Peirce, Miss M. E.	Pennsylvania	South Carolina
Percy, H. C.	Watertown, Connecticut	Norfolk, Virginia
Perkins, Frances A.	Portland, Maine	Beaufort District, South Carolina
Perkins, Frances W.	Middlefield, Connecticut	Washington, D.C.
Perkins, Mary E.	E. Walpole, Massachusetts	Baltimore, Maryland
Peterson, Miss J. J.	New York, New York	Montgomery, Alabama
Pettibone, Rev. Ira	Winchester, Connecticut	Savannah, Georgia
Pettibone, Miss M. L.	Winchester, Connecticut	Savannah, Georgia
Pew, Martha	Mercer, Pennsylvania	Fortress Monroe, Virginia
Pew, Sarah	Mercer, Pennsylvania	Fortress Monroe, Virginia
Phelps, Carrie S.	East Rockport, Ohio	Talladega, Alabama
Phelps, Millie	Ashbury, New York	Lynchburg, Virginia
Phelps, Sarah D.	Worcester, Massachusetts	Baltimore, Maryland
Philbrook, Elizabeth A.	Portsmouth, New Hampshire	Washington and Raleigh, North Carolina
Phillips, Miss A. W.	Boston, Massachusetts	St. Mary's, Georgia
Phillips, Miss H. N.	Philadelphia, Pennsylvania	Atlanta, Georgia
Phillips, I. N.	Tinmouth, Vermont	Gallatin, Tennessee
Phillips, Samuel D.	Boston, Massachusetts	Port Royal, South Carolina (d.1862)
Pierce, Almira C.	Appleton, Wisconsin	Pine Bluff, Arkansas
Pierce, Rev. Edward S.	Chicago, Illinois	Corinth, Mississippi
Pierce, Mrs. Edward S.	Chicago, Illinois	Corinth, Mississippi
Pierce, Mary E.	Lynn, Massachusetts	Washington, D.C.
Pillsbury, Antoinette Francis	Ludlow, Massachusetts	Hilton Head, South Carolina
Pillsbury, George	Ludlow, Massachusetts	Hilton Head, South Carolina
Piper, Mrs. E. L.	Lowell, Massachusetts	Wilmington, North Carolina
Piper, John W.	S. Parsonfield, Maine	Staunton, Virginia
Piper, Rebecca G.	New Bedford, Connecticut	Chestertown, Maryland
Plummer, Evelyn E.	Palermo Center, Maine, or Irvington, Iowa (?)	Murfreesboro, Tennessee, and Columbus, Georgia
Pond, Rev. Benjamin W.	Brunswick, Maine	Newbern, North Carolina
Pond, Mrs. Benjamin W.	Brunswick, Maine	Newbern, North Carolina
Pond, Mary E.	Irvington, New York	Wilmington, North Carolina, and Macon, Georgia
Porter, Mrs. Lizzie F.	Wasioja, Minnesota	Houston, Texas
Porter, Miss M. Y.	Clark, Pennsylvania	Fortress Monroe, Virginia
Post, Mary	Mecca, Ohio	Chattanooga, Tennessee
Potter, Martha J.	Wilmington, Delaware	
Potter, Mary A.	Wilmington, Delaware	Columbus, Kentucky
Potter, Mrs. S. C.	Bridgeport, Connecticut	Arlington, Virginia
Powers, Miss P. E.	Greenwich Village, Massachusetts	Albany, Georgia
Pratt, Mrs. A. S.	Pembroke or Quincy, Massachusetts	Orange, Virginia
Pratt, John W.	Quincy, Massachusetts	Orange, Virginia
Pratt, Julia M.	Shelburne Falls, Massachusetts	Clarksville, Mississippi

NAME	HOME	STATION
Prescott, Sarah F.	Boston, Massachusetts	Charleston, South Carolina
Primus, Rebecca	Hartford, Connecticut	Royal Oak, Maryland
Prince, C. H.	Buckfield, Maine	Augusta, Georgia
Prince, Mrs. E. A.	Buckfield, Maine	Augusta, Georgia
Proctor, Miss S. M.	Towsend Harbor, Massachusetts	Macon, Georgia
Purington, Mrs. M. H.	Keokuk, Iowa	Nashville and Memphis, Tennessee
Pyne, H. A.	Boston, Massachsuetts	
Quaiffe, Eva	Washington, D.C.	Baltimore, Maryland
Rankin, J. E.	Detroit, Michigan	
Ranstead, Cynthia C.	Thetford, Vermont	Petersburg, Virginia
Reed, Ellen	Bath, Maine	Newbern, North Carolina
Reed, Henry L.	N. Easton, Massachusetts	Baltimore, Maryland, and Richmond, Virginia
Remington, Esther	New Britain, Connecticut	Edenton, North Carolina
Renne, Miss Z.	Crown Point, New York	Richmond, Virginia
Richardson, Miss H. H.	Cleveland, Ohio	Montgomery, Alabama
Richardson, Rev. W. T.	E. Cleveland, Ohio	Montgomery, Alabama, and Beaufort, South Carolina
Richmond, Miss E. E.	Lansingburgh, New York	Columbia, South Carolina
Roberts, Cynthia	Farmers Inst., Indiana	Clarksville and Edgefield, Tennessee
Roberts, Emma A.	Springfield, Massachusetts	Washington, D.C.
Roberts, John L.	Farmers Inst., Indiana	Clarksville, Tennessee
Robertson, Helen	Brooklyn, New York	Alexandria, Virginia
Robinson, Mrs. M. A.	Pawtucket, Rhode Island	Catlettsburg, Kentucky
Robinson, Miss S. H.	Providence, Rhode Island	Athens, Georgia
Rockwell, John A.	Norwich, Connecticut	Macon, Georgia
Rodgers, Mrs. Margaret	Governeur, New York	Norfolk, Virginia
Rogers, Miss Maria L.	Topsham, Maine	Newbern, North Carolina
Root, Miss Maria L.	Sheffield, Ohio	Andersonville, Georgia
Roper, Miss Ella	Worcester, Massachusetts	Roanoke Island and Newbern, North Carolina
Rosecrans, Miss H. G.	Rockford, Illinois	Mobile, Alabama
Rossiter, Mrs. Clara	Hinsdale, Massachusetts	Augusta, Georgia
Rowell, Miss M. S.	Brooklyn, New York	Richmond, Virginia
Rowell, Mary	Saratoga County, New York	Malta, (?)
Rowland, Fannie A.	Springfield, Massachusetts	Norfolk, Virginia
Ruggles, Amanda S.	Milton, Massachusetts	St. Helena, South Carolina
Ruggles, Mrs. Harriat W.	Philadelphia, Pennsylvania	St. Helena Island, South Carolina
Ruggles, T. Edwin	Milton, Massachusetts	Port Royal, South Carolina
Russell, Miss Hattie H.	Washington, D.C.	Washington, D.C.
Russell, Miss S. E.	Pittston, Maine	Brunswick, Georgia
Sampson, Sarah A.	New York, New York	New Orleans, Louisiana
Sands, Mary E.	Saco, Maine	Milledgeville, Georgia
Sargent, Letitia	Gloucester, Massachusetts	Charleston, South Carolina
Sautty, Mary	Charlestown, Massachusetts	Mobile, Alabama
Saxton, Mary G.	Boston, Massachusetts	Beaufort, South Carolina
Scofield, Miss	Willett, New York	Camp Nelson, Kentucky
Scofield, Rev. A.	Willett, New York	Camp Nelson, Kentucky

NAME	HOME	STATION
Schofield, Martha	Darby, Pennsylvania	St. Helena, South Carolina
Scott, Cornelia	Yonkers, New York	Wadmalow Island, South Carolina
Scott, John	Naugatuck, Connecticut	Beaufort, North Carolina
Searing, Annie H.	Poplar Ridge, New York	Farmville, Virginia
Sears, J. H.	Ohio	Selma, Alabama
Segur, Carrie	Four Corners, Ohio	Grenada, Mississippi
See, A. W.	Toledo, Iowa	Georgia
Seely, Miss M. E.	Weedsport, New York	Jacksonville, Florida
Semple, Miss C. M.	Cincinnati, Ohio, or Vincennes, Indiana	Nashville, Tennessee
Seymour, Mrs. Ellen	New Haven, Connecticut	Hilton Head, South Carolina, and Helena, Arkansas
Seymour, Livinia E.	Madison, Wisconsin	Mobile, Alabama
Shackford, Carolina N.	Philadelphia, Pennsylvania	Okolona, Mississippi
Shadd, Addie E.	Washington, D.C.	Georgetown, D. C.
Sharpe, John L.	Montreal, Canada	City Point, Virginia
Shaw, Miss	Boston, Massachusetts?	Charleston, South Carolina
Shaw, Mrs. Anna M.	Thorndike, Maine	Lexington, Virginia
Shearman, Mrs. Alice C.	Marshall, Michigan	Louisville, Kentucky
Shearman, Caroline A.	Salem, Massachusetts	Liberty, Maryland
Shearman, Cecelia B.	Salem, Massachusetts	Liberty, Maryland
Shearman, Julia A.	Brooklyn, New York	Augusta, Georgia, and Lexington, Virginia
Shephard, Kate	Richfield, New York	Alexandria, Virginia
Shockley, Mary J.	Bridgewater, Connecticut	Baltimore, Maryland
Shoemaker, Elizabeth	Pennsylvania	Nashville, Tennessee
Shoemaker, Miss M. B.	Newton, New Jersey	Beaufort, South Carolina
Shuart, Mr. B. F.	Footville, Wisconsin	Fortress Monroe, Virginia
Silsby, Rev. J.	Beloit, Wisconsin	Selma, Alabama
Simmons, Abby S.	Essex, Connecticut	Washington (D.C.?) and Norfolk, Virginia
Simmons, Helen A.	Essex, Connecticut	Washington (D.C.?) and Norfolk, Virginia
Sinclair, Caroline F.	Waltham, Massachusetts	Columbus and Jonesboro, Georgia
Sisson, Cora R.	Downers Grove, Illinois	Galveston, Texas, and Griffin, Georgia
Skelton, Miss N. C.	Hartford, Connecticut	Augusta, Georgia
Skinner, Sarah	Beloit, Wisconsin	Houston, Texas
Sluby, Rev. M. F.	Wilmington, Delaware	Alexandria, Virginia
Smith, Abby O.	Cambridgeport or Somerville, Massachusetts	Baltimore, Maryland
Smith, Miss C. E.	Walden, New York	Trent River, North Carolina
Smith, Carrie A.	Exeter, New Hampshire	Selma, Alabama
Smith, Carrie E.	Manchester, New Hampshire	Beaufort, South Carolina
Smith, D. Edson	Vesper, New York	City Point, Virginia
Smith, Cornelia J.	No. Pitcher, New York	St. Augustine, Florida
Smith, Mrs. D. E.	Vesper, New York	City Point, Virginia
Smith, Eliza J.	Syracuse, New York	St. Augustine, Florida

NAME	HOME	STATION
Smith, Ella	Walden, New York	Trent River Camp, North Carolina
Smith, Elvira P.	Brooklyn, New York	Alexandria, Virginia
Smith, Francelia	Sturbridge, Massachusetts	Roanoke Island, North Carolina
Smith, Mrs. Frances S.	Vesper, New York	City Point, Virginia
Smith, Harriet R.	Brooklyn, New York	Alexandria, Virginia
Smith, Miss J. B.	Oneida, New York	New Berne, North Carolina
Smith, J. F.	Marblehead, Massachusetts	East Tennessee
Smith, Miss J. F.	Hickory, Iowa	Montgomery, Alabama
Smith, Jane B.	Hanson, Massachusetts	Charleston and Sumter, South Carolina
Smith, Julia A.	Charleston, Massachusetts	Still Pond, Maryland, and Washington, D.C.
Smith, Juliet B.	Sutton, Massachusetts	Trent River Camp, North Carolina
Smith, Miss L. A.	Greenfield, Ohio	Memphis, Tennessee
Smith, Mrs. M. E. F.	New London, Connecticut	Wilmington, North Carolina; Augusta and Macon, Georgia
Smith, Mrs. M. W. L.	Wells, Maine	Harrisonburgh, Virginia
Smith, Margaret R.	Beverly, Massachusetts	Newbern, North Carolina, and Nashville, Tennessee
Smith, Miss R. W.	Philadelphia, Pennsylvania	Portsmouth, Virginia
Smith, Robert N.	New York, New York	Port Royal, South Carolina
Southworth, Lucy M.	Brookfield, Massachusetts	Charleston, South Carolina
Spain, Minnie	Bellefontaine, Ohio	Nashville, Tennessee
Spees, Clara	Oberlin, Ohio	Portsmouth, Virginia
Sproat, M. L.	Taunton, Massachusetts	Charleston, South Carolina
Stanley, Sara G.	Cleveland, Ohio	St. Louis, Missouri, and Louisville, Kentucky
Stansbury, Miss S. W.	Rahway, New Jersey	Columbus and Cuthbert, Georgia
Stanton, Elmira B.	Lowell and Springfield, Massachusetts	Edisto Island, South Carolina
Stearns, Ellen J.	Bedford and Fitchburg, Massachusetts	Baltimore, Maryland
Stebbins, Miss L. W.	South Wilbraham, Massachusetts	Washington, D.C.
Stephens, Elizabeth A.	Germantown, Pennsylvania	Aiken, South Carolina
Stephens, George E.	Philadelphia, Pennsylvania	Tappahassock, Virginia
Stephens, Lydia W.	Norristown, Pennsylvania	Farmville, Virginia
Stetson, S. U.	Radnor, Pennsylvania	Washington, D.C.
Stevens, Miss J. A. G.	St. Johnsbury, Vermont	Louisville, Kentucky
Stevenson, Jennie H.	Bellefontaine, Ohio	Nashville, Tennessee, and Atlanta, Georgia
Stevenson, John O.	Rice Lake, Minnesota	Houston, Texas
Stevenson, Lizzie	Bellefontaine, Ohio	Atlanta, Georgia
Stevenson, R. P.	Pennsylvania	Murfreesboro, Tennessee
Stevenson, Sue	Bellefontaine, Ohio	Nashville, Tennessee
Stewart, Sarah H.	North Abingdon, Massachusetts	Baltimore, Maryland

NAME	HOME	STATION
Stewart, T. C.	Constantia, Ohio	Marion, Alabama
Stinson, Lydia G.	Wiscasset, Maine	Roanoke Island, North Carolina
Stone, Harriet F.	Chesterfield, New Hampshire, or Milford, New York	Gordonsville, Virginia
Stowe, C. Emelie	New Haven, Connecticut	Selma, Alabama
Stowe, Emily C.	New Haven, Connecticut	Red House, South Carolina
Stradling, James H.	Mechanicsville, Pennsylvania	Lynchburg, Virginia
Stratton, Elmira	Unionville, Ohio	Milledgeville, Georgia
Stratton, Miss M. E.	New Haven, Connecticut	Jacksonville, Florida
Streeker, Mrs. Hannah M.	Pottsville, Pennsylvania	Murfreesboro, Tennessee
Strong, Alice	S. Manchester, Connecticut	Raleigh, North Carolina
Stuart, Jennie	Cameron, New York	Fortress Monroe, Virginia
Stuart, Laura	Cameron, New York	Fortress Monroe, Virginia
Stuart, Marion D.	W. Barnet, Vermont	Darlington and Camden, South Carolina
Stull, Matilda R.	Beloit, Wisconsin	Grenada, Mississippi
Sturges, Lina	Mosherville, Michigan	Athens, Alabama
Sturges, Miss M. C.	Mosherville, Michigan	Athens, Alabama
Suliot, F. E.	Kent, Portage County, Ohio	
Summers, Eliza A.	Woodbury, Connecticut	Hilton Head, South Carolina
Sumner, Arthur	Cambridge, Massachusetts	Charleston and Port Royal, South Carolina
Swails, Stephen A.	Columbia, Pennsylvania	Kingstree, South Carolina
Swails, Mrs. S. A.	Columbia, Pennsylvania	Kingstree, South Carolina
Swallow, Miss H. M.	Nashua, New Hampshire	Nashville, Tennessee
Swift, Susan A.	Bridgeton, Maine	Tallahassee, Florida
Tade, Mrs. A. L.	Utica, Iowa	Chattanooga, Tennessee
Tade, Rev. E. O.	Utica, Iowa	Chattanooga, Tennessee
Tade, Mollie	Utica, Iowa	Chattanooga, Tennessee
Talford, P. C.	Michigan	Cairo, Illinois
Tambling, C. L.	Oberlin, Ohio	Natchez, Mississippi
Tambling, Nellie F.	Oberlin, Ohio	Natchez, Mississippi
Taylor, Mr.	New York, New York	Charleston, South Carolina
Taylor, Alice D.	Claridon, Ohio	Lexington, Kentucky
Taylor, James E.	Andover, Massachusetts	Port Royal, South Carolina
Terry, Miss Cate B.	Piano, Illinois	Pine Bluff, Arkansas
Terry, Miss E. A.	Sutton, Massachusetts	Macon, Georgia
Teunis, John	Evansville, Indiana	Evansville, Indiana
Teunis, Mrs. J.	Evansville, Indiana	Evansville, Indiana
Thayer, Miss L. E.	South Lima, New York	Albany, Georgia
Thayer, Miss S. A.	New Ipswich, New Hampshire	Fortress Monroe, Virginia
Thomas, Charity C.	Hudson River, New York	Trent River Camp, North Carolina
Thomas, Miss D. D.	Bellefont, Pennsylvania	Liberty, Virginia
Thomas, Sarah	Toronto, C.W.	Washington, D.C.
Thompson, S. Grace	Boston, Massachusetts	Richmond, Virginia
Thorpe, David F.	Providence, Rhode Island	Port Royal, South Carolina
Tilley, R. S.	Chatham, Ohio	Alabama
Todd, Miss S. D.	Wakeman, Ohio	Lexington, Kentucky

NAME	HOME	STATION
Tomkins, S. W.	Radnor, Pennsylvania	Georgetown, D. C.
Towne, Laura M.	Shoemakertown, Pennsylvania	St. Helena, South Carolina
Towne, Sarah P.	Danvers, Massachusetts	
Trask, Amanda	Hudson, Michigan	Memphis, Tennessee
Turner, Antionette	New Haven, Connecticut	Hull's Landing, North Carolina
Tuttle, Lizzie	Mount City, Ohio	Ashland, Ohio
Twitchel, Miss E. H.	Saratoga, New York	Fortress Monroe, Virginia
Twitchel, Miss S. J.	Plantsville, Connecticut	Charleston, South Carolina
Twoguors, Miss H. E.	Brant, New York	Milledgeville, Georgia
Tyler, Miss M. E.	Greggsville, Illinois	Memphis, Tennessee
Upton, E. P.	Maine	Macon, Georgia
Upton, Mary A.	Wellesley or Boston, Massachusetts	Charleston, South Carolina
Vannest, Sarah	Spencerport, New York	Athens, Georgia
Varner, Alvin	Berwick, Pennsylvania	Liberty and Appomattox, Virginia
Varnum, Elizabeth W.	Portland, Maine	Jacksonville and Chattahootchee, Florida
Vaughan, Sarah E.	Chesire, Ohio	
Vaughn, Helen	Richfield, New York	Alexandria, Virginia
Veckery, Libbie E.	Burlington, Vermont	
Venning, R. E. D'R	Philadelphia, Pennsylvania	Mt. Hope, Maryland
Vogelsang, Peter	New York, New York	Roanoke Island, North Carolina
Wadsworth, Lois G.	Nashua, New Hampshire	Richmond, Virginia
Wager, Miss M. A. E.	Ludlowville, New York	Richmond, Virginia
Wakefield, Dr. A. Judson	Boston, Massachusetts	Port Royal, South Carolina
Wakeman, Mary E.	Manhattanville, New York	Mitchelville, South Carolina
Walker, John	Maine	Richmond, Virginia
Walker, Susan	Pittsburgh and Philadelphia, Pennsylvania	Beaufort, South Carolina
Walrad, Miss M.	Little Falls, New York	Raleigh, North Carolina
Walton, Wilmer	New Brighton, Pennsylvania	Stevenson, Alabama
Wangh, Miss C.	Oswego, New York	James Plantation, North Carolina
Ward, Miss E. A.	Monson, Massachusetts	Savannah, Georgia
Ware, Rev. E. A.	Norwich, Connecticut	Atlanta, Georgia
Warfel, Melinda S.	Cadiz, Ohio	Columbus, Kentucky
Warner, Miss E. A.	Lowell, Massachusetts	Roanoke Island, North Carolina
Warner, Mrs. E. W.	New York, New York	Augusta, Georgia
Warner, Miss J. G.	Jericho Center, Vermont	Milledgeville, Georgia
Warner, J. K.	New York, New York	Augusta, Georgia
Warner, Julia	Danbury, Connecticut	Montgomery, Alabama
Warner, Yardley	Germantown, Pennsylvania	
Warren, Emma E.	Richfield, New York	Alexandria, Virginia
Warren, Esther C.	Exeter, New Hampshire	Newbern, North Carolina
Warren, George A.	Exeter, New Hampshire	Newbern, North Carolina
Warren, Mrs. Helen J.	England	Piedmont, Virginia
Watson, Mary E.	Newport, Rhode Island	Darlington, Maryland

Name	Home	Station
Way, Miss E. E.	Chatham, Pennsylvania	St. Helena, South Carolina
Webb, Mrs. Hattie S.	Orwell, New York	James Island, South Carolina
Webster, Clara P.	Cleveland and Elyria, Ohio	Montgomery, Alabama
Webster, Miss M.	Binghamton, New York	Petersburg, Virginia
Weller, Josie	Lowville, New York	Cairo, Illinois
Wells, George M.	Providence, Rhode Island	Port Royal, South Carolina
Wells, Miss M. F.	Ann Arbor, Michigan	Athens, Alabama
Wells, Miss S. M.	Tecumseh, Michigan	Milledgeville, Georgia
Wentworth, William F.	Stoughton, Massachusetts	Dalton, Georgia
Wesselhoeft, Selma	Dorchester, Massachusetts	Hilton Head, South Carolina
Weston, Rev. Jacob	St. Charles, Missouri	
Weston, Mrs. M. J.	St. Charles, Missouri	
Wheeler, Addison	Canterbury, Connecticut	Good Hope, D. C. (S. C.?)
Wheeler, Miss L.	West Rosendale, Illinois	Galveston, Texas
Whitaker, Anna F.	Ashford, Connecticut	Lynchburg, Virginia
White, Almira P.	Exeter, New Hampshire	Charleston, South Carolina
White, Fannie L.	Menasha, Wisconsin	Galveston, Texas
White, Laura C.	Saratoga, Minnesota	Nashville, Tennessee
White, Miss M. E.	Hinsdale, New York	Nashville, Tennessee
Whitehouse, Phineas P.	South Hampton, New Hampshire	Muirkirk, Maryland
Whiting, Mr. S. K.	Winthrop, Maine	Petersburg, Virginia
Whiting, Mrs. S. K.	Winthrop, Maine	Petersburg, Virginia
Whitney, Miss S. J.	Westboro, Massachusetts	Macon, Georgia
Whiton, Rev. S. J.	Westford, Connecticut	Beaufort, North Carolina
Whittemore, Mrs. B. F.	Fitchburg, Massachusetts	Darlington, South Carolina
Whitton, D. E.	Wolfboro, New Hampshire	Charleston, South Carolina
Whitton, O. F.	Wolfboro, New Hampshire	Charleston, South Carolina
Wight, Miss M. A.	Nanuet, New York	Beaufort, South Carolina
Wilder, Mary E.	Plymouth, Wisconsin	Galveston, Texas
Wildes, Mrs. Mary T.	Portsmouth, New Hampshire	Jacksonville, Florida
Wilkins, Annie R.	Boston, Massachusetts	Hilton Head, and Bluffton, South Carolina
Willetts, Georgiana	Jersey City, New Jersey	Lynchburg, Virginia
Williams, Miss C. E.	South Deerfield, Massachusetts	Kendall Green, D. C.
Williams, Esther A.	Lowell, Massachusetts	Roanoke Island, North Carolina
Williams, Miss Lincoln E.	South Denfield (Massachusetts?)	Richmond, Virginia
Williams, Miss M. D.	Greenfield, Massachusetts	Beaufort, North Carolina
Williams, Mrs. W. M.	New York, New York	Jacksonville, Florida
Wilson, Caroline	South Salem, Ohio	Memphis, Tennessee
Wilson, Leonidas A.	Cleveland, Ohio	Yazoo City, Mississippi
Wilson, Luthera	Edgerton, Ohio	Gallatin, Tennessee
Winsor, Mrs. Abbie R.	Greenwich, Connecticut	Oxford, North Carolina
Winters, Emily	Dundee, New York	Atlanta, Georgia
Wiswell, Harriett	Chicago, Illinois	Mobile, Alabama
Withington, Carrie	Dorchester, Massachusetts	Washington, D.C.
Withington, G.	Dorchester, Massachusetts	Washington, D.C.
Withington, L. E.	Dorchester, Massachusetts	Washington, D.C.

NAME	HOME	STATION
Withington, Miss M. H.	Newbury, Massachusetts	Augusta, Georgia
Wolf, Miss A. V.	Cincinnati, Ohio	Covington, Kentucky
Wolf, Miss H. F.	Cincinnati, Ohio	Covington, Kentucky
Wolfe, Helen J.	Cincinnati, Ohio	Houston, Texas
Wood, S. Fanny	New Bedford, Connecticut	Culpepper, Virginia
Woodward, Miss R. J.	Amo, Indiana	Gallatin, Tennessee
Woodworth, Sarah F.	Lowell, Massachusetts	Darlington and Camden, South Carolina
Woolsey, Jane S.	New York, New York	Richmond, Virginia
Woolsey, Julia	New Castle, New York	Norfolk, Virginia
Worthington, Miss E. P.	Vineland, New Jersey	Morehead City and Roanoke Island, North Carolina
Wright, Mrs.	Clinton, Massachusetts	Washington, D.C.
Wright, Annie A.	Montpelier, Vermont	Lexington, Virginia
Wright, E.	Huntingdon, Massachusetts	Hilton Head, South Carolina
Wright, Lavinia (Savira?)	Clinton, Massachusetts	Washington, D.C.
Wright, Mrs. M. C.	Groton, Massachusetts	Memphis, Tennessee
Wright, Martha	Nanuet, New York	Port Royal, South Carolina
Wright, Miss S.	Clinton, Massachusetts	Washington, D.C.
Wright, Rev. S. G.	Oberlin, Ohio	Portsmouth, Virginia, and Columbus, Kentucky
Wright, Mr. Theo G.	Huntingdon, Massachusetts	Columbia, South Carolina
Yarnall, Miss	Darby, Pennsylvania	St. John's Island, South Carolina
Yauger, Christine	Union Springs, New York	Washington, D.C.
Yenter, Mary A.	Grantville, Massachusetts	Norfolk, Virginia
York, Miss C. L.	New Bedford, Massachusetts	Great Mills, Woodville, Maryland
Younger, Thomas E.	Boston, Massachusetts	Chestertown (Maryland?)
Zachos, John C.	Cincinnati, Ohio	Port Royal, South Carolina
Zelie, J. H.	West Camp, New York, or Hudson, New Jersey	Fortress Monroe, Virginia, and Washington, D.C.
Zelie, Mrs. Susan A.	Hudson, New Jersey	Fortress Monroe, Virginia, and Washington, D.C.
Zoll, Emma	Spring Garden, Pennsylvania	Huntsville, Alabama

BIBLIOGRAPHY

PRIMARY MATERIALS

Manuscripts

Bureau of Refugees, Freedmen, and Abandoned Lands, Manuscripts of the Educational Division. The National Archives, Washington. (An extensive collection, comprising several thousand reports and letters, both official and private.)

Chase, Salmon P., Manuscripts. Manuscripts Division, Library of Congress, Washington.

Hawks, J. Milton and Esther, Letters. Manuscripts Division, Library of Congress, Washington.

Port Royal Correspondence. The National Archives, Washington.

Letters, Memoirs, Diaries

Abbott, Lyman, *Reminiscences*. New York, Houghton Mifflin Company, 1915.

Ames, Mary, *From a New England Woman's Diary in Dixie in 1865*. Springfield, Massachusetts, The Plimpton Press, 1906.

Bates, Edward, *Diary*. Edited by Howard K. Beale. American Historical Association, *Annual Report, 1930*, Vol. IV.

Coffin, Levi, *Reminiscences of Levi Coffin, the Reputed President of the Underground Railroad, being a Brief History of the Labors of a Lifetime in Behalf of the Slave, with the Stories of Numerous Fugitives, who Gained their Freedom through his Instrumentality, and many other Incidents*. Cincinnati, Western Tract Society, 1876.

Haviland, Laura S., *A Woman's Life-work: Labors and Experiences of Laura S. Haviland*. Chicago, C. V. Waite and Company, 1887.

Higginson, Thomas Wentworth, *Army Life in a Black Regiment*. Boston, Fields, Osgood and Company, 1870.

Forbes, John Murray, *Letters and Recollections of John Murray Forbes*. Edited by Sarah Forbes Hughes. 2 vols. Boston, Houghton Mifflin Company, 1899.

Pearson, Elizabeth Ware, editor, *Letters from Port Royal, Written at the Time of the Civil War*. Boston, W. B. Clarke Company, 1906.

Pierce, E. L., *Memoir and Letters of Charles Sumner*. 4 vols. Boston, Roberts Brothers, 1877–1893.

Towne, Laura M., *Letters and Diary of Laura M. Towne: Written from the Sea Islands of South Carolina, 1862–1884.* Edited by R. S. Holland. Cambridge, Riverside Press, 1912.

Walker, Susan, "Journal of Miss Susan Walker, March 3—June 6, 1862." Edited by H. N. Sherwood. *Quarterly Publication of the Historical and Philosophical Society of Ohio,* VII (January–March, 1912), 3–48.

Weld, Theodore D., *Letters of Theodore Dwight Weld, Angelina Grimké Weld and Sarah Grimké, 1822–1844.* Edited by Gilbert H. Barnes and Dwight L. Dumond. 2 vols. New York, D. Appleton-Century Company, 1934.

REPORTS

Alvord, John Watson, *Semi-Annual Reports on Schools and Finances for Freedmen, 1866–1870.* 10 Reports. Washington, Government Printing Office, 1866–1870.

American Freedmen's Union Commission, *First Annual Report.* New York, 1866.

American Union Commission, *The American Union Commission: Its Origin, Operations and Purposes.* New York, Sanford, Harroun and Company, 1865.

Convention of Freedmen's Commissions, *Minutes of the Convention of Freedmen's Commissions, held at Indianapolis, Indiana, July 19 and 20, 1864.* Cincinnati, Methodist Book Concern, 1864.

Freedmen's Aid Society of the Methodist Episcopal Church, *Reports, 1866–1875.* Cincinnati, Western Methodist Book Concern, [July, 1893].

Freedmen's Aid Society of the Methodist Episcopal Church *12th Annual Report, 1879.* Cincinnati, [Methodist Book Concern?], 1880.

Friends' Association of Philadelphia and its Vicinity, for the Relief of Colored Freedmen, *Report of the Executive Board.* Philadelphia, 1864.

Friends' Association of Philadelphia and its Vicinity, for the Relief of Colored Freedmen, *Statistics of the Operations of the Executive Board of the Friends' Association of Philadelphia, and its Vicinity, for the Relief of Colored Freedmen, as Presented to a Public Meeting of Friends . . . 1st month 19th, 1864. Together with the Report of Samuel R. Shipley, President of the Board, of his Visit to the Camps of the Freedmen on the Mississippi River.* Philadelphia, Inquirer Printing Office, [1864].

Pennsylvania State Anti-Slavery Society, *Proceedings of the Pennsylvania Convention, Assembled to Organize a State Anti-Slavery Society at Harrisburg, on the 31st of January and 1st, 2d and 3d of February, 1837.* Philadelphia, Merrehew and Gunn, 1837.

United States Congress.
Report of the Joint Committee on Reconstruction at the First Session, Thirty-ninth Congress. Washington, Government Printing Office, 1866.

Report of the Joint Select Committee Appointed to Inquire into the Condition of Affairs in the late Insurrectionary States, so far as regards the Execution of the Laws, and the Safety of the Lives and Property of the Citizens of the United States and Testimony Taken. 13 vols. Washington, Government Printing Office, 1872.

House Executive Documents, 38 Cong., 1 Sess., no. 11 (Serial 1255). Report of the Commissioner, Bureau of Refugees, Freedmen, and Abandoned Lands, December [19], 1865.

House Executive Documents, 41 Cong., 2 Sess., no. 142 (Serial 1417). Report of the Commissioner, Bureau of Refugees, Freedmen, and Abandoned Lands, October 20, 1869 and February 15, 1870.

House Executive Documents, 41 Cong., 3 Sess., no. 1 (Serial 1450). Report of the Commissioner, Bureau of Refugees, Freedmen, and Abandoned Lands, July 1, 1870.

House Miscellaneous Documents, 40 Cong., 3 Sess., no. 52 (Serial 1385). Condition of Affairs in Georgia, 1869.

Senate Executive Documents, 39 Cong., 1 Sess., no. 27 (Serial 1238). Reports of Assistant Commissioners, Bureau of Refugees, Freedmen, and Abandoned Lands.

NEWSPAPERS AND MAGAZINES

American Freedman. New York, April, 1866–July, 1869.
American Missionary Magazine. New York, 1846—.
Augusta (Georgia) *Chronicle and Sentinel,* 1785—.
Augusta (Georgia) *Daily Press,* 1866–1869.
Augusta (Georgia) *National Republican,* 1867–1868.
Columbus (Georgia) *Daily Sun and Times,* 1865–1873.
Congregationalist. Boston, 1816— [Title varies].
De Bow's Review. New Orleans, 1846–1864, 1866–1870, 1879–1880.
Freedmen's Journal. Boston, 1864–1869.
Freedmen's Record. Boston, January, 1865–April, 1873 [Vol. I as *Freedmen's Journal*].
Freedmen's Reporter. Cincinnati and Indianapolis, 1867.
Harper's Monthly Magazine. New York, 1850— [1850–1900 as *Harper's New Monthly Magazine*].
Independent. New York, 1848–1928.
Indiana History Bulletin. Fort Wayne, 1915–1923; Indianapolis, 1923—.
Nashville (Tennessee) *Daily Press and Times,* 1863–1869.
Nashville (Tennessee) *Dispatch,* 1862–1866.
Nashville (Tennessee) *Republican Banner,* 1837–1875.
Nation. New York, 1865—
National Freedman. New York, 1865–March, 1866.
New York *Times,* 1851—
New York *Tribune,* 1841— [Title varies].

North American Review. Boston, May, 1815—.

Pennsylvania Freedman's Bulletin. Philadelphia, February, 1865–February, 1867.

OTHER PRINTED MATERIALS

Atlanta University, *The Atlanta University Bulletin, Catalog Number, 1937–1938.* Series III, No. 22, April, 1938. Atlanta, Georgia.

[Atkinson, Edward], *Cheap Cotton by Free Labor: by a Cotton Manufacturer.* Boston, A. Williams and Company, 1861.

Calhoun School, *Catalog, 1937–1938.* Calhoun School, Calhoun, Alabama, [1937].

Claflin College, *Sixty-ninth Annual Catalogue of Claflin College 1937–1938.* Claflin College, Orangeburg, South Carolina, [1937].

Congressional Globe, 108 vols. Washington, Globe Office, 1834–1873.

Fleming, Walter L., editor, *Documentary History of Reconstruction.* 2 vols. Cleveland, Arthur H. Clark Company, 1906–1907.

French, Mrs. A. M., *Slavery in South Carolina and the Ex-Slaves, or the Port Royal Mission.* New York, William French, 1862.

[Gannett, W. C.], "The Freedmen at Port Royal," *North American Review,* CI (July, 1865), 1–28.

Mather School [Bulletin, 1937]. Mather School, Beaufort, South Carolina.

National Education Association of the United States, . . . *Journal of the Proceedings and Addresses of the . . . Annual Meeting. . . .* Albany, New York, etc., 1858—.

Penn Normal, Industrial and Agricultural School, *Annual Report, Seventy-Sixth Year,* 1938. [Penn Normal School, St. Helena Island, South Carolina, 1938].

Pierce, E. L., "The Freedmen at Port Royal," *Atlantic Monthly,* XII (September, 1863), 291–315.

Slaughter, Linda W., *The Freedmen of the South.* Cincinnati, Elm Street Publishing Company, 1869.

Stowe, Harriet Beecher, "The Education of the Freedmen," *North American Review,* CXXVIII (June, 1879), 605–615.

SECONDARY MATERIALS

Appleton's Cyclopaedia of American Biography. Edited by J. G. Wilson and John Fiske. 8 vols. New York, D. Appleton and Company, 1887–1889 (Vol. 8 edited by J. E. Homans. Press Association, 1918).

Bacon, Alice M., "The Negro and the Atlanta Exposition." The Trustees of the John F. Slater Fund, *Occasional Papers. No. 7.* Baltimore, 1896.

Beard, Augustus F., *A Crusade of Brotherhood, A History of the American Missionary Association.* Boston, Pilgrim Press, 1909.

Bond, Horace Mann, *The Education of the Negro in the American Social Order.* New York, Prentice Hall, 1934.

Bowers, Claude G., *The Tragic Era.* Boston, Houghton Mifflin Company, 1929.

Brown, William Henry, *The Education and Economic Development of the Negro in Virginia.* Publications of the University of Virginia, Phelps-Stokes Fellowship Papers No. 6. Charlottesville, Virginia, Surber-Arundale-Company, Inc., 1923?

Davis, William W., *Civil War and Reconstruction in Florida.* Columbia University, 1913. *Columbia University Studies in History, Economics and Public Law,* Vol. LIII.

Dictionary of American Biography. Edited by Allen Johnson and Dumas Malone. 20 vols. New York, Charles Scribner's Sons, 1928–1936.

DuBois, W. E. Burghardt, *Black Reconstruction.* . . . New York, Harcourt Brace and Company, 1935.

DuBois, W. E. Burghardt, "The Freedmen's Bureau," *Atlantic Monthly,* LXXXVII (March, 1901), 354–365.

Encyclopedia Americana. 30 vols., New York, Americana Corporation, 1937.

Fairchild, James H., *Oberlin, the Colony and the College.* Oberlin, E. J. Goodrich, 1883.

Fleming, Dale S., Development of Elementary and Secondary Schools in Mississippi During the Reconstruction, 1865–1875. Unpublished M.A. thesis, University of Mississippi, 1939.

Fleming, Walter L., *Civil War and Reconstruction in Alabama.* New York, Columbia University Press, 1905.

Fleming, Walter L., *The Sequel of Appomattox.* . . . New Haven, Yale University Press, 1919.

Garner, James W., *Reconstruction in Mississippi.* New York, Macmillan Company, 1901.

Hamilton, J. G. deRoulhac, *Reconstruction in North Carolina.* Columbia University, 1914. *Columbia University Studies in History, Economics and Public Law,* Vol. LVIII.

Harlow, Ralph V., "Gerrit Smith and the John Brown Raid," *American Historical Review,* XXXVIII (October, 1932), 32–60.

Harlow, Ralph V., *Gerrit Smith, Philanthropist and Reformer.* New York, H. Holt and Company, [1939].

Harper, Ida H., *The Life and Work of Susan B. Anthony.* . . . 3 vols. Indianapolis, Hollenbeck Press, 1898–1908.

Heckman, Oliver S., The Penetration of Northern Churches into the South, 1860–1880. Unpublished Ph.D. Dissertation, Duke University, [1938?].

Hibben, Paxton, *Henry Ward Beecher, An American Portrait.* New York, George H. Doran Company, 1927.

Hinds, William A., *American Communities and Co-operative Colonies.* Chicago, Chas. H. Kerr and Company, 1908.

Holmes, Dwight O. W., *The Evolution of the Negro College.* Columbia University, 1934. *Teacher's College, Columbia University, Contributions to Education No. 609.*

Howe, M. A. De Wolfe, *Boston, the Place and the People.* New York, Macmillan Company, 1903.

Jackson, L. P., "The Educational Efforts of the Freedmen's Bureau and Freedmen's Aid Societies in South Carolina, 1862–1872," *Journal of Negro History,* VIII (January, 1923), 1–40.

Johnson, Guion G., *A Social History of the Sea Islands, with Special Reference to St. Helena Island, South Carolina.* Chapel Hill, University of North Carolina Press, 1930.

Kendrick, Benjamin B., *The Journal of the Joint Committee of Fifteen on Reconstruction, 39th Congress, 1865–1867.* Columbia University, 1914. *Columbia University Studies in History, Economics and Public Law,* Vol. LXII.

King, Moses, *Philadelphia and Notable Philadelphians.* New York, Moses King, 1901.

Mathews, Lois Kimball, *The Expansion of New England, the Spread of New England Settlement and Institutions to the Mississippi River, 1620–1865.* Boston, Houghton Mifflin Company, 1909.

Moore, David Hastings, *John Morgan Walden: Thirty-fifth Bishop of the Methodist Episcopal Church.* New York, The Methodist Book Concern, 1915.

National Cyclopaedia of American Biography. 13 vols. New York, James T. White and Company, 1893–1906.

Oberholtzer, Ellis P., *A History of the United States Since the Civil War.* 5 vols. New York, Macmillan Company, 1917–1937.

Parmelee, J. H., "Freedmen's Aid Societies." United States Department of Interior, Office of Education, *Bulletin,* 1916, No. 38, pp. 268–295.

Pearson, Henry G., *The Life of John Andrew.* 2 vols. Boston, Houghton Mifflin Company, 1904.

Peirce, Paul S., *The Freedmen's Bureau.* Iowa City, 1904. *State University of Iowa, Studies in Sociology, Economics, Politics and History,* Vol. III, No. 1.

Reynolds, John S., *Reconstruction in South Carolina, 1865–1877.* Columbia, The State Company, 1905.

Rhodes, James Ford, *History of the United States from the Compromise of 1850.* New York, Macmillan Company, 1920.

Rust, R. S., *The Freedmen's Aid Society of the Methodist Episcopal Church.* (Society Series, No. 6) New York, Tract Department, [1880].

Siebert, Wilbur H., *The Underground Railroad from Slavery to Freedom.* New York, Macmillan Company, 1899.

Siebert, Wilbur H., *Vermont's Anti-slavery and Underground Railroad Record.* Columbus, Ohio, Spahr and Glenn Company, 1937.

Simkins, Francis B., and Robert H. Woody, *South Carolina During Reconstruction*. Chapel Hill, University of North Carolina Press, 1932.

Smedley, Katherine, The Northern Teacher on the South Carolina Sea Islands. Unpublished M.A. thesis, University of North Carolina, 1932.

Stanton, Elizabeth C., Susan B. Anthony and Matilda Joslyn Gage, editors, *History of Woman Suffrage*. 6 vols. New York, Fowler and Wells, 1881–1922.

Staples, Thomas S., *Reconstruction in Arkansas, 1862–1874*. Columbia University, 1923. *Columbia University Studies in History, Economics and Public Law*, Vol. CIX.

Still, William, *The Underground Railroad*. Philadelphia, Porter and Coates, 1872.

Stuart, Julia M., Whittier, As an Abolitionist, 1833–1863. Unpublished M.A. thesis, Vanderbilt University, 1939.

Taylor, Alrutheus A., *The Negro in the Reconstruction of Virginia*. Washington, The Association for the Study of Negro Life and History, 1926.

Thompson, C. Mildred, *Reconstruction in Georgia, Economic, Social, Political, 1865–1872*. Columbia University, 1915, *Columbia University Studies in History, Economics and Public Law*, Vol. LXIV.

Webster, Laura J., "The Operation of the Freedmen's Bureau in South Carolina." *Smith College Studies in History*, edited by J. S. Bassett and S. B. Fay, Vol. I, No. 2 and No. 3 (October, 1915–July, 1916), Northampton, Smith College, 1916.

Wiley, Bell I., *Southern Negroes, 1861–1865*. New Haven, Yale University Press, 1938.

Williamson, Harold F., *Edward Atkinson, the Biography of a Liberal*, 1827–1905. Boston, Old Corner Book Store, Inc., 1934.

INDEX